# A First Class Life on a Third Class Ticket

## The Edwardian memoirs of
## Ronald Gray, artist and traveller.

EDITED AND ANNOTATED BY RICHARD GOCHER

SilverWood

Published in 2022 by SilverWood Books

SilverWood Books Ltd
14 Small Street, Bristol, BS1 1DE, United Kingdom
www.silverwoodbooks.co.uk

ISBN 978-1-80042-180-6 (paperback)
ISBN 978-1-80042-181-3 (ebook)

British Library Cataloguing in Publication Data
A CIP catalogue record for this book is
available from the British Library

Page design and typesetting by SilverWood Books

# A First Class Life on a Third Class Ticket

**The Edwardian memoirs of Ronald Gray, artist and traveller.**

# Dedication

With thanks for the support of my sister and brother-in-law Sue and Carey Coombs, my friend Simon Twiston-Davis for advice and support and to Stephen Bartlett, Archivist of the Chelsea Arts Club, for his encouragement in bringing these memoirs to publication.

For an opportunity to see more of Ronald Gray's work,
and in colour, please visit: ronaldgrayartist.com

# Contents

# Introduction

Ronald Gray's Father, James Gray, was born in Edinburgh on 11 April 1810. His father remarried after his mother's death and James never got on with his stepmother, running away from home several times to live with his grandparents.

Aged 13 he sailed from Leith to London and led a rough life for a few years until getting a job in East Anglia, probably working on the installation of hot houses on an estate at Dullingham near Cambridge where he met his first wife Clara. They moved to London where he started his own business as a Horticultural Builder and Engineer in Chelsea in 1841. Clara died in 1853 leaving four surviving children, James, Clara, Alex and Arthur.

James then married Elizabeth Burrell aged 26. Elizabeth had nine surviving children, including Ronald born in 1868 and Jane who married Fred Pegram. She herself died in 1917 aged 87. Another daughter was Susy who married my grandfather, Henry Gocher. He was appointed Rector of Port Darwin in 1901 in the Northern Territories of Australia and they were married on Thursday Island by the Bishop of Carpenteria in 1902.

Nearly all the material for this memoir of my Great Uncle Ron, as he was known in the family, has come to me from Marjory Pegram, the only daughter of Fred and Jane Pegram who inherited all Ronald Gray's papers and also from my aunt, Mary Gocher who was a constant explorer of the family's history.

During the 1970s when I was first working in London, they shared a flat in Drayton Gardens. Among the papers which I inherited from Marjory were Ronald Gray's memoirs, written in 1943 whilst he was staying at High Ham, a village near Taunton. They cover his life up to the end of the First World War in 1918 and describe the many fascinating people he knew in the world of art and literature in London, as well as his extensive travel abroad.

Marjory had written an introduction to the memoirs:

9

*Ronald Gray, one of the founder members of the Chelsea Arts Club, had the most interesting life imaginable, full of sharply defined contradictions. He was sensitive, highly strung and nervous, yet of immense courage, both moral and physical. His capacity for suffering was great, but he would tackle anything, however unpleasant or dangerous if the necessity arose. He had a deep affection for his family and friends, yet he thoroughly enjoyed a row, and could not resist 'trailing his coat' in order to start one. If the Conservatives were in power, he was a left-wing socialist, and if Labour were in power, he was a diehard Tory.*

*Although he professed to despise the usages of the society of the early 1900s, he had an adolescent horror of any of his family doing the wrong thing; this was a great trial to his extremely unconventional family, who did not care a bit if they were socially taboo or not, and it made the young lives of his various nephews and nieces, to whom he was devoted, very difficult indeed.*

*He had many love affairs, but in spite of these, and the Bohemian world in which he lived; he had a strong vein of Victorian puritanism which made him admire and respect youthful innocence and which sometimes caused him to be shocked when least expected.*

*Like most gifted people, he was very modest about his work, and he despised all forms of self-advertisement; yet he well knew that because of this he never attained the position in the world that his beautiful paintings entitled him. He was a generous critic of the work of others and was passionately enthusiastic about fellow artists whose work he admired; and although he had no patience with what he considered bogus 'new art' and 'abstract' schools, he instantly recognised sincerity and real talent, no matter in what unusual form it might be manifested.*

*His scorn for what he called the 'nonsense' which was being foisted on the public led him into perpetrating a successful hoax which made him unpopular in certain quarters for many years. He persuaded a doctor friend who had never in his life held a paint brush in his hand to paint a large picture in oils, which naturally looked like the painstaking effort of a ten-year-old. He himself with immense gusto, did an absurd picture in the prevailing fashion of the day; and these two masterpieces, signed with assumed names, were sent to a London exhibition which featured modern art. Both were hung on the line and caused a considerable stir, and it was some time before the hoax was discovered. His triumph at having 'got away with it' amply compensated him for the anger that his crime aroused. 'There you are' he would say. 'I told you the whole thing was a lot of nonsense!'*

*Despite his difficult and often uncompromising nature, he inspired an incredible amount of affection, and many lifelong and devoted friendships. He was irresistible to women in spite of often being extremely rude to them – indeed,* this appeared an added attraction! He loved all his large family, particularly his mother, his brother Alfred, and perhaps most of all, his youngest sister Jane. Jane was the only person in the world who could manage him, and her, 'Now Ron, don't be silly' was enough.

His last years were tragic. When over 80 he developed cancer which was ignored until it was too late. In spite of a major operation, performed with the utmost skill, he grew steadily worse, and had years of terrible suffering which he faced with his usual indomitable courage. His friends helped him and stood by him to the end. He died, mercifully and suddenly, in the Charterhouse infirmary on 16 November, 1951, aged 87.

His own summing up of his long life was neat. He said, 'I've had a first-class life on a third-class ticket.'

# Editorial note

The language of the memoirs is distinctively that of a writer who was educated in the 1870s. I have left the memoirs, and the letters quoted, unchanged as I wanted the voices to retain their historical distinctiveness. Some of the opinions and comments may sound strange to a modern readers ear, but I felt that I should not make any changes, except a few minor ones. I have also not made any changes to the punctuation of the memoirs and the letters. They remain as they were written.

# Chapter 1

# Early Life in Chelsea

A wise old lady once said to me, 'never talk about yourself, people don't want to hear.' Her remark saddened me, for I was young and enjoyed talking about myself. I risk writing my memories, however, because I was born and lived in Chelsea during an artistic and literary period which seems to interest later generations. To suggest the atmosphere in which I was born I must speak of my parents, brothers and sisters, and our home in Chelsea.

Father was the son of an Edinburgh architect and was born in 1810. His Mother died and his father remarried, but the second wife did not take kindly to her stepchildren. My father was miserable, and at the age of thirteen escaped to London in a fishing boat, and never saw or heard of his parents ever again. In London he lived as best he could, at one time selling matches in the streets. He became acquainted with another young Scotsman named Veitch, who later founded the famous nursery gardens in Chelsea. At Veitch's suggestion Father began building and heating greenhouses, and in 1841 took premises in Danvers Street, Chelsea, an old house surrounded by a large garden. He built works in the garden and installed steam machinery. This business, now over a hundred years old, still functions in the same premises. He lived in the house with his first wife and children; his wife died, and he married my mother. Her name was Burrell, and her people were farmers in Huntingdonshire. He had sixteen children, five by his first wife and eleven by my mother. My childish recollections are of many brothers and sisters, Nurse Alice (who was with us until were all grown up, and died at the age of ninety-two) and a young girl, Nurse Ellen; and of comfortable nurseries and a happy life. My first distinct memory is of sitting on a cushion in front of the nursery fire when a piece of hot coal shot out and lodged inside my frock and burnt my back, the scar remaining until today, more than seventy years later. I have a dreamlike memory of my first smell of the sea, when the family spent the summer at Brighton in 1871, and my hatred of a fat old bathing woman who tried to make me duck my head under the waves.

In Chelsea our life was full of interest. Most afternoons Alice took us to the Apothecaries Gardens where we had permission to play. The bigger children walked, and Alice pushed us smaller ones in a vast perambulator. Our way went past the wharves at the bottom of Danvers Street and under an old archway over which were rooms – we always shouted under the arch to hear our voices echo. Then along Cheyne Walk, where the river came almost up to the old church; and there were trees, and boats for hire drawn up on the banks. There were green fields beyond the Apothecaries Gardens towards the town. In the gardens were two large Cedars of Lebanon, under which we played and made daisy chains. There were some high iron gates looking onto the river, and through these we watched the passing barges. One day we were interested to see workmen shovelling mud about and were told they were going to build an embankment. Sometimes on Saturday afternoons we were taken to King's Road to see the Prince and Princess of Wales drive past on their way to Hurlingham; there was always a number of poor people and working men to watch the procession of fine carriages and horses.

Our great delight was Derby Day when we watched the people returning from Epsom. There were whiskered dudes driving coaches, dressed in grey frock coats and wearing toppers around which were stuck wooden dolls and streamers of coloured muslin and pretty women sat beside them. There was every kind of conveyance, including the old four-wheeler cabs and coster carts drawn by dressed-up donkeys – these sometimes wearing white drawers. Derby Day was a great day at Cremorne Gardens, though it was only the balloon ascents which affected us. I remember an excited group of us standing in our back nursery watching a balloon cast free; the poor 'flying man' fell like a stone and was smashed, with all his flying contraptions,

*Ronald Gray as a boy. From the author's collection.*

14

outside St. Luke's Church in Sydney Street. The last owner of Cremorne Gardens was a man Baum who had as his 'chucker out' a prize fighter called Plantagenet Green. When the gardens were closed in 1877, Baum took a small tobacconist shop in Fulham Road.

Battersea Park was also one of our playgrounds. It was a wilder place then than it is now; indeed, some parts were considered unsafe because of footpads and other bad characters. The attraction there was the lake, for on it were rowing boats which might be hired. These boats were owned by two brothers named Greaves, whose father had a boathouse in Cheyne Walk, near the bottom of Milman Street. Either one of the brothers would row us about the lake and I did not know then that this was the beginning of an acquaintanceship with Walter Greaves which would last until he died in the Charterhouse Alms house in Smithfield, London. Indeed, when I was honorary secretary of the Chelsea Arts Club, I helped to get him into this institution. The Greaves brothers painted in their spare time and became Whistler's faithful satellites. They rowed him on the river and painted with him, but I will tell more of Walter Greaves later.

(This is the first of many mentions of James MacNeill Whistler, most famous for his portrait *Whistler's Mother*. There are many further references in the memoirs to this American born artist.)

In those days Father drove a high dogcart, and on rare occasions took one of us with him on his journeys. He was a strict Presbyterian, and his outlook was puritanical to an extent which the young of today would hardly believe. I can still feel the torture suffered on Sundays, when we were big enough to be marched off to Halkin Street Presbyterian Church to listen to an hour-long sermon preached by one Dr Saphir, a converted Jew. Mother was our kind teacher and told us tales before hearing our prayers. One of her tales thrilled me; it was of a young cousin of hers who was caught be the sail of a windmill and killed. I became interested in the Bible, and never forgot my prayers. I imagined that repetition of a request must have a better chance of success than merely asking once, and my prayers became formidable. I would start with Mother and Father and go right through the family of twelve, asking God to make, 'Good, good, good, good, happy, happy, happy, happy,' finishing modestly with myself. My prayers became longer and longer, until Nurse Alice would tap me on the shoulder and say, 'That's enough, Master Ronnie,' and bundle me off to bed.

There were four of us in the nursery at this time, and we were much intrigued with something we had learned at a Bible lesson, which was that if we really believed, then our prayers would be granted. In our playroom we were well supplied with wooden bricks from Father's sawmill. With these we had built a diminutive village of about twelve houses, and we thought how good it would be if only there were real,

15

live people to live in them. Talking of the possibilities, we agreed that our faith was strong, and that prayer would accomplish the miracle. That evening, each prayed with fervent intensity, and got into bed feeling quite certain that our village would be peopled in the morning. We awakened with the dawn, and my two sisters from one room and my brother and myself from the other hurried down the corridor to the nursery. Too nervous to open the door, we listened. Not a sound from the room. After some minutes we motioned Helen, who was the eldest, to enter first, and we followed. Our cottages were as we had left them, without inhabitants! This was a shock to my faith, and a great disappointment. I began to doubt much that we were taught.

Then there was the carping worry of the 'unforgivable sin' of which we were told. The thought of this sin got on my nerves, for no-one could tell me what it was. The fear that unconsciously I might have committed it haunted me for some time. Then it was drummed into us that ambition was a bad thing, and that we should be modest and remember that 'the last shall be first.' This teaching has coloured all my life, for I can truthfully say that I have never been ambitious except to paint well, and the modesty which got into my soul forced me to think that everybody could do things better than myself. I have yet to learn that the last shall be first!

I was about four I think, when I began to take an interest in 'pretty ladies.' There was a Spanish singer who sometimes came to tea with Mother, and we were brought down from the nursery to see her. Nurse Alice had a job to get me back again, I was so enraptured by the singer's face. I dreamt of her, and pictured walking a tightrope high above an excited, cheering crowd – the Spanish lady cheering louder than the rest. And so our childish lives went happily on, and the Chelsea Embankment materialised and was opened in 1873.

When my brother Kenneth and I were respectively five and seven years old we were sent to a small boy's school in Oakley Street, kept by two nice creatures, the Misses Quiller. There were about twelve pupils. Among them was a boy whom we made our friend, whose name was Ronald Philip. He was the son of the sculptor Birnie Philip, who was responsible for the panels on the Albert Memorial.

John Birnie Philip was born in 1824 and died in 1875. He lived at Merton Villa in Chelsea, not far from the Gray family at Danvers Street. He had a large family of ten children, one of whom, his daughter Beatrice, married Whistler in 1888. After Beatrice's death her sister Rosalind became his housekeeper, secretary and companion. Philip was a well-known sculptor and did much work for Sir George Gilbert Scott, including work on the podium frieze and allegorical statues on the spire for the Albert Memorial opposite the Albert Hall in Kensington. He also did a lot of work for churches and cathedrals including St. Georges Chapel Windsor and Lichfield, Ely and Canterbury Cathedrals.

They lived in a rambling old house surrounded by a large garden in Manresa Road. The public library and L.C.C. technical schools are built on this land. There were wooden gates cutting off Manresa Road from what was then called Trafalgar Square. Most Saturday afternoons Kenneth and I spent at this house. Hide-and-seek played in the overgrown garden was a delight, and there were many sisters whom I thought angels. The eldest whom I loved, (I was only seven), was engaged to that gentle voiced, good looking young painter, Cecil Lawson, who was usually there when we all sat down at a long table for tea. After tea my divinity sometimes took me to the garden when she was accompanied by Cecil, and she would put her arm round my neck or take my hand. I remember my frenzy of jealousy and rage when I saw that Cecil had his arm round her waist. One of these charming creatures married Godwin, the architect, and after his death, became Mrs Whistler.

> Godwin was born in Bristol in 1833 and died in 1886. He was an architect and designer and became closely identified with the Anglo-Japanese characteristic of the Aesthetic Movement and with Whistler's group of friends in the 1870s. His first wife died in 1865 while he was having an affair with Ellen Terry the well-known actress and they lived together and had two children. At the end of the affair, he married Beatrice Birnie Philip who was working in his office and who went on to marry Whistler two years after Godwin's death. Godwin was a frequent contributor to the periodical *British Architect* and published a number of books on architecture, costume and theatre.

When Ronald Philip came to tea with us, my elder brother Alfred, generally walked with him. Alfred told us that when they came to a certain lamp post in King's Road, Ronald always asked whether he thought God was as tall as that lamppost.

After attending the school in Oakley Street for a year or two, Kenneth and I were sent to the Chelsea Grammar School, which was kept by the Rev Mr Wilson, a red-faced, fiery man of whom, at first, I was mortally afraid. The school was a big, one-storied building standing in the centre of a large garden which was the playground. This remarkable old house, which was in Smith Street and faced Burton Court, was later pulled down to make way for an ugly red brick house built by an Irish member of parliament, which is still there.

In those days I was a nervous, delicate boy suffering much from aches and pains, and was often at home, ill. Life did not seem pleasant. Our walk from Danvers Street to school took us along Cheyne Walk and Royal Hospital Road, and at a certain corner, most mornings tiresome rough boys from a Church School gathered. They threw things at us and pushed us as we passed. One day it went too far, and a boy hit Kenneth with a string of metal buttons and hurt him. I knew I ought to fight this boy, but possibilities of defeat went through my mind. We were late for school, and I made that the excuse for hurrying away; but my night was wakeful and restless, and the thought of my cowardice haunted me. When we set off next morning I was pale but determined. The boys were at the usual corner, and our enemy was preparing for mischief. I rushed at him with that 'compelled valour' referred to by Hamlet when he tackled the pirates. The fight was short as, to my relief, it was stopped by a policeman; but it lasted long enough for me to get in some good ones on his face, and our morning walk was peaceful for some time afterwards.

I do not remember much about school life except that I disliked everything they tried to teach me with the exception of the drawing lessons, which I much enjoyed. The drawing master's name was Varley – a son of John Varley, the well know water-colour painter. He was a strong, handsome man, as I have read his father was also. His teaching was simple. He gave each of us a coloured reproduction, which we copied in colour. I did not learn much, but a desire to become an artist was the result of these lessons.

Varley had a small lump on the side of his nose which intrigued me. It looked whitish green, and I once had the bad taste to ask what it was he put on it. He said that he dipped a copper coin in vinegar and rubbed it on the spot, as he had been told that this was a cure for such things. Years later I heard that he died from cancer of the face.

An older boy at this school, whose face I can visualise but whose name I forget, a delicate, thin boy not good at games, surprised us years after by winning the VC in India, at a fight in Chitral. Because so many artists lived in Chelsea it was natural that some sent their sons to this school. It was there that we met the brothers Hughes. Their father was a painter of still life – mostly fruit – and was known at the Savage Club as 'fruity Hughes.' There were three boys, William, Herbert and Sydney. William became a painter and an expert on old costume, and the collection which he formed is now in the Victorian and Albert Museum. Herbert changed his name to Hughes Stanton when he began to exhibit because so many painters were named Hughes. He became an RA and President of the Royal Society of Painters in Water Colour and received a knighthood. They lived in one of the charming old houses in Cheyne Road, named Orange House. This was pulled down to make way for the hideous Roman Catholic Church which now dominates that corner. They were hospitable people, and their house was visited by many artists. Possibly the beautiful daughter, Blanche, may have been part of the attraction. It was boring to find that handsome sculptor, Lawes, so often singing duets with Blanche. He was the Lawes of the 'Belt versus Lawes' case which caused much public interest at the time.

In 1882 Charles Lawes, a well-known sculptor in London, was involved in a libel case after he had imputed in the magazine *Vanity Fair* and elsewhere that another sculptor, Richard Claude Belt, was dishonest for taking credit for work done by someone else. The long trial, the last to be heard by the High Court of Justice in Westminster Hall, occupied the court for 43 sittings and excited much public interest at the time. The question at issue was how much a sculptor may be aided by others in work to which he attaches his name. Eventually the case was decided against Lawes, and Belt was awarded £5,000 damages (about £500,000 in today's money).

A.B. Haughton, one of the best illustrators we ever had (indeed I heard Whistler say that he was one of the best artists England had produced) was a frequent visitor. He and Lawes helped with the plays which the Hughes gave each Christmas, in which several of our family took part. It was when acting in one of these plays that I first met the Carter brothers, with whom I continued to be friendly until they died. William, the eldest, became a successful portrait painter, and when a student at the Royal Academy Schools was chosen by Millais to assist him. He had great knowledge of traditional technique, and some of his portraits were of high quality – though not quite the quality he himself thought, for he often told us that his pictures held their own with Rembrandt and Velazquez! His brother Howard Carter, also painted, but soon went to Egypt where he became interested in archaeology. He was the discoverer of the Tomb of Tutankhamun.

A strange playground where we sometimes larked about was the tower of Chelsea Old Church. Randal Davis, the rector's son, enabled us to get there. The wooden staircase which went to the top of the tower was then in a ruined condition. It was our delight to clamber up this death trap, fortunately without tragedy. Randal's eldest sister Etta was a power in the parish, and sometimes arranged entertainments in the parish room adjoining the church. These were called 'Penny Readings', and we children were roped in for the choir. Once she asked me to sing a solo, and my sister Elizabeth coached me for some weeks. I felt dreadfully nervous, and when the evening came, I was beside myself with terror. However, I thought I had done well until a small boy sitting beside me said, 'Why didn't you sing Ron?'

The more I became acquainted with artists and studios, the stronger became my desire to be a painter. My childish enthusiasms made gods of them all. I badly wanted to be that kind of god, so I discussed the possibility with Kenneth, and he advised me to speak to Mother. She, of course, was anxious to help me and wrote to a painter she knew, George Holmes, for advice. I knew him from a drawing he had done in Elizabeth's autograph book of a picture which had been much reproduced and had given him a certain popularity. The subject was a tiny girl talking to a collie, and he called it 'Can't you talk?'. Under his very careful pencil drawing he had written 'No time to do more than a scribble' and later I realised that the drawing must have taken him nearly a week.

He recommended Mother to send me to Heatherley's school, and Mother thought it would be best for me to ask Father myself. This was an ordeal not to be lightly undertaken, and it took me some time to brace myself for it. Father had had a stroke, and was a semi-invalid. He always breakfasted in bed, and then went to his study where he sat all day, smoking a clay pipe and reading *The Times*. We children never entered the study unless for an important request such as money for the swimming baths, and even this took some courage, but to ask if one might be an artist was a terrifying prospect. For several days, as we passed the study, Kenneth would ask, 'Are you going in?' and I would say, 'No, tomorrow.' At last tomorrow came, and I went in. Father was sitting in his chair reading *The Times*. I could not see his face, but I knew that he was conscious of my presence. A long pause, and I could hear my heart beating. At last I blurted out 'Please, Father, my I be an artist?' Father turned his paper over and just said 'No.' I left the room quickly, and the tears which I could not hold back answered Kenneth's question 'How did you get on?'

Mother did her best to comfort me. She gave me paints, which I used during winter evenings to colour prints in *The Young Ladies' Journal*. I hated the winter, I always felt cold. However, there were compensations, for I looked forward with pleasure and excitement to the Christmas pantomimes at the Hughes's, and also at the Mossop's. The Mossops were a large family who lived in Upper Cheyne Row. For several years their pantomimes had finishing touches added by John Clayton and his wife, who were both well-known actors of that time. I worshipped Mrs Mossop, she had a sweet face.

There was an old actress living in Chelsea. Her stage name was Sarah Woolgar and her married name Mellon. She had been one of the most popular actresses in the 1860's, and I was taken to see her in one of her rare appearances during the 80's. She lived with her two daughters in The Vale. The Vale at that time was like a tiny country village. Every house was separated from the road by a wooden railing,

Sarah Woolgar was born in 1824 and died in 1909, and was an actress long associated with the Adelphi Theatre in London. She took over the supervision of the theatre in 1867 and appeared in plays by Charles Dickens and Wilkie Collins.

and at the back of each was a good-sized garden. Mrs Mellon seemed to enjoy having us to play in her garden, the attraction for us was that from there we could watch fallow deer grazing in the grounds of a house in Church Street, which I think was owned by a Mr Barrett who had a brush and ivory shop in Piccadilly.

Looking at The Vale as it is today, it is difficult to realise that at the end opposite King's Road was a nursery garden with greenhouses, and that beyond was Elm Park, now built over and known as Elm Park Gardens. Many years after Mrs Mellon's death her house was taken by the painters Ricketts and Shannon.

When Chelsea Embankment was opened in 1873 there was little traffic, and the wide pavements were good for bowling hoops and running races. On wild, stormy nights my brother Alfred had the strange fancy to put on running clothes and do a mile or two along the embankment in the pouring rain; he said it hardened him.

On sunny mornings, on a seat near Cadogan Pier, a sombre man in loose, dark clothes and vast black hat would sit in a pose suggesting deep thought. Kenneth and I were rather afraid of him, but sister Susan was interested, and one morning she went to him and peered up into his face. From that day he usually called her, talked to her and patted her head. He was Thomas Carlyle.

There were some curious old men who sometimes sat and smoked with Father in the evening; we were told that Father 'helped them'. The one I remember best always looked dirty, and his hands were stained brown. His name was Hedderley, and he was a photographer and poet. It was he who took the interesting pictures of Chelsea, some of which are now to be seen in the Chelsea Library. He gave Elizabeth letters from many artists, mostly of the pre-Raphaelite group. One was from Dante Gabriel Rossetti asking Hedderley to go into the country and take some photographs of lambs for a picture he was painting. Not an easy thing to do in the days of wet plates and long exposures. Rossetti was the last painter one would have thought likely to use photographs.

Elizabeth had a charming friend, Kate Bishop, who when first I remember her was acting in a play called *Our Boys* which had the longest run then known. Later Kate went to Australia and married Lohr, manager of the theatre in which she was playing. She returned to England with a pretty baby named Marie, who has grown up to be the well-known actress, Marie Lohr.

Marie Lohr was born in Sydney Australia in 1895 and died in the UK in 1975. One of her last appearances was in *Play of the Week* in 1967 with Peter O'Toole and Honor Blackman.

When about ten years old I had my first experience of travel. As usual I had been ill most of the winter and Mother arranged with an old school friend, Mrs Pryde, that I should visit them in Edinburgh. A friend of Father's was going to Edinburgh by sea about that time, and I travelled with him. After going aboard at Tilbury he took to his cabin, and I did not see him again until the ship arrived at Leith. My host, Dr Pryde, was head of a large girls school in Edinburgh (Edinburgh Ladies College).

The Prydes were a big family, about six girls and a boy, James, who was attending one of the Edinburgh boys' schools. We used to sketch together – he said he was going to be a painter, but I could not then know how good a painter he was to become. He and I had a common dislike of Sundays in Edinburgh. In the mornings we walked sedately to Greyfriars Church, endured a long sermon and returned to a darkened house with the blinds half down. After lunch, no games or interesting books, though we were allowed to look at religious pictures. It was not until after tea that we began to live, for then Jimmy and I were allowed to go for a walk.

> James Pryde was born in 1866 and died in 1941. With his business partner, and son-in-law William Nicholson, Pryde formed the Beggarstaffe partnership in 1893 which became well known for its innovative poster designs which had a major impact on graphic design for a long time. The partnership lasted until 1899. Pryde tried his hand at acting but contemporaries felt strongly that his talent was as a painter, not an actor.

But in spite of Sundays, I look back on that summer with the Prydes as a happy one, and I returned reluctantly to London and school. Jimmy stayed with us several times and we corresponded for years, but when, much later, he settled in London, his pace was too quick for me and it was usually by chance that we met. William Nicholson married Jimmy's youngest sister, Mabel.

# Chapter 2

# Father's Death and work in the family business

I returned to a changing home. Father had had another stroke and was more of an invalid, and Mother now devoted all her time to him. My step-brothers, who had been running the business during Father's illness, had made a bad job of it and were to go, and Alfred left the firm he was with and took their place; and although he knew nothing about it, with pluck and hard work he kept it from failing. We had to keep Father's brougham and coachman because he couldn't walk; otherwise it was a case of cutting down expense all round, and life became hard. I stayed on at school and worked at drawing when I could persuade my sisters to pose.

When I was thirteen, Alfred thought it would be a good idea for me to leave school, go into the works and thoroughly learn the business. I pleaded that I did not want to learn the business, but wanted to be an artist; but it was no good. I was put into the carpenter's shop, and had to be there at six o'clock each morning and work nine-and-a-half hours. The misery of the next two years was greater than anything I have suffered since. During the winter the cold of the workshop nearly killed me; my arms and hands swelled, and the doctor kept me indoors for a time, but directly I was well, out I had to go again, and I was made to keep far stricter hours than the workmen.

I liked most of the carpenters, they were an amusing lot if a little coarse. They were snobs in their way. Some wore silk hats and frock coats on Sunday, and they and their wives considered that the painters belonged to a lower strata of society. Their pay was only ninepence-halfpenny an hour, but many owned their little houses. If they held extreme left views, I saw no sign of it, except that one very hot day a carpenter, planing a deal board at the next bench, did say that he could 'imagine the Prince of Wales, lying in his hammock at Marlborough House and laughing up his sleeve at us poor blighters!' I remember that there was a painter who continually tried to get me to look at ulcers on his leg.

I was paid twopence-halfpenny an hour, and with my earnings had to clothe myself. When I bought a new hat my boots wanted renewing, and with the new boots, my shirts would be worn out; I could never get straight. Being very self-conscious, I imagined that everyone noticed my frayed cuffs and shabby hat.

When I was fifteen my father died. It was our first experience of death, until then it had been the mystery of birth which had intrigued us. It was foggy, cold weather. A sister told us to go up to Father's bedroom. There, in the gas light, Mother was sitting by Father holding his hand, and quiet people were standing round the bed. Father realised that he was dying. He had known the previous day, because he told Kenneth and me to be good to Mother always. He suddenly told the doctor that when an old friend of his was dying he got out of bed and smoked a pipe, and he would do the same. There followed a tugging and lifting, and his frail body was put in a high-backed chair, and a pipe put into his mouth and lighted. In a few minutes he asked to be put back. We waited silently, listening to his heavy breathing. I felt tired, and went downstairs to the office where I scribbled sketches of girls. A school friend called and sat with me, and I forgot that Father was dying until a sister came to tell me he was dead. I went upstairs and saw him lying quite still, and Mother sitting by the bed crying. That night I lay awake trying to think what dying meant, and why someone who had the power to speak and move should suddenly lose it. I later discovered that this was not a unique enquiry. On most days before the funeral I managed to creep into the room to look at Father and wonder. The excitement of the funeral took my mind from thoughts of death. I had seen in a shop a silk hat which I coveted and bought, and the pleasure of wearing this hat outweighed the sadness of the funeral.

Mother, after Father's death, filled the blank in her life by devoting herself to all of us. Mothers are wonderful people. I was taken from the workshops and sent about the country overlooking building and heating jobs. It was a common occurrence for drunken workmen to offer to fight me. After about a year I was brought back to the office, which suited me better for I could attend evening drawing classes.

# Chapter 3

# Becoming an Artist

In about 1885 I became acquainted with Jacomb-Hood, whose studio was in Manresa Road. He proved to be a good friend and helped me in my efforts to become an artist. Jacomb-Hood at that time was looked upon as one of the most promising of young artists. There were notices and interviews in the press, and his studio was a centre where one met many well-known men and women. Through him I got to know other painters in the nearby studios.

> George Percy Jacomb-Hood was born in 1857 and died in 1929. Well known in his lifetime as a painter, etcher, illustrator and photographer, he and his wife lived in Chelsea and had a house in Tite Street. He regularly worked for *The Graphic* magazine who sent him overseas on several commissions which often involved travelling with royalty.

I devoted my only free time on Saturdays and Sundays to visiting and probably boring them. During one of these visits I first met Fred Brown, who was then headmaster of Westminster School of Art. I asked him about his evening classes and he invited me to join. This was thrilling, for Brown was revolutionising the teaching of drawing, and students were flocking to his school. Until he came along the method followed was the stippling of drawings with paper stumps and spending endless hours working them up, a lazy process which never got a student anywhere.

> Born in 1851 and died in 1941, Brown was one of the foremost art teachers of his generation. From 1877 to 1892 he was headmaster of the Westminster School of Art and from 1893 to 1918 he was Slade Professor of Art.

It was a great moment for me when I went with Brown into the life room at

Westminster. We passed through a large, dimly lit hall full of dingy plaster casts, which was the architectural room. He opened a door on the left and we entered a room crowded with men. On a throne a nude girl was standing, flooded by light from a powerful central lamp. My first impression was that the students were a queer looking lot. Most were smoking. I sat on a 'donkey' and nervously began to draw. When a rest was called, the model got down and went behind curtains, and the students talked together. I felt lonely, and thought of a saying I had read somewhere, 'A stranger to a stranger is not a man'. Naturally I did not realise that among those young men whom I thought so odd looking were some with whom I was to be friends for the rest of my life.

One pale boy, who looked about fifteen and smoked innumerable cigarettes, was a centre of interest. During rests, students clustered round to look at his work. He was incredibly clever, this Fred Pegram, and later became one of our best known illustrators, and married my sister Jane.

This is the foreword Ronald Gray wrote for the memorial exhibition for Fred Pegram in February 1938. Pegram married Jane Gray, Ronald's sister and this writers Great Aunt. They had one child, Marjory.

*Pegram began drawing when very young. At the age of 16 he was the infant prodigy of the Westminster school of Art at the time Frederick Brown, afterwards Slade Professor, was master. This was about 1886, when wood engraving was going out of fashion and zinc block reproduction was coming in. Pegram's facility at drawing with a pen quickly got him the job of making sketches for the Pall Mall Gazette, then edited by W.T. Stead. Photographs at that time were rarely used in journals, and sketches of plays and all kinds of public events, had to be made quickly. No subject dismayed Pegram and the experience he gained before he was 18 enabled him later to illustrate stories, draw and paint portraits and become a popular contributor to Punch magazine. These were pleasant days for artists; it was possible to draw what one saw without adverse comment; 'isms and abstractions were not yet fashionable. Pegram enjoyed drawing the world about him and I think that examples in this exhibition show a delightful understanding of humanity. He had a great influence on contemporary illustrators. Many well-known artists have told me that, when young men, they collected all the reproductions of his work they could get. His drawings made a wide appeal to the public and all throughout his life letters came to him from admirers in many parts of the world. Looking through his papers lately I found a letter from some lonely man in Central Africa thanking him for the pleasure his drawings had given. Pegram was a member of the Royal Institute of Painters in Water*

That evening I spoke to a student of about my own age. He was a dark, good looking boy, and evidently a star turn, for one of his life studies hung on the wall. His name was Walter Russell, and he is at the time of writing, Sir Walter Russell, Keeper of the Royal Academy. After the class that night I walked back to Chelsea elated by the thought that I had now begun to live.

Foolish puritanical training caused me to believe it wicked even to think of sex problems. A young curate who prepared a friend and myself for confirmation, when warning us of the danger of 'sexual sin', blushed, turned his head away and seemed so uncomfortable that I wondered whether I was the only culprit to be haunted by such ideas. Later I found that what is called 'Romance' came to most young people. In retrospect my first romance amuses me. At a party I met a pretty, vivacious girl who was in London studying music. She asked me to dine with her at her rooms in Warwick Square, where she lived with an elderly chaperone. She was probably about twenty-two, and I was seventeen. It was my first experience of dining with strangers, and my nervousness at dinner spoilt all my enjoyment. However, after coffee she asked if I would like to hear her play. We went into a large, dimly-lighted room. She sat at a grand piano and told me to bring a chair and sit by her. The chaperone had disappeared, and we were alone. I listened to her music with joy, but after half an hour of melody she suddenly clasped me tightly in her arms. I was leaning forward with my face pressed hard against her breast. I became conscious that the buttons of her bodice were hurting my face, but I sat patiently. I suppose she realised my inexperience, for she slowly relaxed her embrace and continued with her interrupted rendering of Beethoven. We met several times afterwards, and once she took me to call on Lord Leighton, but I was not asked to dine again. My handling of this incident has been a matter of amusement and regret in later years.

For several years after Father's death we were really poor, and Mother had a difficult job to run our large house and family. We did what we could to earn; my elder sisters went as governesses, which they disliked intensely. Alfred started what he called a 'debt fund'. Each week we added as much as we could spare. Years of mutual help started the good habit of saving, and it certainly did us no harm. My attendance at Brown's classes three evenings a week saved me from morbid introspection which made me afraid of the future. It gave me fresh interest and a new circle of acquaintance; Pegram, Russell and I became intimate friends, and Tonks joined us later.

I well remember the evening Tonks first appeared at Brown's. A tall, thin, loose-jointed man came into the studio, looked round nervously and took a vacant donkey next to me. He smelt strongly of carbolic, an unusual smell for an art student, but understandable when he told us that he was house surgeon at the London Hospital.

He became fascinated by Pegram's skill, and for some time tried to emulate him.

Henry Tonks was born in 1862 and died in 1937. 'Tonks' as Gray called him in his memoirs is a fascinating man, combining as he did great talent as a surgeon and teacher of anatomy with painting and teaching at the Slade School of Fine Art. His pupils are a roll call of British artists who gained fame in the early 20th Century, including Augustus John and Rex Whistler among many, and his influence cannot be underestimated.

During the First World War he resumed his medical career and then combined his medical and artistic talents making drawings of facial injury cases working with the father of modern facial surgery, Harold Gillies. In 1918 he became an official war artist. Tonks, was to be a lifelong friend of my Great Uncle and appears many times in the memoirs, including on many painting trips at home and abroad. He also makes an appearance in Pat Barker's novel *Toby's Room* where he plays a major role in his two famous incarnations, artist and surgeon. The novel has two parts, the first set in 1912 and the second in 1917 when Tonks was working with Gillies making drawings of wounded soldiers to assist in their reconstructive surgery.

In Part 1 Tonks is teaching at the Slade and he is described at his first appearance as follows. 'Professor Tonks had arrived early and was leaning against the wall at the end of the room: a tall, formally dressed, thin, ascetic man with the face of a Roman emperor. Or a fish eagle. Behind him, the wall was covered in palette-knife scrapings, the colours cancelling each other out, so that his black suited figure was outlined in swirls of shimmering grey. Like birds' feathers. It was actually rather a remarkable sight. You wouldn't need a plumb line to draw Tonks: his body was a plumb line. How tall would he be? Six five? Something like that.' I have included this in these memoirs with kind permission as it is so much more meaningful than any of the photographs I have seen of Tonks.

There was an interesting collection of young men in the classes. One of the strangest looking was Aubrey Beardsley. He was terribly thin, had a cadaverous face, and wore his light, metallic-coloured hair cut in a straight fringe across his forehead. He was at that time working in a bank.

Aubrey Beardsley was born in 1872 and as Gray mentions studied at the Westminster School of Art under Professor Fred Brown in 1892. The posters of Toulouse Lautrec and the interest there in Japanese prints discovered on a visit to Paris had a major influence on his artistic development and he was soon seen as one of the most controversial artists of the Art Nouveau Movement. Themes of mythology and history were illustrated with erotic illustrations some of the most famous being for an illustrated version of Wilde's play *Salome*. He suffered from tuberculosis from an early age and was to die from the disease in 1896 in the South of France aged 25.

D.S. MacColl, Charles Furse, Anning Bell, Frampton, David Muirhead, Hartrick, Sullivan and many others came to that evening class.

There was one Smith, a cobbler, who attended regularly. To help him many of us gave him orders for boots and invited him about. Neither his boots nor his drawings were good, but he made the safest criticism of a picture I ever heard, and one of which no one could complain. He looked at it from every angle, he went down on his knees, putting his face close to the canvas, then he raised himself slowly and said, 'Old chap, *you don't know what you've done!*'

In these Victorian days riches and grandeur were flaunted unashamed. The West End was always crowded with fine carriages, and elegantly dressed men and women with time on their hands. God so ordained it, and the poor more or less accepted their own hard lot. Now and then, however, discontent became evident, and in memoirs of the time which I have read indignation is expressed by the writers because their carriages were stopped by angry crowds from the East End, who had spent a cheery morning breaking shop windows.

My own reactions to the possessors of wealth and privilege were envy and resentment. It angered me that some were able to do as they wished while I could not, as I wished, spend all my time painting. I was cheered, however, when given a commission to make a drawing of a tombstone in Brompton Cemetery, and another, a portrait of a young girl in pen and ink, for which I got three guineas. The tombstone drawing caused me some disappointment. I made it for some people whose children my sister taught. I took it to them in fear and trembling, and was given a good tea. My hostess said that my drawing was 'exquisite, just what she wanted', but she gave me no money for my pains! I have suffered all my life from want of self-confidence, whether a physical condition or the result of my early religious training I do not know, but it has been a handicap to feel, every time I struggled with a drawing or painting, that it was no good. I have often hidden paintings for years, and on finding them again thought them rather good, and sent them to exhibitions. I was reminded of this weakness when looking through an early sketch book. Under a drawing I had made of a horse's head I had written 'Bad' about a dozen times, and my brother Alfred had added 'Hear, hear!'

It was during the winter of 1886 that I first met Wilson Steer. When I was skating on what was known as the Ladies' Pond in Battersea Park with Clare Wright, a student at Kensington, she stopped in front of a tall, thin man, saying, 'Why, there is Mr Steer', and introduced him, and we have been close friends ever since. My memory of the incident is that he was on skates, but he assures me that he was walking on the ice, because he never skated.

Wilson Steer, born 1860 and died 1942, is a regular in these memoirs. He and Gray studied together at the Academie Julian in Paris as well as in London and regularly travelled together on painting expeditions in England and France. In his time in France Steer was greatly influenced by the impressionists and developed this style as his own in England. Later he would develop a more realistic style which was much appreciated. Professor Brown appointed him Professor of Painting at the Slade School of Art. Lord Beaverbrook, in his role as Chairman of the British War Memorials Committee, recruited him during the First World War to paint pictures of the Royal Navy. Gray was an executor of Steer's will.

This same year, Jacomb-Hood invited me to join a class which he held in his studio two evenings a week – luckily on the evenings I did not go to Brown's. These evening were heaven to me. Most of the artists from adjoining studios came, Steer, J.J. Shannon, Stirling Lee, Llewllyn, Davidson Knowles, Frank Short and many others. Several times Whistler looked in, attended by witty Mortimer Menpes. They did not come to work – I never quite knew why they *did* come, unless to pay Jacomb-Hood a friendly visit. Once, when I was drawing next to Steer, he surprised me by saying that he could not see lines in nature, only tones. This was upsetting, because I was being taught by Brown to concentrate on lines! Office work was getting more and more distasteful. I longed to break away, and I persuaded Alfred, when work was slack, to give me Saturdays off to attend the class at Brown's. They were jolly days, and I would not have changed our luncheon at an A.B.C. in Parliament Street for food at the best hotel. Pegram and Russell both came to the Saturday class, indeed, Russell was able to give all his time to study. My Saturdays off continued for some months, but our firm was getting busy, and Alfred told me that I must now be at the office on Saturdays as well. I pleaded with him to let me off, but he was always a stubborn fellow, who thought it weakness to give way on any point. He simply said 'If you don't come to the office on Saturday you may consider yourself dismissed.' This gave me something to think about, for without the office I should have no money. I knew that Mother would let me stay on at home, but it was an awkward situation which gave me a sleepless night. However, by morning I had made up my mind, and off I went to the class. That night, when Alfred and I met, he looked grim. He asked me to his room, and when I had closed the door he said 'You understand that you don't come back to the office again.' A pause, and then he broke down and between his sobs he said, 'Ron, you might have stayed and helped me.' That my leaving proved a good move both for him and for myself shows how little one can for see the result of one's actions.

Here was I, at the age of eighteen, without job or money. Pegram, (who was sixteen) became my saviour. He was at that time retained to draw for the *Pall Mall Gazette* and the weekly *Pall Mall Budget*. W.T. Stead was the editor of these papers, with Charles Morley as art editor.

William Henry Stead, born 1849, pioneered the way for the tabloids of today. As Deputy Editor and then Editor of the *Pall Mall Gazette* (the forerunner of the *London Evening Standard*) from 1883 to 1887, he introduced many innovations such as using illustrations, maps and subheadings to make the articles more interesting. He also started campaigns bringing the dreadful condition of the poor and destitute to the nation's attention and used the interview with great effect. In every way he was a campaigning journalist, whether attacking the Government over General Gordon's death in Khartoum or going after Sir Charles Dilke which led to Dilke's ultimate ruin. After many other journalistic ventures at the age of 63 Stead was sailing to the United States to take part in a Peace Conference when he drowned on the Titanic in 1912. Charles Morley, journalist and editor, he preceded Stead as Editor of the *Pall Mall Gazette*.

Pegram busied about, with the result that I got a few commissions. As I had no experience, want of confidence cramped my style. The zinc block process of reproduction was coming into fashion. This was quicker than the wood block process previously used, and daily papers were for the first time printing pen sketches of topical interest. This meant much work to be done and not many people to do it. New plays, opening ceremonies and all kinds of illustration kept Pegram busy.

Alfred Harmsworth was publishing a new series of magazines to supply a want created by the board schools. Through Pegram's introductions I got work for Harmsworth's paper *Home Chat* and also for a religious publication *The Sunday Companion*. The stories for the latter gave us much amusement. They had the ordinary type of plot, with a touch of religion added by a man employed for that purpose. A sameness ran through all. There was always the lovely daughter of the squire, a villain and a handsome young parson who beat the villain to the post.

Alfred Harmsworth, 1st Viscount Northcliffe, was a giant of the publishing world of late Victorian and Edwardian England. He began his career as the publisher of cheap but appealing periodicals as referenced by Gray in his memoirs. He then went on to build a business empire with publications like the *Daily Mail* and the *Daily Mirror* and by 1914 dominated the popular newspaper business.

Calling on the *Home Chat* Editor one day I was told that Harmsworth wished to see me. The editor warned me that Harmsworth had a way of beginning an interview with a newcomer by staring him out. I went into his room in fear. His manner was Napoleonic. Sure enough, before he spoke he glared. Being forewarned, I returned his glare. When he considered that I was sufficiently pulverised (I was certainly jumpy) he began about the drawings I was doing for his papers. He told me that the old people I drew never looked as though they had been through the wear and tear of life. I replied that I was surprised he thought that, because after my old people had been through the wear and tear of his printing press one might believe anything of them. He rang the bell, and I was politely shown out. That was the only time I ever met this Emperor of the Press, but he bore me no ill will, for I continued to get jobs for his papers.

Mother gave me the use of our old playroom at Danvers Street for a studio, and Pegram worked there with me. We attended dress rehearsals and functions. Though this quick sketching was not at all in my line I floundered on, helped over the more difficult stiles by Pegram. Dress rehearsals were amusing, but dreadfully tiring, for they went on until all hours. I regret not having been at Her Majesty's Theatre with him when he heard the following incident. Beerbohm Tree was dissatisfied with one of Mrs Tree's entrances, and he made her repeat it several times. At last she happened to touch his face with her outstretched hand, and he suddenly lost his temper, 'Blast you, Maud,' he screamed, 'haven't I sat up night after night *trying* to teach you to act, and now you put your thumb in my eye – *blast* you, Maud!'

Beerbohm Tree, 1852 to 1917, was one of the great actor managers of the 19th Century. By 1887 he was manager of the Haymarket Theatre and was famous for the scale of the spectacles he favoured in his productions. His success enabled him to preside over the rebuilding of Her Majesty's (later His Majesty's) Theatre. A mix of Shakespeare, classics and new plays ensured the success of the Theatre and he was often the leading man opposite his wife Helen Holt who appears in the Gray memoirs along with her husband.

Charles Morley commissioned me to make some full page drawings for the *Pall Mall Budget*. Mrs Langtry, Lady Bancroft and Sir George Lewis, the lawyer, were those with whom he arranged sittings. That I was to be introduced to Mrs Langtry was almost too remarkable to be true. She was playing in *As You Like It* at, I think, the Haymarket Theatre, and my instructions were to go to the dress rehearsal and ask for Lionel Monckton. He took me to Mrs Langtry's dressing-room and introduced me. She was busy putting finishing touches to her dress. She must have noticed my miserable nervousness, so to relieve the strain she said, 'Now Mr Gray, buckle my garter.' I nearly fell flat, but I pulled myself together and buckled it. It was a cross garter which came from the shoes to the knee over tights. Her costume being complete, she said that we must watch the next scene from the front, and taking my hand she ran down a flight of stairs, across the stage and through the pass door into the auditorium, pulling me after her, until we reached the stalls where Oscar Wilde and others were sitting. Wilde was evidently an intimate friend. For he called her Lily and she called him Oscar. I had already met him several times at Jacomb-Hood's. My meteoric entrance with Mrs Langtry surprised him, for he said 'What are you doing here, Ronald?' We sat together and watched the act. Mrs Langtry was so exceedingly pleasant and kind that in my youthful ignorance I thought I had made a friend for life, but I was soon to discover my mistake. On this occasion she gave me a photograph of herself, and later I thought it would be a good idea to get her to sign it. One evening I went boldly to the stage door and sent up my name with the request that Mrs Langtry would sign the photograph. I was expecting to be bowed up to her dressing room, but instead I was kept waiting some time in a draughty corridor until her dresser came along with the photograph, signed, but no invitation to 'step this way and see Mrs Langtry'.

Lily Langtry, 1853 to 1929, was a famous society beauty, lover of the Prince of Wales and actress of renown on both sides of the Atlantic. She started acting in 1881 when in need of money, at the suggestion of her great friend Oscar Wilde. This is reflected in the episode narrated by Gray in his memoirs. Gray was susceptible to beautiful women but his shyness and low opinion of himself is reflected in this anecdote and one cannot help feeling slightly sorry for him in this circle of gigantic personalities. Sir George Lewis was lawyer to the Prince of Wales and played an important role in protecting the Prince's reputation when scandal developed linking the Prince in a possible divorce between Lily Langtry and her husband in which he would be cited as a co-respondent.

Lady Bancroft sat to me at her house in Berkeley Square. She was making a reappearance, after some year's absence from the stage, in one of her old successes. She was a plump and pleasant little lady. She said she was glad to be working again, for she loved 'her public'.

Making a drawing of Sir George Lewis was a more business like affair. I was taken to his office by a clerk, who examined my credentials with care. At my entrance Sir George, who was sitting at a large desk, looked up, nodded and said, 'I can spare you a quarter of an hour, so you had better start at once.' Leaning back in his chair he sat perfectly still until the clerk showed that the sitting was ended. He then said, 'Time's up,' and with a thank you and a good day I left.

Pegram was commissioned to make a drawing of Ellen Terry when she was playing Lady Macbeth, and he took me with him to the Lyceum Theatre. We were shown into her dressing room, which was dark except for a strong light over a big looking glass, in front of which Miss Terry was putting finishing touches to her make-up. Surely no woman had ever had greater charm. Her voice was most seductive, and her manner gracious and delightful. We drew hard for about twenty minutes, until with a tap at the door a call boy sang out, 'Your call, Miss Terry.' 'That's all right' she told us, 'you can have a few minutes more.' But very soon there was a louder tap at the door, which opened, and Irving's sonorous voice said 'Your call, Miss Terry.' She jumped up, shook hands with us, gathered together her voluminous skirts, bowed and smiley coquettishly and left us staring at each other, quite overcome! We went dreamily from the theatre and drank whisky and soda at a nearby public house.

Ellen Terry, 1827 to 1928, was an actress of great renown on both sides of the Atlantic. For 6 years she lived with the architect and theatrical designer Edward Godwin (see details earlier) who was the father of her three children. Returning to the stage in 1878 she joined Henry Irving at the Lyceum Theatre and they created one of the most famous theatrical partnerships in the history of the English theatre. She played Lady Macbeth in 1888 which probably gives a reliable date for these stories.

The next time we were at the Lyceum Theatre was for a dress rehearsal of *Henry VIII*.

Aubrey Beardsley was one of the many artists present. Most men in those days wore silk hats and frock coats, artists included, but Beardsley was really exquisite. He was arrayed in a light grey frock coat, grey top hat and lemon coloured gloves. (There is a slight painting of him in this kit by Sickert, which I last saw at the Tate Gallery.) He looked bored and moved wearily. The result of this visit was an unconventional portrait of Irving, much like a design for a stained glass window. I forget in which journal it appeared.

*Ronald Gray as a young man at about this time from the author's collection.*

One night we went to Covent Garden to make drawings of Jean de Reszke. He and his brother Edouard were then at the height of their fame. Pegram and I stood in the wings whilst the brothers were taking call after call from the excited, cheering audience. When the curtain finally fell we were instructed to follow Jean – and he took some following. We dashed after him through a door which opened into a long corridor filled with ballet girls returning to their dressing-rooms, de Reszke, singing the chorus of a popular song – 'Ri tiddleo i ti' – at the top of his enormous voice, seized and danced round with one girl after another until he came to the stairs which led to his dressing-room. He rushed up there, Pegram and I panting after him. His first words to his dresser were 'Une cigarette, s'il vous plait,' and having lit it he turned to us with a bow, saying 'A votre service Messieurs.' He could talk no English nor we French, so our conversation was limited.

Jean de Reszke, 1850 to 1925, was born in Warsaw. Initially singing as a baritone he became famous as a tenor after further study. In 1888 he sang his first season at Covent Garden and became associated with French and Wagnerian operatic genres there for many years. It looks increasingly clear that these meetings were all in 1888 when Gray was only 20 years old.

At the first night of a play at Drury Lane, Russell and I saw an off stage drama which was premeditated though unrehearsed. We were at the back of the dress circle. In the front row Whistler was sitting with Charles Brookfield, a well-known actor of the time. During the first entr'acte we all trooped out to smoke and stretch our legs. I noticed that Whistler, followed by Brookfield, appeared to be looking for someone. Suddenly they found him. He was Augustus Moore, editor of a paper called *The Hawk*, and a brother of George Moore, the writer. Whistler walked quickly up to him and gave him three sharp blows with his cane, shouting 'Hawk, Hawk, Hawk,' with each blow. The crowd rushed towards them, and Whistler was dragged back by several men, his top hat falling to the floor. I heard the manager saying that 'he should remember that he was a guest in Augustus Harris' house, and that it was bad manners to attack another guest,' etc, etc. During his harangue Brookfield was leading Whistler, rather bedraggled, out of the theatre. In the meantime another man, smart and tough looking, had approached Moore, and we heard him saying that he had been several times to *The Hawk* office without having the pleasure of seeing him, but now he would like to know what Moore meant by allowing that disgraceful libel on his wife to appear in *The Hawk*. Without waiting for a reply he aimed a hard punch which caught Moore fairly on the face. Moore staggered back, shouting 'How many more of them?' Again a crowd rushed between them, and if they had not restrained the tough attacker I imagine that Moore would have been laid out.

Not long after this Pegram and I were at a first night at the Lyceum. During the performance, high words from the stalls disturbed the audience, then a loud bang, caused by one gentleman bashing another on the head with his opera hat. These war like disturbances at theatres suggested a drawing which appeared soon after in *Punch*. It represented a man in full armour, complete with vizer and plumes, saying good-night to his wife, the caption read:

Wife 'Where on earth are you going, darling, in that absurd get-up?'

Husband 'Only to a first night at the – Theatre.'

One of the great changes since I was young is in dress. During the '80s and '90s – indeed, almost until the Great War, most men wore silk hats with cut away or frock coats when about town. We poor, untutored young men who made the illustrations were evidently considered ignorant of social conventions, for when Cust was Editor of the *Pall Mall Budget* he caused a notice to be hung in the waiting room which read, 'will artists please remember that gentlemen do *not* wear tall hats when in the country.'

Another change is in the method of running journals and weekly illustrated papers. High finance was not at that time interested. The papers reflected the personality of the editors rather than of the owner. Our relations with editors were pleasant and free-and-easy. I cannot remember that there were agencies then who employed clever young people to make drawings at so much a week, working long hours in agency studios.

The *Daily Graphic* was, I think, the first daily paper to print drawings of current events. The process block which was replacing the wood engraving made it possible to reproduce and print a drawing quickly. This paper was a pleasant, bright one as I remember it, and the advertisement manager was less in evidence than he is nowadays. Reginald Cleaver was the star turn, and he went everywhere and drew almost everything. He told us of his discomfiture when at Windsor to sketch a Royal Wedding when, rigged up in court dress and sword, he had to stand on a small platform, head and shoulders above the guests, to do his work. His output for a time was enormous, indeed, he knocked himself up by overwork and afterwards spent much time abroad. Hartrick and E.J. Sullivan both worked for this paper, and later, when he returned from Australia, Phil May was for a time on the staff. At a function at the Crystal Palace we first met F.H. Townsend. I had seen much of his clever work in various weeklies, and was surprised to find him so young. He worked principally for *The Ladies' Pictorial*, a paper which much enjoyed a large circulation. Later he married my sister Helen.

There is a drawing by Reginald Cleaver of the wedding between Princess Marie Louise of Schleswig-Holstein and Prince Aribert of Anhalt at St George's Windsor on July 6 1891 in The Royal Collection and may be the one referred to in the text. The *Daily Graphic* was first published in 1890 and was the daily paper of the long-established *Weekly Graphic*. The latter had been created to take on the famous *Illustrated London News* at which it had proved successful. Both papers were innovative in their use of illustrations and the new printing processes of the day as Gray states. F. H. Townsend married Ronald Gray's sister Helen on June 4, 1892. So there were now three artists in the family, Pegram, married to Jane, Townsend married to Helen and Ronald.

We continued to attend the evening classes at Westminster, and Tonks attached himself more firmly to our group. When he left the London Hospital he was appointed house surgeon to the Royal Free Hospital. His free afternoons he liked to spend with me in Chelsea. He had no other artist acquaintances, and enjoyed going with me to different studios. Walking with him one day in Manresa Road we met Steer, and I introduced them. They were a couple of tall, thin young men of about the same age –older than myself by seven years. Tonks continued a devoted friend and admirer of Steer for the rest of his life.

Tonks was in a different category from anyone I had known. He had a strength of purpose greater than most people, and was very ambitious. Even in those days he mapped out his day almost to the minute, and continued to do so until the end. He wished to be efficient as a horseman, and later as a fencer. He and I took a recruit's riding course at the Knightsbridge Barracks, and one summer, when Pegram and I were staying at his home in Warwickshire he bought a horse, a brute which ran away with me when I first rode it, and nearly killed Tonks when he tried to follow the hounds. He was a delightful companion, something amusing always happened when one was with him. Soon after his appointment to the Royal Free Hospital he invited me to dine. He sat at the head of the table with assistant doctors around him. He was gay and in his best form whilst carving the chicken, then came a knock at the door, and a porter entered. 'Please, sir' he said, 'there's a man at the door with a cut 'ead.' Tonks, somewhat dampened, told him to go down and cut the patient's hair off. The porter replied, 'Please sir, I 'ave cut 'is 'air off.' Tonks sprang up, plunged the fork into the table and shouted 'Damn the bloody man!' But after attending to him he returned, and calmly went on with his dinner. One day an urgent telegram summoned me to the Royal Free Hospital. When I arrived Tonks took me quickly to his room, shut the door and, walking mysteriously towards me and pointing at himself said 'I've been called a murderer. *Me* – a *murderer!*' The accusation was more than he could bear.

During the summer of 1889 Tonks joined Pegram, Townsend, Russell and myself at Marlow. That summer in retrospect had more sunny days than wet, indeed, my memory is that they were all sunny days. Like happy school boys we swam in the river each morning before breakfast. Between breakfast and lunch we worked at our illustrating, the afternoons we spent on the river, rowing to Hurley for tea on the lock, and making sketches of any country children we could persuade to sit. There was one charming little girl who used to hover round, watching us. I was much taken with her, and spent a long time trying to coax her to come nearer. At last she came confidingly up to me, and nestling against my shoulder she whispered coyly in my ear, 'I've got the measles!' This little scene later appeared in *Punch*.

Often some of us hired horses and rode to Cookham or Marlow Common.

K.J. Gregory and Clausen were living at Cookham Dene, and Gregory, who was fond of tennis, invited us to play. At that time I admired him as a painter. He painted river scenes, charming girls in punts and canoes. Whether it was that I reacted to the beauty of the pictures or the allure of his pretty models I do not remember; anyway, I felt proud to be his friend.

Then there was the weekly excitement when the lovely 'Maud' came to sit. Maud was a really beautiful girl, and we looked forward eagerly to her visits. Each of us wished to please her, I tried so hard, but without success. Townsend and I on fine mornings, used to box on the lawn, and Maud usually arrived by an early train and watched us. It was disheartening to hear her shout to us to stop when I hit Townsend and applaud when he hit me. Maud married a fat watercolour painter who wore lemon coloured gloves. When tired of him she ran off to Venice with a well-known young man who, Whistler said, was 'living in pawn' there.

In the late '80s Chelsea was full of enthusiastic young artists. A revivalist feeling was in the air, much as there was among young writers. Any old workshop was turned into a studio, and rents were low, £40 a year was considered extremely expensive. Bordering the garden where now stand the public library and L.C.C. technical school was a ramshackle row of old buildings. These were used by Stirling Lee and La Thangue and, when they came up from the country, by George Clausen and James Charles. It is amusing to remember that Clausen (now Sir George Clausen) in those days tied his trousers below the knee, like a navvy, and asked to be addressed as 'Citizen Clausen'.

*(In the margin of the manuscript, D.S. MacColl has written, 'He denied all this to me' D.S.M. Under this is pencilled, 'But it was true all the same' R.G)*

On the other side of the road, Trafalgar and Wentworth studios had already been built. Among the artists working there were Wilson Steer, Brangwin, J.J. Shannon, Jacomb-Hood, W. Llewellyn (later President of the Royal Academy), Alfred Hartley, Frank Short, Markham Skipworth, Pomerey and Trood. When visiting London from Italy, Harvard Thomas also worked in one of these studios. Walter Russell, Fred Pegram and I took one of the glass shacks in Glebe Place, opposite Bramerton Street, and had as neighbours A.J. Walker and Conrad Dressler. Carlyle Studios in King's Road were much as they are today. Fred Brown built a studio in the garden of his house in Natherton Grove, and later moved to Richmond. Many young men were working in rooms.

Among this extraordinary collection of artists and sculptors are five Associates of the Royal Academy and five Members. In addition, one was awarded the Order of Merit and three were knighted. W. Llewellyn served as President of the Royal Academy and is buried in Westminster Abbey.

At that time some of the artists in Chelsea living south of Fulham Road were members of the Royal Academy – indeed, the feeling was pretty hot against that institution. La Thangue and Clausen usually had their pictures chucked, and most other Chelsea painters were treated in the same way. La Thangue called and addressed meetings in their studios to demand the reform of the Royal Academy. During one of these meetings, which was held on the same night as the banquet at Burlington House, an excitable painter named Britten, standing on his chair and putting one foot on the table, gave a great harangue and finished by calling on the meeting to follow him 'as one man' to the Academy and threaten to overturn the dinner tables unless a promise was given to treat the younger men more generously. This suggestion was not greeted with enthusiasm, and the meeting broke up mildly. It was at one of the meetings that someone suggested the holding of an opposition exhibition, and thus the New English Art Club was born.

Chelsea was buzzing with vitality. Most of the painters back from Paris were under the influence of Bastien Lepage, and the cry was 'back to nature' as opposed to the studio picture. Work of the period shows also the influence of Whistler – the full length, low toned portrait painted on a narrow canvas was in evidence at exhibitions. The first picture I remember seeing in Wilson Steer's studio was a full length Whistlerian portrait of Jennie Lee, the actress. La Thangue and Clausen were both Bastien Lepage whole hoggers; they thought it was sinful to put anything into a picture which was not painted direct from nature. The following story, told me by Marchant of the Goupil Gallery, shows that Whistler also held this view. One morning Marchant called on Whistler at his studio in Carlotte Street. Whistler at once asked if Marchant would pose for a few minutes; he only wished, he said, to get the highlight on the boot of a full length portrait of a man. Marchant took the pose, expecting to be free in ten minutes, but Whistler worked on, hour after hour, painting and wiping it out. After a pleasant luncheon poor Marchant was posed again, and it was fully six hours before Whistler was satisfied with the highlight on that boot!

> Bastion Lepage was born in 1848 and died in 1884. In his short life he took impressionism and added a natural realism that increased its general appeal. He was also a noted portrait painter and one he did of the Prince of Wales was exhibited at the Royal Academy in 1880. His love of painting outdoors also influenced the young English artists as these memoirs demonstrate.

J.J. Shannon was at the beginning of his very successful career. He was extremely good looking, and before he left Manresa Road for the luxurious house he built in Holland Road he had made a reputation as a painter of pretty women. In later years Shannon and his wife gave delightful dinner parties and dances, which I always felt it a privilege to attend.

W. Llewellyn was also making a success with portraits of women. At that time I am sure neither he himself nor any of his friends thought he was to be President of the Royal Academy.

Of all the painters in Manresa Road, Jacomb-Hood was looked on as the most promising. Whistler seemed to think so, and was often at his studio. He had been one of Legros' favourite pupils at the Slade School, and I often came across his photograph in papers and read glowing accounts of his powers. It was at his studio that I first met Oscar Wilde and W.H. Hudson, the South American traveller and writer. The latter was a pleasant, bearded man.

> W.H. Hudson was born in Argentina in 1841. He settled in England in 1874 and became a naturalised citizen in 1889. He built a reputation as a naturalist, ornithologist and author. In 1910 he published *A Shepherds Story*, a rare appreciation of the life of those who lived and worked on the land in 19th Century rural Britain. James Rebanks acknowledges this as the inspiration of his book of the same title, published in 2015.

Brangwyn, who usually dressed as a sailor, had come from Cornwall with some charming small pictures of boats and fishermen, which he was selling very cheap. He and another painter of nautical subjects, Ernest Dade, (an engaging person) were noted for their knowledge of bargee language, of which they gave a sample one evening at Hood's when they were asked to have a word battle.

I knew Oscar Wilde as an acquaintance for many years, and my experience of him was a happy one. I never heard him say or saw him do anything in bad taste. He was always charming to Pegram and me. We were surprised that this well-known man took any notice of two unknown boys, and once when we went to tea with him in Tite Street we were intrigued by our fellow guests. They were good looking young men, foppishly dressed, self-confident and talkative. Pegram and I felt out of place, and sat dumbly in a corner. Once, when my brother and I were at Paddington Station, Wilde was waiting for the Oxford train and talking to a very handsome, elegant young man, who was dressed in the usual costume of smart young men of the time, grey frock coat and tall hat. Wilde came across and talked pleasantly, he asked whether my brother and I had seen his play, *Lady Windermere's Fan*, which was then running. I regretted that we had not. 'Then I will send you tickets' he said, and in a few days two stalls came, with a charming note which unfortunately I have lost. I asked the name of his good looking friend and he told me it was Lord Alfred Douglas.

Sophisticated young people of the present time would find it difficult to believe that anyone of over twenty could be surprised at Oscar Wilde's downfall. I can only say that I was both surprised and shocked, knowing nothing about homosexuality.

Another writer of a different stamp from Wilde was in Chelsea in those days. Morley Roberts. He had lived as a cowboy in America, and once figured in a knife and flowerpot throwing incident, which happened at a local restaurant much patronised by painters before the formation of the Chelsea Arts Club. I saw a good deal of him because he lodged in Danvers Street, near our house, which he called 'The Moated Grange'. He said he was writing a story in which it played a part, but I never knew whether it materialised. There was something very human and loveable about him. I have heard that he was a good writer, though I never read any of his books.

Stirling Lee, the sculptor, was a saint if ever there was one. He wanted everyone to be happy. He collected down and outs, and was forever helping lame girls over high stiles. Before coming to Chelsea he had worked for some time in Paris. He was deeply religious, but unlike most religious men, he enjoyed light-hearted gaiety. He was responsible for the Mardi Gras dance which was held each year at the studios in Manresa Road, where a throng of be-wigged and costumed people danced the night through. I was about eighteen when first invited, and I remember the thrilling moment when I entered a brightly lit studio and saw my friends dancing with lovely girls. Far too nervous to ask any of them to dance, I watched with envy. Jacomb-Hood took pity on me and told his beautiful model, Nelly, to give me a dance; and next morning gloom gripped me because the glorious evening was past.

Stirling Lee was given the commission for panels to be placed on Liverpool Town Hall. The many years he spent executing the job were made miserable by the interference of the Town Council – the usual quarrel between the artist and the business man. Lee made a bust of Wilson Steer, which Steer bequeathed to the Tate Gallery, but when Steer died, the bust was refused by the Tate Gallery committee.

'Show Sunday' was a great event in those days. Chelsea would be full of smartly dressed people visiting the studios, and I have seen Manresa Road blocked by the throng of carriages. Society seemed to take an interest in pictures, or in the men who painted them. Now 'Show Sunday' is hardly noticed, and very few men are at home to their friends on that day. The change was referred to by a Chelsea milkman with whom I spoke lately. 'When I was a boy' he said, 'Father used to sell about twenty quarts of cream in Manresa Road alone, for Picture Sunday. Now I don't sell a pint!'

In spite of the worry my illustrations caused me, the life I now led was happy compared with the drudgery of office work. The companionship of young men with similar aims was a joy, but I was troubled by the thought that I was not learning to paint. During the autumn of 1890 we decided to go to Paris for the winter, and work at Julian's – the aim of most students at that time. We talked the scheme over at Brown's, and Pegram, Walter Russell, Salmon, Swanwick and I decided to take the plunge.

One evening, arriving home late, I found my brother Alfred waiting for me. We stood in his bedroom by the fireplace over which a gas jet threw a flickering light onto his pale face. He told me a disjointed tale of how he had gone into the country on business, and how suddenly his memory had failed and his mind become a blank. He had no idea what had happened, or of how he had got home. He sobbed as he told me. I had to undress him and get him into bed. For months I had felt elated and happy, but all through life I have found that tragedy waits on happiness. That night I did not get much sleep for wondering what was best to be done. In the morning I told Mother that Alfred was not well and that I would take up breakfast. I feared to tell her the whole story. I took him to see Dr Rouse at St. George's Hospital – the father of a school friend. He made a careful examination and advised me to take Alfred at once to Brighton for a complete rest. A tall order, for it meant both of us giving up our work. However, Alfred's manager said that he could carry on the business without him, so away we went to Brighton that same afternoon.

I did not know where to stay, but a kind fate and a railway guide took us to an address where the proprietress proved to be understanding and kind. It was in the old part of the town, near the house where we had lived when we all stayed in Brighton many years before.

The first night we had dinner in our rooms, but the next day I made my invalid take meals with me downstairs. For the first week these meals were an ordeal; not knowing that he was ill, people would talk to Alfred and ask him questions he did not understand and could not answer, which meant that I had to be alert to answer for him. I saved my reason by a flirtation with a girl staying in the house – in many tragic episodes I have found a love affair a great solace. Luckily the weather was fine, the sun and sea air were taking effect, and I could see that my brother was better. He even spoke now and then to our fellow boarders. Pegram, with unfailing kindness, came for long week-ends. We hired horses and took our invalid to gallop on the downs. He enjoyed these rides immensely, and they certainly did him good. We stayed in Brighton for a month. Alfred was better, but not yet fit for work, so as I was due to meet the others in Paris, there was nothing for it but to take him along too. A few days at home followed, with visits to the doctor, who told me that Alfred would get quite well if he continued to rest and be amused. Neither of us had been abroad before, and this trip to the unknown was looked on as a great adventure.

# Chapter 4

# La Vie in Paris

It was freezing hard the day we left for Paris. The ship rolled horribly during the long crossing from Newhaven to Dieppe, but we were not seasick. At Dieppe the quays were covered with ice, and we slithered across to the refreshment room for welcome hot coffee and rolls. Porters in blue smocks seemed very foreign and odd to me, though I must have appeared the same to one of them when I tried to ask the way to the lavatory. Not knowing a word of French, I was reduced to dumb show in my effort to explain our pressing need. He was kind, and watched my actions with patient interest, but with no understanding; for he looked bewildered, and after some minutes left us with a gesture of despair.

I remember arriving at our apartment in the Boulevard des Batignolles and our welcome from a pleasant, plump little French lady to whom I had been recommended by a fellow student. It was a well-kept and well furnished apartment in a large block built, in the old fashioned French way, round a courtyard which had large gates giving onto the boulevard. A grumpy old concierge and his wife answered the bell when they felt like it. Madame was a widow with three sons, two living at home and one in the army. Boarding with her was an American Lady and her small son. This lady was very plain, but had a soft southern voice. She was studying music, and played the piano charmingly. She was a strange creature, and the thick layer of white powder with which she covered her face gave her an odd look. Not long after our meeting she told me of a romantic episode on her journey from America; though it was difficult to follow the whole story, I gathered that the ship's doctor had been attending her for some complaint, and she coyly told me that the night before the ship arrived in France this doctor bit her neck, and she wished to know if I thought this a sign of affection. Being inexperienced, I really did not know what to answer, but looking at her, I thought it a case of blind affection, and told her so. She was pleased with this reply, and I thought I had got out of the difficulty pretty well.

My four friends had established themselves in a barn of a studio in a cul-de-sac off the Rue Lepic, not far from our lodgings. (When in Paris a few years ago I found that this cul-de-sac had been roofed over and was being used as a garage.) The Rue Lepic runs up the hill behind the Moulin Rouge, through the somewhat dilapidated district called Montmartre, not then full of night clubs or exploited as of late years.

The Moulin Rouge was at the height of its popularity, one could dance and watch dancing for a small payment. We all enrolled as students at Julian's studio in the Rue Constans in the same neighbourhood. The class started at eight am and finished at noon. Madame gave me coffee and rolls at seven thirty, and I got back to dejeuner at twelve thirty. My brother rested in bed all the morning, and we spent the afternoons together, exploring Paris. It was a thrilling experience, seeing places about which I had read and heard so much. Paris then was one of the few places which came up to one's expectations; it had not been exploited by those sinister foreigners who vulgarise every town in which they settle. Great placards were not then put across the houses in the Place de l'Opera, advertising wares as one sees of later years, and the shops were more personal – not so much chromium plate. During one of our walks we unexpectedly met Arthur Blunt, a son of the rector of Chelsea, and the outcome of this meeting was that he joined our party in the studio off the Rue Lepic, and another bed was hired, making five in a row – luckily the studio was big.

The professors under whom we worked at Julian's were Flameng and Ferrier. The former, was a successful portrait painter, dressed immaculately; the latter was older, and not so smart. A student who spoke French acted as interpreter for the professors when criticising the work of the English and American students. I doubt if I learnt as much in Paris as at Brown's in London, but I was thrilled by the new experience. To keep me fixed on earth was the worry of my brother's illness, for although better, he was far from normal. One day we met Harry Irving, son of Sir Henry, with whom and his brother Lawrence, we had acted in amateur theatricals a short time before Alfred's illness. Harry was a good looking edition of his father, and full of energy and fun. He was so beautifully dressed when we met in Paris, silk hat and cut away coat, gloves and stick that we felt conscious of our shortcomings in that line.

Gabriel Ferrier and Francois Flameng were lecturers at the Academie Julian. Both were noted portrait painters and Flameng had commissions in Paris, London and New York. His portrait of Queen Alexandra hangs in the White drawing room at Buckingham Palace. He designed the first bank notes in France and was a notable war artist in the First World War.

I suppose that we did much the same as most young men who went abroad to study. In retrospect I feel that our behaviour was not perfect, for some of the English students were assertive and arrogant; quite rightly, this attitude annoyed the French students, and in several ways they showed that they did not love us. One way was their criticism of our accent, when in the studio, we called to the garcon for the bread which was used for rubbing out purposes. One of us would call, 'Du pain, s'il vous plait' and this simple request would call forth shouts of 'du pang, du pong, du pint, du peng, du pung' from the French fellows. Arthur Blunt was touchy about his accent, he thought it good. One morning he called for 'du pain' and an unfortunate Frenchman, fat and middle-aged, sitting on a low donkey just in front, turned his bald hear and, looking up at Blunt, started the usual 'ping, pong' business. This was more than Arthur could bear, he took up his easel and bashed his critic on the crown, knocking him to the floor. Blunt, calm and unperturbed amid the hubbub which followed, slowly collected his things and went on with his work. He was not again bothered by this form of criticism.

Anyone reading a paper during a rest was as likely as not to find himself enveloped in flames, because there was always someone who could not resist putting a match to it. Anyone entering the studio with his hat on was greeted with shouts of 'chapeau' and unless he reacted quickly the hat would be torn from his head.

An attractive model inspired tender feelings in the heart of an English boy. He sometimes brought her chocolates or a bunch of violets. One morning he presented his violets after she had undressed and stepped onto the throne. She gracefully took and kissed them, and placed them where I had never seen a posy before. The class showed approval of this charming act with a round of applause, and our work proceeded. Some wag told this model that the English boy was the son of a duke, and fabulously rich. Is there a girl in the world that would not be interested in the son of a fabulously rich duke? This girl certainly was, and my friend was astonished at his many successes, as were all who did not know the reason. Walking to the studio one morning this young man confided in me that he was afraid he would have to break this pleasing friendship, for he found it too expensive; indeed, he told me that he had spent the whole of his month's allowance on a petticoat.

It was at Julian's studio that I first met Will Rothenstein. He gives a description of the studio in his first book. I do not at all mind that he put me among the also runs, but I was a little hurt that he did not spell my name correctly. At that time 'probity' had not crippled his style as a man about town. The tales he told of his escapades filled me with envy. He looked so young and small that one did not suspect so much vitality and intelligence. He was apparently on terms of intimacy with most well-known people in Paris; I was jealous, for I knew no-one there at that time. It was at Rothenstein's studio that I met Conder, who was to become so well-known in London. He struck me as looking a weary young man with an interesting face. I was to see a great deal of both Rothenstein and Conder in Chelsea during the following years.

William Rothenstein, 1872 to 1945 is best known as a portraitist, writer on art and war artist in both World Wars. He was at the Academie Julian in 1889 to 1893 and shared a studio in Montmartre with Charles Conder. Rothenstein was knighted in 1931.

Charles Conder, 1868 to 1909, was born in England and sent by his Father to Sydney Australia in 1884 to work with his engineer Uncle. Two years later he left to study painting and in 1888 moved to Melbourne where he became involved with the early days of the Heidelberg school of artists.

The whole of that winter the cold was intense. The Seine was frozen over the for the first time since 1870. Harold Swanwick had a curious desire to walk across it on the ice, but the gendarmes seemed against it. He spent much time hanging about the river banks looking for an opportunity, and made several abortive attempts. At last he did get across, but he had to run pretty fast, with gendarmes in pursuit.

One of the joys of winter was skating in the Bois. The frozen lake, dotted with happy people on skates, and burning braziers were one could warm one's hands, reminded me of Dutch pictures of winter subjects. Then there was the steaming hot 'Grog Americain' made of rum, which we drank before coming home, and the foolish game we invented for the return journey. This game could be played on snowy days, when sounds were muffled, for the idea was, after five or six of us had crowded into a cab, to try to get out of it as it went along, leaving the loser to pay the fare.

Walking to the studio in the morning was a delight. Paris awakened early, midinettes (*shopgirls*) hurried along to work, men in blue aprons flushed the gutters with streams of water from long, snake like hoses, and shutters were removed from shops. The air was keen and invigorating, and how gay and bright it all was! Paris was free from the gloom and sadness of yellow fog; perhaps that is why French people begin the day earlier than the English. I can't imagine English students getting to London studios as eight o'clock in the morning, and yet we found this no hardship in Paris.

My brother and I continued our explorations during the afternoons. The Louvre and the Luxembourg thrilled but rather frightened me, for it seemed futile to try to paint when so many masterpieces existed. Students react differently to masterpieces, some set their teeth and determine to do better – which is all right

47

when one is built that way. I was not.

The gaunt ruin of the Hotel de Ville, wrecked in the communal rising after the Franco-Prussian war of 1870, brought a memory of our Chelsea nursery when we were small children, for we were made to pick pieces of silk for making soft pads for the French wounded.

Mrs Georgina Weldon, an old friend who was living at Gisors, came to stay in Paris while we were there. I first remember her when as a small boy I came down to breakfast and saw a beautiful lady sitting by the fire. Helped by my sister Elizabeth she had that morning escaped by the back door from her house in Tavistock Square whilst men from a lunatic asylum were knocking at the front. She was a clever, headstrong, very beautiful woman, with whom nevertheless it was possibly difficult to live. She was a fine singer, and devoted herself to music and good works, filling her house with orphan children whom she trained as a choir. Her husband, Captain Weldon, got tired of these activities, with the result that he persuaded two doctors to give a certificate of insanity. Then the fun began. She brought actions against the doctors, against the newspapers for libel, and against anyone who had had anything to do with business. She conducted her cases herself and won most of them, and became known as the 'modern Portia'. When someone brought an action against her for libel, and won damages, she refused to pay, saying that she would rather go to prison, and to Holloway she went. When she was released she was met by a triumphal procession. 'Women's Rights' enthusiasts, women's societies, and numbers of strange people who are against everything, met their heroine at the jail gates and dragged her carriage back to Tavistock Square. To gain money for carrying on her law cases she sang religious songs at the Pavilion music hall, which then occupied the site of the present Pavilion Cinema, Piccadilly Circus. Her success was remarkable. I have been told that to get a seat on the nights she sang one had to queue for several hours. In her youth she was very popular in Victorian society. She was much painted and sculpted, the best portrait of her being by Watts. Charles Gounod lived with the Weldons during the years he spent in England, and the songs and music he wrote at that time were dedicated to her.

When she came to see us in Paris she was still beautiful, though she had grown rather stout. She knew many people, and took me to several studios of artists whose names I forgot. From the grandeur of their surroundings I concluded that they were popular, for their studios were very different from those I knew in Chelsea. She also introduced me to the director of the Opera, whose name I think was Galliard. Mrs Weldon told him that I was in Paris with several friends, studying at Julian's. He asked for my address, and several times sent me eight tickets for different operas. Each ticket was always made out to 'Monsieur George'. Mrs Weldon told him that we were not called George, but he said, 'Nonsense, every Englishman is called George!'

The eight Georges were delighted when he sent tickets for the Opera Ball. I had read in novels of these gala nights at the Opera House, and expected – I don't quite know what – a brilliantly lit heaven perhaps. My first impression was that the auditorium was dimly lit, that there were a great number of black coated men and not nearly enough gaily dressed angels, indeed, the scene was rather dingy. We wandered more as spectators than participants. On the dancing floor crowds of laughing, shouting people surrounded girls dancing pas seuls. I found myself in a group around 'La Goulue', then the most famous dancer in Paris. Her technique looked simple, though was possibly difficult to do well. Poised on the toes of one foot and holding her other leg as high as human anatomy would allow, she turned slowly round, and I gathered that the interest of this came from the fact that she wore lace drawers. (Not long ago I heard that 'La Goulue' had died in a caravan, very old and poor.)

*Louise Weber, nicknamed La Goulue for her habit of downing the drinks of patrons as she danced past their tables, was a famous can-can dancer at the Moulin-Rouge in Montmartre in the early 1890s. While there at the height of her fame she was a favourite subject for Toulouse-Lautrec. Public domain.*

I had no one with whom to dance and feared to approach a partner, it might cost money which I had not got. No partners approached me. I realised that night, as I have many times since, that thoroughly to enjoy a party of that kind one should be slightly drunk, then the silliest joke seems a gem of wit.

Our time in Paris was drawing to a close. My brother was better, though not yet well enough for work. Something would have to be done, but what? The pleasure of getting home was overshadowed by a mountain of difficulty – what to do to get our invalid well. He longed for a sea voyage, so we therefore took that line of inquiry.

Pleasure cruises were in their infancy, but an Orient Company's advertisement told us that their S.S. *Garonne* was going on a twelve week cruise in the Mediterranean. This would be perfect if we could find the money. The cheapest fare was a hundred pounds, between all of us we might manage that, but he could not go alone, and therefore I should have to go with him but until I had called on the editor of a paper for which I worked, *The Pictorial World*, I had not an idea how I was to find my fare. I told this editor my difficulty. He was most sympathetic and promised to help, with the result that the Orient Line sent me a ticket for the voyage. Instead of cash payment I was to make sketches of places and events, which were to be published in *The Pictorial World*, to advertise the Orient Company's cruises. What an excitement! It was strange how this sad illness of my brother's was causing me to gain new and interesting experiences. A voyage to the Holy Land was indeed a widening of our horizon. We only had a few days to make arrangements. Our poverty prevented our getting suitable clothes for quick changes of climate, but that did not worry us for long, there was so much to which we could look forward.

# Chapter 5

# Fresh Fields

I felt rather superior when I returned from my winter in Paris, but the idea of this voyage to the Holy Land eclipsed all that – it was incredible! It seemed more dreamlike than real to find myself sitting next to my brother on the deck of the S.S. *Garonne* holding tight to the back of a seat while the ship rolled angrily in a nasty channel sea. At each roll I held my breath –would she be able to right herself? It got dark, and still we sat there. It was cold, but hours passed before we gathered courage to go to our cabin. In my travel dreams there had been no unpleasant moments, this first night of cold, damp depression was unexpected. In contrast to the cold and foggy England we had left, the sunshine which greeted us in Madeira, the scent of flowers, the sight of the fruit, and the gay dress of the natives who rowed us out to the ship, raised everyone's spirits. After we left Madeira the passengers became beings with personalities, and gradually, like attracted like. We had the excitement of trips ashore, Morocco, Spain, Monte Carlo and Cyprus on our way to Palestine. Whether it is usual for strong winds to blow at Cadiz I do not know, but the day we landed a gale rushed through the town, and whilst we sheltered behind dock buildings we saw a cab, horse and driver blown completely over. It was evening before it abated and we were able to return to the ship.

The smell and sight of white robed Arabs at Tangier convinced us two Cockneys that we were really abroad, and what a thrill we had later when exploring Monte Carlo. Here, new passengers joined the ship. Among them I noticed a small, elderly man with a well-trimmed white beard. He was neat and precise. We saw little of him, but sometimes he would ask me to show him my drawings, and that ended it. I should have thought then that he was one of the most unlikely people with whom I should become friends. The captain was responsible for much of our enjoyment. I always remember Captain Tuke with affection; he looked after my brother and myself like a kind father. He was a cousin of Tuke the painter, with whom later I became acquainted.

Foolish self-consciousness has always made me shy of drawing or painting in public, and we were in the Mediterranean before I plucked up courage to start. Once started I drew everyone and everything in the ship. I had no difficulty in getting people to sit and I made portraits of most of the passengers and officers.

It was March when we arrived in Palestine. I found it difficult to realise that it was I, myself, walking in places of which I had read in the Bible. In 1891 things had not changed much since Biblical times; no railways had been bult to hurry thing up; at Beirut, Arabs in blue garments ploughed between mulberry trees with wooden ploughs, and there were many camels, mules and donkeys. From Beirut most of the passengers went on excursions to Damascus. These excursions were expensive and so were not for us, though we were determined to do the trip to Jerusalem from Jaffa. It would be silly to visit Palestine and not see Jerusalem. We had about a week in Beirut. The ship, with most of the passengers away, made a pleasant hotel. When the captain went on an excursion he took us with him. Omar, a young dragoman who spoke English, was most helpful. We could get good horses, he said, if we cared to ride at any time. We did care, so he arranged to have horses on the quay at a certain hour.

Approaching the quay in the ship's pinnace to keep this appointment, we saw a large crowd of Arabs surging backwards and forwards. My enthusiasm waned, for the horses we were to ride were the cause of this excitement – two snorting stallions! We were for it! It took at least five minutes for willing hands to get Alfred mounted, and at once his horse dashed at full gallop down a crowded, narrow street, and that was the last I saw of him for a couple of hours. Now came my turn. Men were hanging onto the bridle of my horse, whilst the beast pawed the air and kicked out behind. Directly my feet were in the stirrups I also went off at full gallop. I had no control over the horse, but luckily turned onto the road which led up a long hill to Mount Lebanon. At last the pace slackened and I was able to turn back towards the town, where I met Omar, who was coming to look for me. He had heard that Alfred was last seen going flat out for Lebanon. Together we set off to find him, and when we did both he and his horse looked tired. Omar explained that these horses were really good horses, but that the crowd on the quay had excited them. It was only luck that no one was killed.

Riding back through Beirut in the cool of the evening we were intrigued to hear screams and pistol shots when passing the end of a narrow street. Omar said that the commotion was not unusual, it was only a fight between Jews and Arabs!

At Omar's invitation we went with him to see a prison. It was a large, dark room in which were dozing prisoners and a Turkish soldier. We were surprised to see, reclining on a couch, smoking a cigarette and clothed in a clean white garment, an elegant young man who nodded and smiled pleasantly. What on earth was he doing in that milieu of cut-throats? Apparently he was a bit of a cut-throat himself, he had committed murder, they told us, but being rich, would soon go free.

I was surprised that everyone smoked, men, women and children. In England at that time it was unusual for even women to smoke, and certainly children had not acquired that habit. It was unpleasant to see babies in their mother's arms with their eyes black with clinging flies. Omar explained that it was God's will that flies were there, and it would be wrong to disturb them. Many people had diseased eyes in consequence. This was fifty years ago; they are no doubt more hygienic now.

With Omar we visited an old carpet merchant, who was cursed with the name 'Louzy'. Whenever he appeared near the ship the sailors gave him no peace, should 'Good morning, Louzy, how is Louzy today, glad to meet you, Louzy,' until the poor man went nearly crazy. He would amble away waving his hands about his head and muttering, 'Louzy, Louzy, always Louzy.'

I saw Omar the dragoman a few years later. I made a sketch of him in Beirut which I used with others in *The Pictorial World*, and I sent him a copy. A year or so later I was astonished to have a visit from him at my studio, dressed in native costume. He had brought some Arab horses to London, and had got my address from *The Pictorial World*. Luckily there was an exhibition then at Earls Court, so I gave him dinner and took him there. He was entranced. It was a lovely summer evening, the gardens glittered with fairy lights, and gaily dressed people wandered about while a band played light music. He said in broken English, 'Surely this is Heaven, and these ladies are the angels!' I thought it best to let him keep his illusions about the ladies.

These exhibitions at Earls Court were most pleasant. One could dine there in the open air and listen to the band. Fairy lights against a dark blue sky and mysterious figures whose faces were dimly seen in the half-light have always stirred my imagination. It is sad that our uncertain climate put an end to this resort.

Jaffa was our last port of call in Palestine. It was from there that we were to make the journey to Jerusalem. We dropped anchor about two miles from land, there being no proper harbour at that time. A heavy surf broke some distance out. We went from the ship in an enormous open boat, rowed with long oars by a crew of wild looking Arabs who chanted a dismal dirge. Ship's boats were not suited to such heavy surf. An enchanting scent of orange blossom came from the shore, and as we approached, overcame that of perspiring Arabs. Messrs Cook controlled travel facilities in Egypt and Palestine. They had the arrangement of our visit to Jerusalem. Fifty or sixty passengers were packed into many carriages, each drawn by two horses. The dragomen rode on horseback, and I wished I were a dragoman. Our procession was a long one, the carriages at the end of the line were smothered in dust, for the roads were thick with it. It was thrilling to drive through villages bearing Biblical names. We ate a picnic lunch at Ramleh (Ramallah today) – a strange place for a picnic. However, one can only keep one's enthusiasm for a limited time, and after many hours in a bumping carriage, breathing dust, I lost interest and felt bored.

Thomas Cook's guide book to their tours of the Middle East (published in 1876) explains that it took 10 hours by coach and 12 hours by horse to get from Jaffa to Jerusalem. It was quite normal for the journey to be broken at Ramleh for the night, but Gray's tour pressed on to make the trip in one day.

Ten or twelve miles from Jerusalem, whilst the horses were being watered, I asked a dragoman whether he would change places and let me ride his horse. I was surprised by the alacrity with which he accepted the change until I mounted the horse; it was weary and disgruntled and refused to keep up with procession It was getting late and the sun was setting beautifully behind distant hills. I was jogging along slowly and happily when a strong puff of wind took my straw hat and dropped it some distance away amongst white stones which covered this desolate plain. I dismounted, and leading the horse, began to search. Whilst I groped around I became aware that a group of white robed Arabs were watching me, appearing from nowhere. Fearing their intention I approached boldly and began a dumb show act, pointing to my head and then in the direction my hat had taken, and left it at that, happy to remount and get away from them. It was getting dark, the long line of carriages was far out of sight, and I wondered if my horse would find Jerusalem. Luckily it did, and I found my brother installed in an hotel outside the Jaffa Gate.

Hotels were so crowded that two passengers and ourselves shared a large bedroom. A curtain across the entrance divided it, my brother and I in one division and the two other men in the other. I give these details to make clear a later incident.

We dined in a crowded tent, and when drinking coffee we were startled by shouting and struggling at the entrance. Attendants were trying to force an excited Arab from the tent. This Arab was waving a hat, a straw boater, *my* hat. It cost me ten shillings, for the man must have walked at least five miles with it. That evening we wandered about outside Jerusalem. Brilliant moonlight made the Arabs appear ghostly and unreal, a different world from any I had known before. We were both tired out when we got to bed that night, and I was soon sound asleep. How long I had been asleep I do not know, when I became conscious that something touched my head, and my heart thumped when I awoke to see a tall figure silhouetted against the window, creeping towards my brother's bed. Was I dreaming, or was an Arab really about to murder Alfred? Shaking with fright, I reeled across the floor and gripped the man tight around the waist. Instead of being stabbed as I expected, I found I was holding a figure which did not struggle, but remained limp in my arms. This must be a nightmare. But soon I heard one of the men on the other side of the curtain asking what the fuss was about. He brought a lighted candle, and we found the intruder was the man from the fourth bed. The light roused him, and he asked the time. We led him to his bed, and next morning he had no recollection of the incident. His brother told us that 'Pat' had suffered from sleep walking for some years, and that they were travelling in the hope that the change would cure him.

It was Easter week, an interesting time to see Jerusalem and visit the Church of the Holy Sepulchre where, on Good Friday, six different religious denominations worshipped. A company of Turkish soldiers with bayonets fixed kept order. To enter the Holy of Holies one had to squeeze through a small opening, so small that it was a matter of bending almost double. To get out one came backwards in the same doubled up position, and that was the moment when a fellow passenger lost his gold watch. He accused the two priests who stood on either side of the opening of pinching it as he emerged. He was Irish, excitable and noisy, but the priests were unmoved, probably not understanding a word he said. We were shoved along by the press of crowd, our friend hurling back reproaches in good Irish – it was a relief to get out into the sunshine. The Church of the Holy Sepulchre was the last place where one would expect to have one's watch sneaked. The culprit was never found; the Irishman was convinced that the priests knew something about it.

We spent a week in Jerusalem, doing the usual excursions. I have never much cared for sightseeing with droves of other tourists. Sometimes a few of us got away on our own, riding horses or big donkeys. During the day the sun was very hot, but the nights were freezingly cold with the result that when we embarked at Jaffa most of us suffered from sore throats. At Jaffa an elderly lady with a niece joined the ship. I was glad, for the niece was pretty and young, and gave an interest which was lacking on the outward voyage. The passengers taking them all round, were cultured and pleasant people, and before the voyage was over I made some good friends, though I little thought that the small, precise gentleman with the pointed beard was to make quite a difference to my life.

The three or four weeks spent in Palestine, although more than fifty years ago, I remember vividly; the places, the people and the smells. Of the voyage home I have only a slight recollection, but my brother was much stronger, and was anxious to get back to work.

Before landing at Plymouth there was the usual exchange of cards. To my surprise, the little gentleman with the pointed beard gave me his card and asked for my address. His name was Frank D. Brocklehurst, and he lived near Macclesfield. The following day he wired, and asked me to luncheon at his sister's house in Henrietta Street, and so began a friendship which lasted until he died

Frank. D. Brocklehurst, born 1837 and died 1905, was the son of a famous silk manufacturing family in Macclesfield, the original business having been established by his Grandfather. At the age of 21 he set off on a 3 year journey around the world and developed a taste for travel that obviously never left him,

I found Pegram installed in a big studio in Glebe Place which had lately been completed. He invited me to join up with him. I gave an exhibition there of drawings I had made on the ship, and invited the passengers who were available; most of them came. They wanted to buy the drawings, indeed, I could have sold the lot. Self-depreciation, vanity or something equally foolish caused me to refuse to sell. I *gave* them away! In later years necessity forced me to overcome this weakness, though the business side of the profession I have always found unpleasant.

It was not long before I was again making illustrations. An old friend of ours, Jerome K. Jerome, lived in a block of flats behind the Guards Barracks, opposite the Chelsea Pensioners Gardens. He was a kindly soul. His amusing book *Three Men in a Boat* had lately brought him fame. He smoked continually, and I was not surprised that he dedicated his book to his pipe. When I called on him on my return from abroad he told me that he was bringing out a magazine called *The Idler*, and he asked Pegram and me to make drawings for it. Conan Doyle, Israel Zangwill and Eden Philpotts were among the authors he engaged to write. I illustrated some articles by Eden Philpotts which he wrote after a visit to the West Indies.

*The Idler* magazine was published from 1892 to 1911 and Jerome K. Jerome was co-editor and then editor until 1897. The literary and artistic contributors were wide ranging and included Conan Doyle, Rudyard Kipling, Rider Haggard, Mark Twain and H.G. Wells. Gray's brother-in-law Fred Pegram was also a contributor.

Among his contributors Jerome found enough cricketers to form an Idler eleven. Conan Doyle was a first-class cricketer; I believe that he once played for his county. His cricket stood out from that of the rest of us. Zangwill was certainly not a good hand with the bat. He did not bother about dressing the part conventionally; a cut-away coat, tweed trousers and a bowler hat were good enough for him. His style was odd; he bent double and scraped his bat horizontally along the ground. Of course he never hit the ball. Our principal match was against the musician's team, which was a pretty good one. I do not remember that Jerome ever played, he usually kept the score. About this time most of the professions formed cricket elevens.

The Idlers became the Author's Cricket Club, the Musicians had their eleven and the Artists also. Edwin Abbey, the American painter and illustrator, was much interested in the game – he seemed keener to play cricket well than to paint a good picture. His costume was perfect, if extreme. A white cap came down over his eyes, the collar of his sweater covered the lower part of his face, and he wore enormous batting pads. I remember helping Dermod O'Brian to give him practise by bowling for an hour or so one hot afternoon in what is now called Chelsea Square. Abbey was as poor a cricketer as I have known, but he loved playing. Each year he had an eleven to his house at Fairford for a cricket week. I regretted that my cricket was not good enough to qualify me for a place in the team, because they had such a splendid time.

Edwin Abbey was born in Philadelphia in 1852 and died in 1911. He settled permanently in England in 1883 and this was obviously long enough for him to develop a strong interest in the very English game of cricket.. He was elected an Associate of the Royal Academy in 1896 and a Member in 1898. He painted the official picture of the Coronation of Edward VII in 1902 which hangs in Buckingham Palace.

# Chapter 6

# Enter the Chelsea Arts Club

The Chelsea Arts Club was formed because the many painters and sculptors who now lived in Chelsea wished for a place where they might have a good meal at a reasonable price. The Italian restaurants which were patronised by many of the men had nothing cosy about them, and nowhere to sit. A practice had been started of meeting at each other's studios on different nights, the host providing beer, bread and cheese. It was natural that in these circumstances the idea of a club began to take root, a place where we might meet in the evening. Energetic Stirling Lee got on the job, and assisted by Christie, Llewellyn and Herbert Vos arranged a meeting which was held at Christie's studio. A list of artists willing to join was made, with the result that a lease was taken of a house in King's Road in 1890, close to the Town Hall. It was a go-as-you-please affair at first, but Lee and the committee struggled to keep it alive.

The growing pains of the club were many, the principal one being of service. Our first steward was interesting as an human specimen, but not good as a caterer. He was usually drunk, and several times suffered from delirium tremens, and then we never knew what would happen. He had a way of creeping into our sitting room, raising his hand and whispering 'Shhh! *They're after me!*' At other times he had the dignity of a family butler and seemed bored when asked the cost of something he had brought, for instance, I remember that when asked the price of a pot of tea he answered 'Two shillings.' The member said 'Surely two shillings for a pot of tea is a bit stiff?' But our steward merely replied airily, 'All for the good of the club!'

Our next effort was a strong, capable man with dark blood in his veins. He and his wife produced order out of chaos and gave us excellent meals. His weakness was his temper, he was a touchy man. When Carey Elwes (a relative of Simon Elwes) was sleeping at the club he was awakened one night by harrowing screams. He pluckily went into the steward's bedroom, from where the sounds came, and found him trying to cut his wife's throat with a razor. How Elwes was able to prevent this wild man from carrying out his whim we could never understand, but he succeeded, and the little affair blew over.

> Simon Elwes, born 1902 and died 1975, was taught at the Slade School by Tonks and Steer. He became famous as a society portrait painter in the 1930s and later as a war artist. He was also a favourite of Queen Elizabeth the Queen Mother.

The days, now so long ago, when the club was in King's Road are to me like a half forgotten dream, but certain individuals and incidents remain in my memory. James Christie, who had a studio behind the club, was much in evidence. He was a rollicking, jolly man, energetic and always smiling, and suffered a good deal from thirst. Closing time at the club was not strictly kept. Christie and his friends often drank the night through, and he was sometimes able to persuade the others to join him in a morning swim in the Serpentine. One morning I chanced to go to the club early, and met Christie's party returning from their swim after an all-night sitting. J.J. Shannon was with them looking particularly cold and miserable. He said that it had all been horrible!

There was another whom one could not ignore, Hollins, a painter from the Midlands. He was quick witted and argumentative. Two other members were named Rollins and Collins, and the three names were often muddled. Havard Thomas said to Hollins in his slow meticulous way, 'I never know whether you are Hollins, Collins or Rollins.' Hollins, spitting fire and pointing at Thomas, answered 'Oh, you don't, don't you? It is a coincidence that when I see you I can never recollect whether you are Thomas, Jackass or Fatass!'

Whistler came often to the club in those days, and was always charming to us young men. He usually kept a four-wheeler waiting for him at the door. One evening James Charles, up from the country, was with us when Whistler came. Charles, pleased at the prospect of a good talk with Whistler, opened the proceedings by saying, 'Do you remember that time when you were bankrupt, Whistler?' Whistler was taken aback by this unexpected opening. 'This club,' he said, 'seems to be a very frank one.'

We gave a dinner to John Sargent on his election to the Royal Academy, and he rose to make a speech, but after many 'er – ers' he snapped 'Damn it, that's the way I make a speech' and sat down again.

> John Sargent was born in Florence of American parents and spent his life in Europe, based first in Paris and then London. After studying in Paris he began to establish himself as a portrait painter. The scandal associated with his

portrait *Madame X* led to him leaving for London in 1884. He was a founding member of the New English Art Club and was elected associate of the Royal Academy in 1894 and a Member in 1897. After 1910 he concentrated on landscape painting and was a war artist in the First World War. His painting *Gassed* is in the Imperial War Museum. He died in 1925.

Then there were the concerts we gave, when Christie always recited *Tam-O-Shanter* the length of which bored me, and Walter Sickert did his amusing recollection of a scene from *Hamlet* acted by Cockney strolling players. In 1902 the club moved from King's Road to our present comfortable quarters in Old Church Street.

Stirling Lee was fond of getting up fancy dress dances, and for some years had arranged parties to celebrate Mardi Gras – and they certainly *were* parties. Getting ambitious, we gave a bigger one at Chelsea Town Hall, which was the forerunner of the Chelsea Arts Club Ball. In the early days, these balls at the Albert Hall were very much more exclusive and far less of a riot than they are today. There was, however, one rule which we invariably broke, which was the taking into our boxes of our own drinks. We found it cheaper to smuggle them rather than buy them on the premises, and were careful to remove the tell tale empties on leaving. A large crowd always collected round the steps in the early morning to watch the departure of the revellers, and once, as I was about to descend these with dignity before the watching multitude, I caught my heel in the top step and rolled to the bottom, scattering empty champagne bottles in all directions from under my cloak. This exit was an enormous success with the crowd, who cheered me to the echo, shouting 'Try a bit more water with it next time!'

My *Garonne* friend, F.D. Brocklehurst, often asked me to say at his home in Cheshire, and generally gave me a commission to draw some member of his family whilst I was there. It was my first experience of riches. I enjoyed everything; the life was so completely different from anything I had known. Each morning I found great entertainment in the entry of a nervous head gardener, who crept into the room to place a single bloom before his master. He was followed by a sturdy game keeper, who was not at all nervous, and who gave a report on the health of the pheasants. Then there was the arrival of the servants after breakfast, who ranged themselves round the room for family prayers, read by my host; when the back view of the huge old house keeper when kneeling to pray engaged most of my thoughts. But these visits made me realise the truth of Wilson Steer's remark, 'Money doesn't make you happy, and neither does the want of it.'

Brocklehurst was a great traveller, and had made many interesting expeditions when a young man. When I first knew him he usually went abroad for part of each winter. The year after the cruise to Palestine he invited me to accompany him to the

West Indies on the Steam Yacht *Victoria* which was going on a twelve week tour. I was becoming used to these unexpected excitements.

One cold morning in February we set off. S.Y. *Victoria* was a vessel of only 1500 tons – rather small, I found, for bad Atlantic storms. She carried forty or fifty passengers, some of whom I had met on the *Garonne* the year before. To my delight there were plenty of young people, and I found pretty models to draw and play about with. Indeed, I was so much occupied with my new friends that my kind host complained that he never saw me. This, I felt was not playing the game, so I arranged to walk with him each morning and evening.

On board the *Victoria* there were one or two people who amused us, the best entertainer, perhaps, being an irascible old colonel who had spent many years in India. He made an unlucky start, for when eating his early morning orange in the Channel he unfortunately spat his false teeth overboard. We thought that possibly his spare dentures were not as comfortable as those he had lost, which might help to account for his extreme touchiness. He took a curious dislike to one young man the moment he saw him. This young man was just down from Cambridge, and we became friends. For some reason I never understood, the colonel, whenever he met my friend, crowed like a rooster, and among other rude questions asked him why he travelled without his nurse. It became intolerable, and got on the boy's nerves. One golden evening when we were returning to the ship after a day ashore, he asked what I thought he should do about it. I suggested that, should the colonel continue his insults when we got back to the ship, he should walk straight up to him and say 'Only your age protects you.' I guessed the possible result, but hoped for the best. We looked anxiously at the group standing near the top of the gangway – the colonel was there, a loud 'Cock-a-doddle-dee' left no doubt of that. I followed my friend up the gangway; he strode over to his enemy and said, rather too dramatically I thought, what I had advised. The result was indescribable. The old man rushed at him, and had it not been for the quick intervention of the captain and several of us, he would have hurled the boy into the sea. The colonel continued his insults until the end of the voyage.

Another incident which sticks in my memory was an effort we made to catch a shark in St. Thomas's harbour. The harbour was full of them. The bosun supplied us with strong lines, shark hooks and pieces of pork. Some of the pork we threw overboard to entice them. Each shark has two small fish swimming on either side of its back fin, 'pilot fish' we were told they were called. When the pork was thrown in the two pilot fish swam to it, sniffed all round, returned and evidently gave a favourable report, for the shark immediately swallowed it. Then we baited the hook and tried our luck. Up came the pilot fish to investigate – with the result that the shark was never caught. Someone suggested having a shot at them, and produced an enormous weapon which he called an elephant rifle. Several of us fired at the sharks, but nothing occurred until a man apparently put a shot in a large shark's eye. The shark leapt from the water and plunged back with a great commotion, when other sharks immediately attacked and tore their mate to pieces.

After touching at Tangier we visited all the important West Indian islands from Trinidad to Cuba, and beautiful most of them are; and there is romance in their history. But I was never happy in tropical climates, the blinding sunshine gave me headaches, and there are many penalties to pay for sunshine in the way of snakes, nasty biting insects and dust. On the way home, however, we came to a place which must be as near heaven as could be. About twenty miles from Ponta Delgada, the port of St. Michael's, an island in the Azores, is a village called Furnas. It lies at the bottom of a played out volcano – the high crater encircles it and prevents a distant view, but the people and the flowers were so lovely that one did not miss distant views. The complexion of the women was a warm olive, and in their pretty clothes they were the most entrancing looking women I had ever seen. The place was full of hot and cold springs, sulphur and all kinds of healing waters, and we were told that it was patronised by Americans for medical baths. Fifty years ago, when I was there, it was primitive, perhaps now it has been developed into a fashionable spa. If so, I am glad to have seen it as it was then.

Furnas is still a very beautiful place. Gray saw it at the height of its 19th Century beauty where much time had been devoted to the development of the gardens and the hot springs. Things declined in the 1930s but today he would probably not be disappointed. Modernised, certainly, but with all the character of the original place in the centre of a large volcano.

A few nights after our return to England, Harry Collison, a young man of my own age with whom we had made many happy expeditions during the cruise, gave a dinner party for Lady Lacon, Mrs Walpole and myself; these ladies were also passengers in S.Y. *Victoria*. We dined at a luxurious club which had just been opened in Dover Street. It was well named the Maison Doree, and the many waiters were dressed to suit their surroundings. The point of this is that after dinner we went on to the Empire, and while we were waiting in the vestibule Lady Lacon said 'Why, there's the Sirdar.' A tall man with a moustache and very bronzed face approached, and Collison and I were introduced; and that was my only meeting with Lord Kitchener.

The Sirdar was a title given to Kitchener as leader of the Egyptian Army in the Anglo-Indian Campaign in the Sudan in the late 1890s and which culminated in the Battle of Omdurman.

Rather unsettled by the cruise, I gradually took up my life in Chelsea, and worked with Pegram at the studio in Glebe Place. More men had joined the club while I was abroad; John Sargent had descended on Chelsea like a meteor and had taken a studio in Tite Street.

Pegram and I thought Walter Sickert the best looking man in the club. Like Whistler, he dressed with care and elegance, indeed, he was rather a fop. One day we were astonished to see that he had shaved off his lovely fair moustache. He said he found it a nuisance when eating thick soup. At his Glebe Place studio he was painting the head of a woman. Mortimer Menpes, looking at it, said 'Very nice, Walter, very nice; don't do much more to it, but don't you think it would be as well if you coaxed the eye back into the face!'

John Sargent's arrival caused quite a stir among the local painters, for he had made a great reputation in Paris. He was big and tall, stood very erect, and wore a beard. Although shy and modest, there was the air of a conquering hero about him. His studio reminded me of the rich studios I had seen in Paris. He was overwhelmed with commissions to paint lovely ladies, and those who thought themselves lovely. Years later he told me that he gave up painting portraits because 'The mouth was always wrong.' He had amazing energy and was never idle. De Glehn said that when they travelled abroad together and had to wait at a railway station, Sargent would make sketches from the platform. When in foreign hotels, on wet days he put in the time copying photographs printed in journals. His sister had a book filled with these pencil drawings.

Another personality had arrived from Scotland, Robert Brough. Good looking, gay and attractive, he had a seductive stutter. He took a studio in the same building as Sargent, and they became friends. Being extremely clever, he soon got commissions for portraits, and became a fashionable painter. No one could be dull while he was about. Once, at a dinner at the club, Brough squirted a soda siphon at J.J. Shannon, who was in dress clothes. The soda water went over his shirt front and made him very angry. He aimed a blow at Brough, who dodged, and the blow caught me. Shannon regretted hitting me, and by way of reparation invited me to the whitebait dinner given each year at Greenwich by members of the Royal Academy. A friend of Shannon's took us from the Temple pier to Greenwich in a small steam yacht. I have a lively recollection of this dinner. A well-known contractor, a tall, bearded man, was the guest of honour and replied to the toast. It was a florid speech; he finished by thanking Alma Tadema, who presided, for his kind words, adding 'I only wish that I 'ad a few 'andfulls of roses from the lovely picture 'e 'as lately painted for me, and I would 'eap them on 'is 'ead!' (Loud cheers.)

At that dinner Edward Stott was also called on for a few words. Stott was sore that he had not been elected to the Academy, and said so. Not long before this, a friend by way of a joke had advised Stott to give a small present to the President and Council just before the election was to be held. Stott, acting on this advice, sent a bottle of sloe gin to each, much to their astonishment. Some years later Stott attained his heart's desire. At the time Edward Stott began exhibiting in London there was another painter called Stott who was also exhibiting there. They met at a gallery, and the elder Stott suggested that it might prevent mistakes if Edward changed his name. He agreed, but later said that this would impossible, as all his shirts and underlinen were marked Stott. So the elder Stott called himself Stott of Oldham.

Robert Brough's death was a tragedy. One winter he was painting a portrait in Scotland, and he booked a sleeping berth to return to London. Arriving at his carriage he found that another man had taken his berth by mistake, and Brough said that it did not matter in the least, and he would go to another; which he did. On the journey there was a bad accident, and the part of the train in which Brough was travelling was thrown from the line, and caught fire. Brough, injured and burnt, was laid in a snow covered field, where he remained for some hours in agony before being taken to hospital. Directly Sargent heard of the accident he went to the hospital in the Midlands to see if anything could be done for Brough, but he was too late.

The Scottish church in Pont Street was crowded for his memorial service, and I noticed that many women were crying. We all felt acutely the loss of the charming, vital young man, and were shocked by the horror of his end. It was a strange fate that caused him to change carriages, the one in which he should have travelled was undamaged.

Robert Brough, born in Scotland in 1872 and died in 1905, was a successful portrait painter and friend of John Sergeant. After growing up in Scotland, Brough studied in Paris at Julian's Atelier and then established himself in a studio in Tite Street near to Sergeant's studio.

Havard Thomas, the sculptor, was an amusing and stimulating member of the club. He was a Welshman, short and potbellied, and spoke wearily in the higher register of his tenor voice. Once, when young, he went to the Royal Academy on varnishing day to see how his exhibit had been placed. To his annoyance he found it in a corner against a wall. He approached Sir Frederic Leighton, the President, and said, 'Sir George Leighton, I believe.' Leighton, ignoring the wilful use of the wrong name, bowed. 'I should like to know, Sir George, why my piece of sculpture has been placed in a dark corner and (pointing to work by Leighton) that bloody group is in the centre for all to see!' Leighton, getting his own back, later enquired, 'who was the fat little man with spirituous breath?'

One evening I heard Thomas discussing sculpture with Conrad Dressler. He was jeering at those sculptors who had their marble pointed by assistants, and he said, 'I always carve the marble myself.' Dressler suggested that he was not the first man to do so, and he had heard that Michelangelo did all his own carving. Thomas replied, 'And a very worthy predecessor.'

Thomas enjoyed telling the following story, in which Trood played the leading role. Trood was deaf and dumb. He had been taught to lip-read, indeed, he was very proud of his prowess in this, although he made many mistakes. One day he and Thomas were talking outside Trood's studio when a stranger approached and asked Thomas to direct him to Sloane Square. Trood doing a bit of lip-reading, shouted, 'He's not here.' The stranger lost his temper and shouted, 'Cui bono, bloody foreigner! Who the hell said he was here!'

A Duchess once called at Thomas's studio to ask if he would give her daughter lessons in sculpture. 'Before I undertake to teach her,' said Thomas, 'I should like to know whether you want her to learn *sculpture*, or the bloody muck they *call* sculpture!'

> Havard Thomas, born 1854 and died 1921, was the first Professor of Sculptor at the Slade School of Art. He first exhibited at the Royal Academy in 1892 but his vociferous support for the reform of that organisation and his participation in the New English Art Club meant that he was never elected either an associate or full member. He is famous for his sculpture *Lycidas* which caused a scandal in 1905 when it was rejected by the Royal Academy. Rated by positive critics as 'unorthodox and rigorously classical' it was too much for Thomas's enemies at the RA. Lycidas is today in the Tate Gallery.

Trood painted animals, and behind his studio kept quite a menagerie, including a fox. One morning the fox escaped into the street, and a hunt began. Trood led a field of milkmen, workmen and anyone who happened to be about that early hour, full cry along Manresa Road, past South Kensington Station, and finally ran it to earth in an area in Thurloe Square. Trood bore his infirmity lightly. His deafness often enabled him to get out of awkward situations. Once he was seen standing at the top of the steps leading to Trafalgar studios; at the bottom stood an irate father, shouting at Trood that he would have law on him if it cost him five pounds. Trood was shaking his head and repeating in his one note voice, 'He's not here!'

# Chapter 7

# Glebe Place in the Nineties

In 1892 or '93 Rothenstein and Conder took studios in Glebe Place. Rothenstein had painted the portrait of (I think) a young girl wearing a fur cap. The canvas was not completely covered, he must have painted with a thin medium, for there were two streaks of paint which had trickled down the canvas. At the time, this seemed to me a mark of genius. His picture *The Doll's House* now in the Tate Gallery, always gives me pleasure.

> Rothensteins's *The Doll's House* is named after the Ibsen play of the same name. The models are Augustus John and Rothenstein's wife Alice Knewstub. The Rothensteins were on honeymoon in a rented cottage in Vattetot, Normandy, where they were joined by John, Bonder and Orpen. The painting was finished in 1900 and presented to the Tate by the artist's brother in 1924.

Despite his youth, he had remarkable assurance. I was at a party at his studio, and with admiration, heard him lay down the law to his guests, who included George Moore, Wilson Steer, MacColl and Tonks, all much older men than himself. One remark he made that evening remains in my memory. They were talking of the prevalent custom of painting and writing about ugly things, and Rothenstein pointed out that if a thing were ugly it did not necessarily follow that it was good. This is useful when judging any of the contemporary arts.

One evening at the Chelsea Arts Club the company was startled when Rothenstein, accompanied by another young man, both in faultless evening clothes, appeared on the stairs leading to the billiard room; they seemed to look with pity on the crowd below as they slowly descended. The stranger moved among them as though unaware of their presence. Rothenstein introduced me to his friend, and I have always felt grateful for this introduction, for he was Max Beerbohm, lately down from Oxford.

Max Beerbohm was born in 1873 and died in 1956. He was a half-brother of the famous Actor Manager Beerbohm Tree. After leaving Oxford without taking a degree in 1894, which must be about when Gray saw him in the Club, he built a friendship with Beardsley and Wilde amongst others and developed a reputation as cartoonist, humourist writer and eventually broadcaster. In 1904 he married an American actress Florence Kahn and they moved to Rapallo in Italy where they were to live for the rest of their lives except for the First and Second World Wars. He was knighted in 1939.

In after years Rothenstein gave me the impression of being a disappointed man; he was certainly worried by the modern painting so popular with the 'Art Boys'. Once, when we were walking round an exhibition of modern art, he stopped before a picture of a blowsy nude woman which looked as though painted with plum jam and marmalade, and said wearily, 'Surely future generations will not take this sort of things seriously.' I heartily agreed with him. I do not know why Rothenstein should have felt disappointed – to me he seemed one of the successful men. He had good appointments most of his life, and his pictures have been acquired by the Tate Gallery.

Conder was a good looking youth. His hair was fair and his eyes were blue; he had a shy way of looking at one, and spoke in a soft voice. He was an artist to his fingertips; not one of those who mapped out his day to the minute, but who painted when he felt like it. When he had nothing better to do he sometimes called on us, his studio being nearby. He had a generous disposition, and liked companions to share his pleasures.

A rich young sculptor, whom we will call A., occupied a studio near ours. Knowing that he had money, unscrupulous people often attempted to get him involved in their projects. One morning he called to ask me to come quickly to his studio and stay till his visitor left. The visitor, a pretty woman, was trying to persuade him to spend the weekend with her. Having been warned that the husband was in on the plot, he was afraid of being alone with her for a moment. I spent an amusing half hour while the pretty creature used her wiles to get me to leave; but I sat tight.

In those days a certain old woman gained a precarious living by introducing models to artists. She once brought to me a beautiful girl who was elegantly and expensively dressed. Naturally, I asked her to sit. She said that she was busy, but might manage the following Sunday morning. I was at the studio early, and waited with hopeful expectancy, but she never came. I felt despondent, and walked to Dover Street for lunch at the Hogarth Club. A. was there, and I told him of my sad disappointment. He was a gay, cheery fellow. He said that one must not let a thing like that rest, and we must look into it. That afternoon we got a hansom cab and drove to a dingy street in West Kensington. A. knocked briskly at the door. A long pause – then he knocked again. Then the door was opened by the old woman who had brought the girl to me. A. was taken aback when he saw her. 'Why, if it isn't Mr A.' she said, 'I am pleased to see you. Pray come in.' We entered, and there on a sofa was my lovely hope of the morning, dabbing her face with scent. The old woman, much excited, said, 'Kitty, here's Mr A. you know, the father of Lizzie's baby!' A. striking a heroic attitude, said, 'How dare you say such a thing! I shall put it in the hands of my lawyer.' 'Oh you were always so good to her' said the old women, 'many's the fiver you've given her.' Then she shouted upstairs, Mary, 'bring those photos of Lizzie,' and we were shown a series of photographs of Lizzie, nude and in various stages of pregnancy. We both said things such as, 'You must get Sir George Lewis on to this, these photos are no proof of parentage – how dare you make this allegation' and so on. As we got into the cab A. said 'Well, I'm damned!' He took me home to dine. His charming mother asked what we had been doing, and to my horror he told her that I had taken him to see a lovely friend of mine. I feared he was about to relate everything, but he said no more. A year or two later the lovely girl on whom we made that afternoon call figured in a divorce case which caused some stir.

Francis Howard also had a studio in Glebe Place. He was a good looking and fashionable young man about town, and he and Sickert were certainly the best dressed artists in our neighbourhood. At the club we usually referred to him as our 'violet eyed youth'. He would stand no nonsense, and often challenged people to fight duels, although I do not remember that he ever fought one. He knew Buffalo Bill, and when that gentleman brought his circus to Earls Court, Howard became one of the cowboys who attacked the Deadwood coach, to the delight of the members of the Chelsea Arts Club, who flocked to see his performance. He painted enthusiastically until his sight became weak and forced him to use his energy in other ways. He founded, and ran until 1941, The International Society of Painters, Sculptors and Engravers, which held interesting and successful exhibitions. Howard befriended many artists, without thought of reward except the satisfaction of helping young talent. I cannot say that he ever got me a commission, though once he nearly gave me a job to varnish some pictures belonging to the King of Greece. However, he evidently thought better of it, and he gave the job to somebody else. When not engaged in writing letters to The Times, buying ruined castles or bidding for pictures at sales, he still, at the time of writing, comes to the Chelsea Club, where he is popular. Personally it always gives me pleasure to meet and talk with him.

Francis Howard was born in 1874 and died in 1954 and was the great grandson of Benjamin Franklin. Buffalo Bill (Colonel William Cody) first brought his Wild West show to London in 1887 as part of the American Exhibition at Earls Court where it was a huge success and played to over one million people. He returned in 1892 and 1903. The reference in Gray's memoirs must refer to the 1892 show when Howard was 18, and this fits in with other dateable references in this chapter.

When Pegram married my sister Jane* he gave up the lease of 64 Glebe Place. I took a pleasant room in a large house which Tonks had leased in Church Street. The house has been pulled down, like most other good old houses in that street. One of its attractions was a big garden at the back. Tonks had installed his old landlady with whom he had lodged in King's Road, and she brought her servant with her. This servant was swollen eyed, short and fat, and always wore a shawl. She frequently had black eyes and bruises, her explanation being that she suffered from fits. We learnt later that 'fits' was another name for gin.

It was an odd establishment. Once, when passing a room, I heard what sounded like young girls crying behind closed doors. One was shouting 'Oh, I wish I was married.' Tonks then discovered that his housekeeper was employed by a Girls Rescue Society. The household became odder still when Tonks let the remaining rooms. He occupied the two rooms on the first floor, I had the front one on the ground floor, and Philip Treherne, a nephew of Mrs Weldon's, the back ground floor room overlooking the garden. As Philip wished to study drawing I introduced him to the Slade School and to Tonks. Another Slade student took the upper room. He was having singing lessons, being taught, he told us, the 'Bencke attack' method. On summer days, with the windows open, we could hear him attack his high notes with a ferocity I had not suspected. A disconcerting noise, and we did not know what to do about it, because he ignored our hints. Treherne thought that he might possibly stop the nuisance by using with discretion a small revolver he possessed. He proposed to fire a shot at his easel each time B. attacked a high note. The next morning, working in my room, I heard B. humming softly to himself. Later the high note attack began. Immediately a bang from Treherne's revolver nearly deafened me; another high note, another bang, and then silence. Then my door opened and the swollen eyed servant clumped into the room shouting, 'Oh lor,' Mr Treherne has shot himself!' It was the last we heard of the Bencke attack.

*They married in 1895, further confirmation of the dating mentioned in this section.

The letter archive has another piece of theatrical memorabilia dated 1895. It is a letter from George Alexander (later Sir George), Actor Manager of the St James's Theatre in London, thanking Gray for a drawings he had done of *The Prisoner*. These must have been publicity pieces for the first performance of the Ruritanian Classic *The Prisoner of Zenda*. The letter, on St. James's Theatre letterhead, reads as follows:-

*Dear Sir,*

*Very many thanks for the charming sketch of the Prisoner, which seems to me quite excellent. Not feeling quite clear as to the manner of the sending. I am sure you will pardon me asking the extent of my indebtedness to you.*

*Believe me, yours truly,*
*George Alexander*

Sadly Gray, in what I fear must have been typical, had neglected to set a price before doing the work!

# Chapter 8

# South Africa, England, France, and illness

Nearly every winter I went abroad with Brocklehurst. At different times we visited the South of France, Italy, and Algeria as far south as Biskra. At first we travelled with a courier, a Swiss, whom we found a bore. He endeavoured to make us visit only the places where <u>he</u> was comfortable. I became tired of sightseeing, preferring to sit in cafes, watching people. In January 1896 we went further afield, and voyaged to South Africa, arriving in the Colony at a critical time. The Jameson Raid had been ignominiously beaten by the Boers, and there were rumours of war.

> The Jameson Raid took place in December 1895 and was an aborted attempt to launch a coup against the Boer government of President Kruger in the Transvaal. The discovery of gold in huge amounts, and the subsequent establishment of Johannesburg, had resulted in an influx of foreigners or 'Uitlanders' who threatened to overwhelm the local Boer population. Cecil Rhodes, Prime Minister of The Cape, saw an opportunity to support an uprising in Johannesburg and the raid was planned under Jameson's leadership to support this. Due to miscommunications and errors of leadership the raid failed, and the participants were jailed. Rhodes resigned as Prime Minister and much controversy persists as to the involvement of the Colonial Secretary, Joseph Chamberlain in London. Four years later, the Anglo-Boer War broke out.

We left the ship *Howarden Castle* at Durban, and after a few days stay, made our way leisurely to Johannesburg. We stopped at Maritzburg to visit Brocklehurst's nephew, Harold Fielden, a subaltern in the 7th Hussars, who was stationed there. It was my first experience of soldiers and I found them rather frightening. Most of the officers kept polo ponies, and were much interested in both horses and polo, as Cavalry men should be. They were dressed in short white coats and white trousers,

71

with long golden sashes round their waists. After dinner we sat outside the Mess tent in the moonlight, listening to their excellent band. The young officers with whom I talked filled me with confidence for the future, for they gave me to understand that their, regiment, unaided, would be able to settle any bother which might occur in the Transvaal. The day on which we proposed entering the Transvaal happened to be Majuba Day, the anniversary of the Boer victory at Majuba Hill.

The battle of Majuba Hill in February 1881 was a resounding defeat of the British Army by the Boers, and which ended the First Boer War. Majuba is just outside Volksrust in the Transvaal.

Colonel Paget of the 7th Hussars advised Brocklehurst to postpone our journey for a day or two because he had heard of the possibility of developments. In spite of this advice, we went off on the day arranged. I personally felt a bit nervous when, on our arrival at Volksrust, the Boer officials examined our luggage. However, though they were not matey or pleased to see us, we had no bother. The journey from Maritzburg to Johannesburg took twenty four hours, a long, tiring spell with inadequate arrangements for food. The line, which followed the old road, went through grim country, past places with names which brought uncomfortable memories to English ears, Majuba Hill and Lang's Nek among others. Charles Furse was in Johannesburg at this time. I had written asking him to get us rooms at a comfortable hotel. He and Charles Sheldon, (an American war artist living in England, and a member of the Chelsea Arts Club) met us at the station and took us to the Goldfields Hotel where we were to stay. The hotel was a rambling, one storied place with bedrooms built round a courtyard, in the centre of which stood the dining room and kitchen. Of course it had its stoep, and sitting there we found some fellow passengers from the ship waiting to greet us. That evening I was taken to the Rand Club, which had the distinction of being the most expensive club in the world. The bar was crowded with men dressed in every kind of costume, from smart dinner jackets to cowboy get up. Barny Barnato was sipping crème de menthe with Melton Prior, war artist of *The Illustrated London News*. The loudness of the check suit Barnato was wearing I can still remember. Someone made Brocklehurst and me honorary members of the club, a kindness I was to appreciate later.

At that time Johannesburg was a strange town; cheap looking two storied buildings built on a sandy plateau, nearly 6,000 feet above sea level. The roads were primitive. Apparently nothing had been done to them except to dig gutters on either side, some of them 3ft deep. This was especially noticeable when driving in a Cape cart. One of the unpleasant characteristics of the place was dust. A strong wind would pick up tons of red sand in one district and bring it, curling high like a water spout, across the town. One was nearly blinded by darkness and filth. Even the native drivers covered their heads with scarves. It was far more unpleasant than a dust storm I once experienced at Biskra in the Sahara, for there the dust was clean and tasted better. At first sight the population seemed to be composed of Africans and Jews.

Shortly before we arrived in Johannesburg a train carrying dynamite had collided with another train, with appalling results. The explosion made a crater a couple of hundred yards long and twenty feet deep. At each end, twisted railway lines stood high in the air. Iron huts in which natives lived and stone buildings were blown flat for half a mile around. It was a scene of desolation. Many people had been killed and hundreds wounded. Gangs of convicts were digging in the debris in search of bodies.

One evening I felt shivery and cold, and went early to bed. Next morning Brocklehurst did not like the look of me and sent for a doctor. The doctor was a sensible, pleasant Welshman named Davies, and was a Reform prisoner whom Kruger had let out on bail because there was so much sickness in Johannesburg. He examined me carefully and told me to stay in bed until he came next day. During the morning the hotel proprietor, hearing of my illness, came to see me. He told me that fever seemed to attack *young* men. 'Why' he said, 'it was only last month that a young man just about your own age took sick *in this very room* – he was dead in a week.' When he was leaving I thanked him for his visit and asked him to be sure to look in again to cheer me up.

Next morning the doctor made his promised visit. He tapped my tummy, listened carefully to my breathing and looked serious. With professional gravity he told me he was afraid I had typhoid fever, and advised me to summon what philosophy I possessed and not to worry. He would make arrangements for me to go to a nursing home the next day.

I was carried on a stretcher to a carriage which moved slowly to a nursing home in the suburbs. Brocklehurst, Furse and Sheldon walked solemnly on either side, reminding me of funeral mutes. I was put to bed in a long, narrow bare room by the matron of the home, a nurse from St Thomas's Hospital in London. To assist her in looking after twelve patients, mostly suffering from typhoid, she had only a pale, delicate looking little woman and two Zulu boys, who, though always smiling, did not understand a word of English.

For the next ten days I was starved, although I craved for food. The doctor then came to the conclusion that it was not typhoid fever which had laid me low, and to my delight I was put onto solid food; but it took me three weeks to get well again. Brocklehurst, not feeling fit himself, had gone to Pretoria with Sheldon, but I had plenty of kind people to enliven my convalescence, and most afternoons I was taken out driving.

One of my oddest experiences was driving to a polo ground along an unmade road across the veldt in a Cee spring carriage drawn by a pair of high-stepping horses. The occasion was a match between the Johannesburg club and the 7th Hussars, whose team had come from Maritzburg. The Wanderers band played light music, and tea was served in a big tent. Most of the women wore dresses made in Paris, and the whole business seemed incongruous and vulgar; coachmen and footmen in smart liveries were too much of a contrast to the waggons drawn by oxen, which we passed on our way. No wonder the Boers looked askance at so strange a site.

> The Wanderers Club was founded in 1888 when a Rugby Club and a Cricket Club joined together. Located in Sandton, north of Johannesburg, it is known today for its first class sporting facilities and especially the cricket stadium where international cricket matches are played.

Furse was staying with Cecil Rhodes at Cape Town when Jameson made his raid. He at once left for Johannesburg. Arriving at the battlefield carrying paintbox, canvas and easel, he had some difficulty in explaining his presence. Furse was a man with an overriding manner. He not only persuaded the Boers to let him paint a picture of the battle, but got many to pose in their original positions among the rocks. This picture he called *The Battle of Doornkop*. During my stay in Johannesburg the picture was in the window of the principal photographer's shop, and Furse took me to see it. He told me that he proposed having reproductions made and was taking the picture to Pretoria with the idea of showing it to President Kruger. Whilst I was in hospital Furse, accompanied by the man who was to work the selling of the reproduction started on his expedition.

The day after they arrived in Pretoria an unfortunate incident occurred which upset their plans. It appeared that Furse had been worried that the men of the Rand had not gone out to help Jameson as had been promised. In a letter to his father he gave vent to his feelings and let himself go without restraint. He said of the Reform Committee that they were 'emasculated, champagne livered gutless men.' His father, pleased with his son's literary ability, sent this letter to *The Pall Mall Gazette*. Copies of the paper containing the letter reached Pretoria at the moment of Furse's arrival with his picture. Naturally, members of the Reform Committee were not pleased with this severe criticism, and one of them wrote to the most popular Pretoria journal a letter in which the following extract occurred. 'Oh, the delectable Charlie, that gay raconteur, who drinks our champagne, takes our money at poker and repays us by saying that we are "emasculated, champagne-livered gutless men,"' The result was that all were in arms against him, and he disappeared from Pretoria without leaving an address. I felt very sorry for Furse. He had written the letter to his father never dreaming that it would be published. His criticism of the Reform Committee was certainly fair with regard to some members, though not all.

Furse had suffered from lung trouble for years, and had gone to South Africa on his doctor's advice. The dust of Johannesburg had not helped his cure. In spite of his energy and loud voice, I thought that he looked ill. He did not live many years after his return to England. What became of his picture *The Battle of Doornkop* (a very good one) is not known, even to his wife. I can only think that some lucky person in Pretoria took advantage of Furse's sudden departure

---

Charles Furse, was born in 1868 and died in 1904. He studied at the Slade School of Art and at Julian's Atelier in Paris. He was a staunch supporter of the New English Art Club and exhibited regularly. His painting of the Battle of Doornkop appears to still be lost, but there is a pen and ink drawing by Furse in the British Museum of dead horses by moonlight on the Doornkop battlefield and the note at the bottom states that this was where Jameson surrendered. The drawing was purchased by the museum in 1907 from his widow Dame Katherine Furse.

---

When I was strong enough to travel, Brocklehurst returned from Pretoria and we made preparations to leave for home. We travelled to Bloemfontein, stayed two nights and then journeyed on to Cape Town. We took rooms in a comfortable hotel in Wynberg, a charming suburb of Cape Town. To my delight we found Furse at the same hotel. He was unhappy, for he could not escape the anger caused by his letter. We were able to take walks together, enjoying flowers and trees again after the bleakness of the Transvaal. After a week of this pleasant life, we went on board the S.S. *Tantallon Castle* and left Cape Town for England.

It was on this voyage that I became acquainted with that strange and interesting writer, Frank Harris. I had noticed a stocky, Jewish looking man walking about the deck looking at the passengers with a ferocious contempt, and I wondered who he was. One evening he spoke to me, and finding that I knew some of his London friends, he became matey. After dinner he often invited me to his cabin to drink liqueur brandy, given him, he said, by Nicol of the Cafe Royal. He was always trouncing somebody. Dr Gill, the Astronomer Royal of Cape Town, was on board, and Harris would not leave him in peace. Listening to their arguments often kept me up half the night. They argued without ceasing about the mathematics of space and time. Dr Gill's scholarly calm made a contrast to the other's theatrical emphasis. Harris's face became shiny and red, and he had a way of thrusting his fingers through his oiled hair until he looked like a golliwog. I came to the conclusion that neither knew much more about the boundaries of space and time than I or anyone else.

Harris broke most of the rules of the ship and got away with it. He even managed to have his deck chair put on the bridge and to sit there, reading. The captain was a very religious man. When off duty he held religious services, playing the flute to accompany the hymns. This annoyed Harris, who one day lost his temper and said derogatory things about the Almighty. The captain was distressed, and told Harris that he could not allow such things to be said on his bridge. 'Why' he added, 'it is to God I pray for the safety of my ship.' Harris replied that it was quite probable that God had as much to do with the ship's safety as the captain – he was certainly a rude man.

> Frank Harris, born 1855 and died 1931, was an Irish born American journalist and author. In London he edited *The Evening News, The Review* and *The Saturday Review* where major contributors were H.G. Wells and George Bernard Shaw. He is best known for his autobiography which is considered very unreliable and was banned in both the UK and USA for its racy content. Gray's assessment of him as rude and ill-tempered seems to be shared by many of his contemporaries.

He told me many things about his past life, when he was employed by the Board of Works. He said he began by being honest and doing his best, but found that it did not pay. Therefore he threw in his lot with the blackguards and found it more lucrative and amusing. This admission, (whether true or not,) gave colour to the rumour that he had come to South Africa with the idea of blackmailing Rhodes, but that Rhodes was too tough a nut to crack. Among the things which Harris told me were his efforts to get Oscar Wilde away from England before his trial. The authorities, not wishing so unsavoury a case to be made public, had helped, and Harris had a steam yacht waiting at the docks. He begged Wilde to go with him, but so great was Wilde's vanity that he felt sure his genius would protect him, and that he would go free. He had not reckoned with Carson, who was prosecuting counsel.

Before we left the ship Harris gave an epicurean dinner to a dozen of us in a small saloon. I still have the menu on which the names of the guests are printed. The purser told me that a private dinner was against the rules of the ship, and I can only surmise how Harris obtained the privilege. I met him occasionally in London for several years after, and visited him at the office of *The Saturday Review*, a famous weekly which he owned and edited. Once I was invited to the weekly luncheon he gave at the Savoy. There were about a dozen guests, and we waited and waited for Harris's lady friend, who was so late that we sat down without her. Before we had finished the first course the pretty creature fluttered breezily into the room, holding a note book. Without any apology she walked up to Harris and said, 'Frank dear, should one use the word "in" or "at" in this sentence?' and showed him the note book. 'At' said Harris loudly, and we went on with our meal. After lunch I offered to take Harris and his friend to the private view of the New English Art Club at the Egyptian Hall in Piccadilly, (long since pulled down.) The three of us squashed into a hansom, and when we arrived Harris strutted among the crowd, frowning. In front of one portrait, the painter of which was standing near, Harris shouted 'Where are we? At the Royal Academy?' This was by no means meant as a compliment. Sometime later he accepted my invitation to dine at the Chelsea Arts Club, and during dinner he made audibly rude remarks about some of the guests. After dinner, which I had thought quite good, he said, 'Now, you boys, come along with me to the Cafe Royal and get something to eat!'

The last time I spoke to him was many years later in Piccadilly. He had become fatter and redder, and was dressed in a tight frock coat and wore a top hat. He did not recognise me or did not wish to, and was passing without a sign. I boldly stopped him, saying I had not seen him for ages, but that the other day Rothenstein had shown me a portrait he had done of Harris, and I thought it good. Harris shouted 'Portrait? Why he made me look like a bloody butcher.' He stumped away, and that was the last I ever saw of him.

Tonks continually changed his lodgings. I never knew anyone who had so many addresses. When I returned from South Africa he was moving to Cheyne Row, where Dermod O'Brian lived with him for a time; a time amusingly recorded in Hone's *The Life of Tonks*. Walter Russell and I took Great Cheyne Studio, close to Tonks' new house. I was still living with my mother nearby. The few years when I was working at this studio were some of the happiest and gayest of my life. I was able to do more painting, though I still had to make my living by illustrating. Pretty models sat for us. We worked, loved and danced through life.

Ethel Walker and Clare Christian, fellow students of my sister Jane at the Slade, built a house on Cheyne Walk. This house was large, and in it were two fine studios. It was built on the site of the old 'Magpie and Stump'. George Moore was usually a guest at their amusing parties, where we sometimes danced and sometimes played roulette. Wilson Steer was fond of dancing in those days, and often came.

There was one model whom some of us found rather too exacting. After a time I avoided her, realising the truth of the saying, 'The inconstancy of those I love is only equalled by the infernal constancy of those who love me.' One night I was talking about this girl, whom I will call Rose, to an ill, and sad looking sculptor. He said that he had something serious to say, and asked me to go with him to his lodging. It was very late, and his room chilled me, in spite of his efforts to coax the embers of a dying fire, and a whisky and soda which we both solemnly and slowly sipped. There was a long pause, then he began, with suppressed excitement, to talk of Rose. He considered her a remarkable girl, but misunderstood. Had I ever seen anyone more beautiful, or with such a lovely figure? He asked. Suddenly he pointed at me dramatically and said, 'I know that you have had her, and A. and B. and C.'

Going through the names of most of the painters in the district; finishing with 'I am not sure about Steer.' Steer had first brought her to my studio. It was a difficult moment for me, but I wriggled out of it somehow. Shortly afterwards this sculptor married Rose, and strangely enough it proved a successful marriage. Rose comported herself with genteel dignity, and was pleased with and proud of her man.

Peter Studd had come from Paris and taken a house in Cheyne Walk where Whistler had once lived with his mother. Studd was one of a family of cricketers. As a boy I had been much interested in the scores made by his brothers when they played for one of the Universities, and I was thrilled when introduced to a member of so renowned a family. Whistler was Peter's god. Indeed, Whistler helped him to decorate his house, and beautiful it was. The sitting room on the first floor had three high windows overlooking the river. The original wooden dado matched the high door. All the woodwork was painted a broken, creamy white; the walls above the dado were a light, cool brown, and the ceiling a lighter brown. From the centre of the ceiling a glass chandelier hung, and a beautiful plain buff coloured Persian carpet covered the floor. For curtains Whistler chose a gorgeously patterned chintz. Later Studd bought three pictures by Whistler, *The White Girl at a Mantelpiece, Fireworks at Cremorne*, and *A River Symphony*. Whistler, who was hard up, would only take a few hundred for them, and Studd hung them in this room. The effect was lovely; the memory of that room keeps fresh in my mind.

Studd gave many dinner parties. Not only was the food as perfect as he could make it, but he spent hours decorating table and dining room with flowers. Certainly the evening I met the French sculptor, Rodin, at one of these dinners, the decorations were better than the conversation, for this distinguished old gentleman, though evidently much pleased with his food, said no more than 'non' and 'oui' the whole evening. Soon after Whistler died, Studd showed me a cable from a collector in America offering him £5000 each for his three Whistler pictures. The American's reply to Studd's refusal to sell was a signed cheque and a request that Studd should fill in his own amount. Studd still refused to part with them – like a good patriot, he left them to the nation.

At this time Whistler's beautiful portrait of his mother and one of Carlyle were both unsold. I think it was Lavery who got the Glasgow gallery to buy the Carlyle for a hundred pounds. The French government bought the picture of his mother for some absurdly small sum.

Phil May returned to England in the '90s after making a reputation in Australia, drawing for *The Sydney Bulletin*. He had been in Yorkshire and lived there until he married, making a precarious living by drawing, and by doing odd jobs for the local theatre. I first knew him when he and his wife lived in a small studio in Holland Park Road. He was then working for *The Daily Graphic*, and soon after was taken on the staff of *Punch*. There is no doubt that May looked and was a 'character'. His face was thin, he had high cheekbones, prominent eyes and a roman nose. He wore his hair cut straight across his forehead in a fringe, like Beardsley. He had great sympathy for humanity in general and the poor in particular. He was vain, and enjoyed popularity. His pockets were usually stuffed with cigars, which he handed out to anyone he met. He had a strong sense of humour, and rarely journeyed to the West End without returned with an amusing story. One day, riding on the front seat of a horse omnibus, next to the driver, he was passing the lodge of Holland House in Kensington. In the small garden, the Lodge keeper's wife had hung out her weekly wash, consisting mostly of red flannel petticoats and drawers. The bus driver casually indicated these garments with his thumb, saying, 'I see 'er ladyship 'as returned.'

Philip May was born 1864 and died in 1903. Known as the Father of modern cartoonists he was able to use his untrained artistic talent to succeed in London and Sydney as a gifted cartoonist with a spareness of style that was quite new at the time. At the age of 21 in 1885 he was hired by *The St Stephens Review*. He met W.H. Trall, the Managing Director of *The Sydney Bulletin* who offered him a job, and he worked in Sydney until returning to London in 1890. He then worked for *The Daily Graphic* and started contributing cartoons to *Punch* in 1893. He was a heavy drinker almost all his life and died at the young age of 36.

I have a copy of *The Parson and the Painter*, which is an amusing account of his wanderings in the Bohemia of both London and Paris with a rather simple parson. It contains May's drawings of most well-known theatrical and sporting characters of the time. This publication gave offence to the Church, and many letters of complaint were written to various daily papers. Two other publications, *Mudlarks* and *Their only Playground* show May's humorous sympathy with the poor children of a city. When walking in Kensington High Street he met three children in fantastic, ill-fitting and ragged clothes. He stopped them and asked the eldest, a girl of about seven years old, whether they had any more brothers and sisters. Hearing that there were seven of them, he told the child to give his card to her mother and say that he would like them all to come to his studio next morning at ten o'clock. Entering his studio next morning he found the seven youngsters sprawling over his furniture, and the girl he had first spoken to sitting apart in tears. ''E's *my* artist, *I* found 'im,' she sobbed. The result of the children's visit was a full-page drawing in *Punch* of a man and woman and a bevy of ragged children singing, 'We're a fair old, rare old rickety rackety crew.'

Phil's wife, Lillie, was a beautiful, fair haired creature with a strong character.

Her life with Phil was difficult. He was usually behind time with his drawings, was out most nights until early morning, and he drank too much. He told me that he drank a bottle of whisky a day before he was twenty. Calling one evening, I found Lillie sad and worried. She had given Phil an ultimatum; if he did not return by twelve o'clock that night, she would leave him. Knowing her character, I felt sure that she would carry out her threat: knowing Phil's character, I knew that he would not be in by twelve. I was surprised, therefore, when I found her there the next evening. As I had expected, he had not returned by twelve, so she packed a bag and went to bed, determined to leave next morning. But when she woke she found that her bed was covered with roses. 'What can you do,' she said, 'with a man like that?'

Phil May took infinite trouble with his work. For what appeared a slight sketch he first made careful pencil drawings, these he traced two or three times, eliminating unnecessary lines.

On his drawing board he had written two slogans to keep him up to the mark. One was 'Spend the day loitering, it will be the same tale tomorrow and the next day.' The other, 'Only engage, and then the mind grows heated, begin it, and the job will be completed.'

Phil employed a man named Utting, a well-known model, to be in attendance for posing and for odd jobs. Having to draw a medieval knight, he dressed Utting in a suit of armour, complete with visor, feathers and steel jointed leg pieces, and when he had securely fastened all the buckles he told Utting that before starting work he wanted him to take a note to Mr J.J. Shannon, who lived at the end of the road. Utting expostulated, pointing out that walking the street in full armour would surely collect a crowd, and that probably he himself would get locked up. Phil disregarded his objections, gave him the note he had scribbled and told him to be back as soon as possible. He then watched Utting's progress from a window. There was no one about when he set forth, but by the time he got to the High Street a crowd had gathered, which waited outside Shannon's while he delivered the note. His return along Holland Park Road was a triumph. A policeman and the crowd followed him back to May's door.

I have a recollection of leaving a party with May, Pegram, Chantry, Corbould, (who drew hunting scenes for *Punch*) and Dudley Hardy. It was early morning when we stopped at a coffee stall, around which men and women derelicts clustered. Phil immediately ordered coffee and tea for the crowd, and we ate and drank with them until the stall was cleared. Phil then proposed that we should walk to his studio for a real drink. On the way Corbould and Hardy quarrelled. Corbould stood over six feet high, was broad shouldered and always carried a revolver. Dudley Hardy was short and thick set and had a fierce aspect. The quarrel continued as we walked. Corbould said he would kill Hardy and Hardy said he would break Corbould's back.

*Philip May self-portrait. Public domain.*

Phil led Corbould ahead and we retained Hardy, who was shouting 'Let me get at him.' When we arrived at the studio Phil, who was very sentimental, took the warring hands and made them shake. He hushed us into the studio, fearing to wake Lillie, and looked for drinks. But Lillie was one up on him, having hidden both drinks and glasses against such an emergency. All he could find was some liqueur and liqueur glasses, and in this we pledged eternal love and affection, and the last we saw of the warriors was when, arm in arm, they stumbled towards their homes.

Phil May was only thirty-nine when he died*. His end was tragic. Tubercle and consequent weakness reduced him to such a state that he could not bear a button to touch his skin, and they wrapped him in the softest silk and cotton wool. He loved life, and did not want to die. In the Chelsea Arts Club hangs a memento of him, it is a framed letter from him to Whistler, asking Whistler to propose him for membership of the Club, and it still hangs in what is 'The Whistler Bar' at the Club.

Walter Russell and I spent several summers painting together. At Swanage we stayed at a teetotal hotel, a sort of glorified ham and beef shop. We had small bedrooms in the roof, which were hot and uncomfortable. In spite of the discomfort, Walter painted a charming picture of trees whilst sitting on the bed with his canvas fixed awkwardly on the pulled out drawer of a rickety chest. The studio in which a picture is painted has little to do with the quality of the result.

*Gray's memory is incorrect. He was 36

There was also a pleasant summer spent at Southwold, where Pegram had taken a house. Several other friends were staying there, and with bathing, picnics and work, we had much amusement. One afternoon we were invited to a birthday tea. Wishing to make a good impression, we both dressed in our best – mine was a new grey flannel suit in which I felt superior. Having an hour to wait before the party, we walked to Walberswick and sat around on the old wooden pier, watching boys bathing. The river joined the sea here, and caused a strong, swirling current. One boy had got into this current, and we were watching with interest what we took to be his amazing stunts – diving, turning over and swimming under water, when an old man shouted to us that the boy was drowning. Walter immediately climbed down to the beach and went into the sea after him. I followed to the water's edge, and paused. I was not in the least afraid of the water, for we were both strong swimmers, but I could not bear the thought of spoiling my new clothes. My coat, at least must be saved, so I threw it onto the beach and went in. When I caught up with Walter he was well out to sea and had turned towards the shore. 'Where's the boy?' I asked. 'I have him under my arm' he spluttered. 'Damn it, you're drowning him' I said, 'give him to me.' I swam on my back and kept the boy's head up, and Walter pushed behind, and so we got to the beach. As we progressed I noticed that foam from the boy's mouth was going over my waistcoat. A crowd had gathered, and a man on horseback had galloped to a cottage for blankets with which they covered the small, dead looking body we handed to them. A doctor was giving artificial respiration when we left for our lodgings a mile away. Walking in wet clothes is unpleasant, they cling, and water oozes at each step. My new coat was safe, but no cleaner was ever able to take the stain out of the waistcoat. When we came down to breakfast next morning, a weather-beaten coastguard was waiting. He said he had come to thank us for saving his boy, and that his wife would like to wash our clothes for nothing! We called to see the boy – he was on a sofa, wrapped in a red blanket. He remembered nothing about his drowning act of the day before. It was more than an hour before the doctor had brought him round.

Another summer I arranged to spend with friends who lived in an old chateau in the Oise department of France.

Tonks had gone to Paris and was to join me later. He wrote telling me it was very hot in Paris, and that he was not happy. On hearing this, Madame S wrote asking Tonks to come to the Chateau and await my arrival, and this he did. A few days later he wrote to me and said 'Come at once, you don't know what you're missing – it is heaven.'

This is a beautiful 12th Century Chateau in the Oise Commune northeast of Paris called the Chateau de Montataire. It was constructed by Count Renaud II on the instructions of the King. In 1848 the Chateau was purchased by the

Baron de Conde who died in 1886. It was inherited by his wife Agnes Anna Cecilia Schultz and I believe she must be the Madame S referred to in the memoir, which dates the visit to before 1891. At her death in 1891 the Chateau was inherited by her brother Naylor Dunbar-Schultze. His son Alfred inherited, and he was married to an English woman, Anna Marie Charlesworth. They both became great friends with Gray.

He was well installed when I arrived. A large family party crowded the house. Tonks and I shared an immense bedroom, which was called the Henri IV room. Tradition had it that Henri IV had slept there. On one side of the room Tonks slept in a canopied bed draped with lovely hangings, and I had a small bed on the other.

*An undated photograph of the Henri IV bedroom and the four poster bed that Tonks slept in. Supplied to the author by the current Chateau owners.*

The Chateau was run luxuriously. A French major domo had bossed the place for years, but an English butler, who had been bequeathed to Madam S. by a relative in England, was beginning to assert authority. This butler was one of the oddest characters I ever met. He ambled around as though in a dream, and although he knew very few French words, he made himself understood and had gained complete control over the French servants. The feeling between him and the French major domo was naturally strained. He waited on one side of the dinner table, and the Frenchman on the other. He took charge of Tonks and myself. Each morning he came to our room and solemnly pulled back the high wooden shutters, saying 'I presume, gentlemen, you have finished with the darkness.'

A dressing bell rang each night at seven o'clock. The younger daughter of the house was always late, and to dodge her son's annoyance, Madam would wait in her room until the unpunctual girl came, so that they might appear together. Tonks and I got wise to this, and always waited for the dinner bell before going to dress. One evening we thought we really had cut it too fine, and running down a corridor, found James standing outside his mistress's room looking heavenwards. We asked if we were late, and he replied, 'No sir, la premiere personne has not descendee encore.' One day I was waiting on the terrace for the pony cart as I was going for a drive with the younger daughter. James came out, looked me up and down and asked, 'Are you driving with Miss V. in that habillement?' 'Yes, James' I said, 'don't you think I look smart?' He made no answer, and wandered away, muttering 'Cricketing suit, or something of that sort.' He had a high opinion of Tonks' judgement on all matters, and referred to him continually. Late one night we were sitting alone when James ambled in, holding a parcel. Walking solemnly up to Tonks he said 'I know you have been a great doctor, and are now a great artist – has, or has not this parcel been opened in the post?' The height of James's expression of admiration for Tonks was reached when he said 'We are now eleven in family, and there is Miss C. (the elder daughter). I should have no objection to twelve in family. Twelve is a good number – and you get on well together.' He then walked away, still looking heavenwards. We wondered what the girl's feeling would have been had she known that the butler had offered her hand in marriage to a comparative stranger.

The local clergy were always welcome visitors, and they took advantage of the good fare which this hospitable family offered. A waxen faced, black bearded priest, whilst waiting to go into dinner, said to me, 'You are an artist, eh? Do you paint in oil collars or water closets?' I said I painted in both, but that I was not really keen on painting in water closets.

Tonks, with his usual thoroughness, decided that he must study French. It was arranged that he should stay with the black bearded priest for a week or two, where he would hear no English. We drove him to an out of the way village and deposited him at the priest's house. It looked pretty grim, and Tonks seemed none too happy when we said goodbye. Certainly it was going to be a change after the comfort of the Chateau. The following day, when we were having tea in the garden, we were astonished to see Tonks hurrying towards us, carrying his bag. He went straight to Madame and said excitedly 'The man has phthisis* – when giving me a lesson he sat in front of me and his head about six inches from mine and shouted "lu, mu, nu, fu" and I couldn't stand it, and escaped when he went out to do

*a kind of tuberculosis

84

the marketing.' So Tonks stayed on with me at the Chateau for the remainder of a happy summer.

A few years ago I visited the Chateau again to stay with Madame's son and his wife, who now own the property. It all looked much the same as it did when we were there thirty-five years ago. (This must have been in the 1930's.) James the butler was no longer there. They had discovered that he was a secret drinker and pensioned him off; drink possibly explained some of his eccentricities. They told me that he had a passion for the younger daughter and had put a rose outside her door each morning. Tonks and I had noticed this when we were there, and I was glad to have it explained, as I had been conscious that everyone suspected me of the romantic act.

> I will return to the Chateau much later. In my Great Uncle's papers is a fascinating letter from Alfred written in early 1945 outlining what happened to him, his wife and his Chateau during the war.

*A modern photograph of the Chateau de Montataire in Winter from current owners.*

When war was declared against the Boers, some of the artists from the Chelsea Arts Club joined the Artists Rifles. Peter Studd, Derwent Wood, Dermod O'Brian and I spent hours at headquarters being put through it by energetic sergeants.

We volunteered for foreign service, but were turned down on account of age – all of us being over thirty! I was relieved, because I did not want to fight the Boers. I had read their history and seen something of their charming old villages, where well designed and well built houses gave evidence of simple and civilised existence.

The Rand stood for moneygrubbing commercialism, which is a poor form of civilisation. I was not feeling well and was losing weight, and a suspicious lump had appeared. Our doctor said that it might be tubercle, but he did not think it likely because I was not the tubercular type. At that time I did not know what tubercle meant. I was to discover later.

> A tubercle is a small, firm, rounded nodule or swelling, such as a swelling that is a characteristic of a tuberculosis lesion.

My bedroom became an operating theatre, Mother the matron, and my sister Elizabeth the head nurse. The anaesthetist told me to 'breathe deeply' and I remembered no more until I awoke to misery and pain. I did not improve in spite of all the tender care. I was sent to Sussex to stay with the Pegrams, where the local doctor who attended me repeatedly told me that I was responding to treatment; I thought it strange that I became weaker and weaker. To make things more interesting, my sister-in-law, playing with a powerful air gun, shot me in the leg while I was reclining in a chair on the lawn. The pellet went through my flannel trousers and embedded itself in my flesh, but did no great harm.

I became so weak that the doctor thought it would be as well if I returned to London for more advice. I could hardly stand when I was taken to St Thomas's Home. A clever surgeon named Abbot, a charming man, examined me. He said he feared that the tubercle had gone too far for another operation to be of any use, but that he would do what he could. I little guessed what was in store for me. When coming out of that condition of nothingness caused by anaesthetics, some hours after my operation, I became conscious of distant music, and asked the nurse what it meant. She told me that C.I.Vs, (City of London Imperial Volunteers, I think it meant) were crossing Westminster Bridge on their way to the Boer War. Then I heard Big Ben strike the hour and I knew that I was back in the world again, having in the interval collected bandages and pain.

> St Thomas's Hospital is just across Westminster Bridge opposite the Houses of Parliament which are on the other side of the River Thames.

At that time St Thomas's Home was one of the large wards of the hospital, divided by curtains into cubicles. The ward overlooked the Thames, and on the balcony convalescents were allowed to sit. Some of the patients had been there for months. They initiated the newcomers into the traditions of the ward. Some of these seemed odd to me. When Big Ben struck the hour for meals, all the patients in unison had to shout 'NURSE, WE WANT FOOD.' The amount of groaning allowed after each operation had been fixed. A Jewish doctor in the cubicle next to mine had groaned the whole night. Next morning the oldest inhabitant – a man, who in spite of not being able to move his head or limbs, was always cheerful – asked what his operation had been. A week voice answered 'Appendicitis.' 'Why you groaned all night, we don't allow that, we only allow an hour's groaning for appendicitis.'

Another patient was Captain de Horsey (afterwards an admiral) back from South Africa, and wounded in the foot. Each morning a man massaged his ankle, and one movement always made de Horsey shout with pain. At every shout the other patients yelled in unison, 'COWARD.'

> Sir Algernon de Horsey was born in 1827 and died in 1922. He was a Royal Navy Officer with a distinguished career throughout the British Empire. He was ADC to Queen Victoria in the 1870's, then Commander in Chief of the Pacific Squadron, followed by Commander in Chief of the Channel Fleet. Promoted Full Admiral in 1885 he went onto the reserve list in 1892. In 1903 he was knighted.

A small boy was put into our ward because they were full up elsewhere, and the poor kid never ceased whining and calling for his mother. During the night he continued calling for 'Mumm' and suddenly he shouted 'Nursey, I wants to pee-wee.' The night nurse must have been dozing, for his appeal continued until a loud bass voice shouted 'For God's sake, Nurse, let the boy pee-wee, and then we can all go to sleep!' The boy was moved next day.

When a patient was on the danger list the curtains of his cubicle were kept closed. One night, in the cubicle opposite mine, I watched a man die; his curtains not being fully closed. A candle was burning. His wife, silhouetted against it, knelt at his bedside. I could hear murmuring, and after a while there was silence. A nurse led the weeping woman away. Late in the night, when all patients were supposed to be asleep, he was carried away in a coffin.

I was at the home for a month. In spite of the pain and surrounding miseries I cannot say it was an unhappy month. The other patients were amusing, I liked the nurses, and I had many visitors, among whom was our old Nurse Alice, who brought me two apples and still called me 'Master Ronnie'.

The surgeon advised that I should spend the winter at Margate. My brother Alfred took me there and settled me in a most comfortable small hotel. My kind family took it in turns to stay and look after me, so that I was rarely alone. Among artists who came for week-ends were Tonks, my brothers-in-law Pegram and Townsend (Fred Townsend), and Philip Treherne. Phil May and Lillie were staying in Margate with the Burnands, and Phil rode over each morning on his horse Punch. Sometimes Lillie came to tea with me. Each morning I was pulled around in a bath chair by an old man named Gale. Mr Gale was an amusing character, and I watched with interest the technique he used to ingratiate himself with clients. I have noticed that each profession has its own method of ingratiation, even portrait painters. The first morning Mr Gale fetched me for my run he asked me, to my surprise, whether I was suffering from kidneys or stomach. He explained that he always likes to know the nature of his patients disease, for then he knew what care to take when pulling his chair over curbs. When on the Parade among dozens of other invalids in bath chairs, Mr Gale whispered 'If you should 'ave a fancy for any particular party I will bump them by accident, and you can make it up with 'er when we apologise.' I pointed out one rather nice looking party, but he said 'I don't recommend 'er, she's a bad case of kidneys.' However Mr Gale's professional help did lead to my acquaintance with a charming 'party' and her family, a friendship which brightened my stay at Margate and which lasted many years.

In this way weeks passed, and the cold, fresh air 'straight from the North Pole' certainly braced me, but I was horrified to find that something was happening to my lately healed wound – another lump was forming. I called on a recommended doctor, hoping against hope that it would not prove serious, but was not reassured when he advised me to get in touch with Mr Abbot again. The result was that I struggled miserably back to St Thomas's to undergo another operation. My nurse sent a telegram to Mother after it was over; the poor dear thought I was still in Margate, almost well, and was upset when she came to the hospital. However, I was able to take her for some lovely drives, for a kind friend sent his carriage and pair whenever I wished. The last drive we took was to see the draping of the streets for the funeral of Queen Victoria.

The surgeon now said that my best chance of recovery would be a long sea voyage, but this meant expense which we could not afford. My kind friend Brocklehurst came to my rescue and bought me a ticket for the longest sea trip possible – to Australia via South Africa, and back round Cape Horn. This would give me some months of sea air. I left St Thomas's and returned home to make preparations for the journey.

---

The funeral of Queen Victoria took place on February 4 1901.

---

# Chapter 9

# Down Under

I was a poor, weak specimen when my brother Alfred took me on board the ship at Tilbury. I felt rather bewildered when we said goodbye and he left me standing on the deck. Then a fair young man in uniform appeared and asked me if my name was Ronald Gray. He told me that the previous night, at a dance given by J.J. Shannon, Kitty Shannon his daughter, had asked him to look out for me, because we were evidently travelling in the same ship. This was luck for me, for he was the ship's doctor, an Australian named Page. (We were friends for many years, for he lived in England for some time after this voyage.) After introducing himself, he asked me to come to the rail and see the bo'sun saying goodbye to his wife. To my surprise he pointed to an enormous black man on the dock below clasping a black woman, and as he kissed her he kept saying 'I'll be true to you, Sal.' I expressed astonishment that a black man could manage a white crew, but Page said that he had them completely under his thumb, in spite of never raising his voice or swearing at them. He had been raised to the rank of bo'sun for bravery, and for standing by the captain when a ship was wrecked. On the voyage I got to know him and liked him. He was a student of Shakespeare, and could quote whole plays.

The ship in which I was to make the long voyage was one of the smaller ones, of only 8,000 tons. It was a disappointment to find that the passengers were all men, and mostly invalids at that. The shipping company had evidently arranged that invalids should travel together, and not be carried in mail boats. After touching at Las Palmas we were to make for Melbourne, a seven week run without a break. The captain was a short, fat Jersey man, and he spoke with a French accent. The officers were pleasant, tough sailor men. The captain proved to be our principal source of amusement. He was excitable, and when things became difficult he retired to his cabin with a bottle of whisky and left the job to his officers. He liked joining in when we played poker, and this led to a regular bust up. Once whilst playing I saw him deliberately pick up one of his discards and quietly throw out another. I accused him of cheating, he exploded with rage, and shouted that he would put me in irons. It was some time before his officers could calm him. He did not put me in irons, and we did not play cards with him again.

In those days there was, of course, no wireless, and we got no news of how the Boer War was going until we reached Melbourne. Near Cape Town a large Red Cross ship passed us on its way to England with wounded. We passed land near enough to see Table Mountain covered with the usual cloud which is called its table cloth. We steered the course of the grand circle which took us far into the southern ocean, an inhospitable ocean, cold and grey, with immense rollers, always rolling in the same direction.

I was glad when we approached Australia. One gets tired of being boxed up with a bunch of uninteresting male invalids. I still have a book filled with their ugly faces. I was certainly stronger than when I left London, but when Page gave me an overhaul, to my horror he said that I must land at Melbourne for 'just a slight operation.' He assured me that I should be well enough to regain the ship when she called back at Melbourne in a fortnight. I was beginning to know what these slight operations meant, for this would be the fourth. I had little money, and hated to worry my overtaxed family again. I knew no one in Melbourne, but I remembered that Ada Crossley, the Australian contralto, had given me a letter of introduction to a friend of hers there. This letter was my salvation.

> Ada Crossley was born in 1871 and died in 1929. She was one of the first famous Australian singers to gain international fame. She was sent to Melbourne to be trained and made her first appearance with the Philharmonic Society of Melbourne in 1889. In 1894 she left for Europe and first appeared in London at the Queens Hall in 1895.

Directly we had booked rooms at an hotel Page drove with me to St Kilda, a suburb of Melbourne, and I presented my letter to Miss Veitch. Page explained my predicament, and she at once telephoned a surgeon friend, and we went to see him. After he had examined me he rang up a nursing home and arranged that I should go in next morning. Again I was caught in a current from which there seemed no escape.

> This section of the memoirs is also well covered in letters he wrote home to his mother in London, and which have survived, and are in the authors collection. They make an interesting check on his memory and also fill in some details, sometimes forgotten by him and sometimes deliberately omitted.

On my return to the hotel that evening, whilst I was going along a corridor to my room, a door opened and a small hand and arm appeared, putting out a pair of ladies' shoes. To my astonishment Page seized the hand, and as I continued on my way I heard him arguing with a voice from behind the door. I lay on my bed, and after a few minutes Page came in and said, 'It's all right, she's going to have supper with me!' This was the oddest introduction I had so far known. Page helped me to bed and tried to be sympathetic and cheery, but I could see that his thoughts were elsewhere.

I spent a wakeful night. Next morning Page came with me to the nursing home. It was a pleasant house, brilliant sunshine came through the French windows of the room I was to use. The home was run by two Roman Catholic nurses, and I found that Dr Ryan, my doctor, was a Catholic also. He had a cheery manner, and he suggested that I should make a will, explaining that if I died without saying what was to be done with my things it would be very awkward for the owners of the home. I told him that I did not feel that I was going to die, adding that it would be rather hard luck if I died at thirty-two. I was surprised when he said, 'Oh well, old chap, you've lived your life!'

I was very ill indeed after the operation, so weak that for a day or two I cried each time Nurse Fitzsimons spoke to me. This kind nurse and Dr Ryan could not possibly have done more to get me well. Miss Veitch and her friends kept my room gay with flowers. I renewed a friendship with Bernard Hall, head of the Melbourne National Gallery, and Miss Veitch introduced me to a fine looking old man named Mitchell, the father of Melba, the singer. He had been a successful contractor. He drove lovely horses, and took me out sometimes in his high phaeton.

Bernard Hall was born in England in 1869 and died in 1935. He studied in London and Europe before working in London for the illustrated papers where he probably first encountered Gray. They were both founding members of the New English Art Club in 1886 and he was appointed Director of the National Gallery of Melbourne in 1891.

Once we went to a station owned by an old Scot, well on in his eighties from which Mitchell was buying some cattle, and I had great entertainment listening to their bargaining before they shook hands on the deal. The Scotsman told me that when young he had been cow keeper to Sir Walter Scott. Mitchell was over seventy but he exuded energy, and a drive with him was a tonic. He rattled on about all kinds of things, and was especially interesting on the subject of gold mining. He advised me never to put money into any Australian gold mining company floated in London. He said that Australians kept the good mines to themselves. He explained that a small mine would be bought in Western Australia for, say £5,000, and at such a price it might pay a dividend; but a promoter would get hold of it and float a company in

London for one or two hundred pounds, and the result the investors would discover later. I have always been suspicious of men who call themselves company promoters; no wonder some of them live in Park Lane.

This is described in more detail in a letter home dated August 6 1901:

*I went for the drive with Melba's father last Tuesday – I think I told you I was going in my last letter. He is great old man and we had an amusing time. He took me to call on people called Laidlaw who have a fine house in the country. They are very old settlers – Mr Laidlaw is 84 and as active and bright as an ordinary man of 60 and Mrs L. is 83! He told me that 60 years ago he watched a tribal fight between natives on the site of his present grounds. He also informed me that before he left Scotland he had the charge of Sir Walter Scott's Castle at Abbottsford. He is now a very wealthy Station owner. These first settlers were a fine tough lot of men – mostly Scotch!*

After a month at the nursing home I stayed a week or two with Bernard Hall, and then moved to a cheap boarding house at St Kilda, to be near Miss Veitch. There I paid 25/- a week. The people were kind, but it was hardly the place for one in my condition. Dr Ryan let me pay his bill with a small portrait I painted of him in Hall's fine studio at the gallery. Most mornings Ryan came to the boarding house to look me over. The wound had not quite healed, and one morning he did not like the look of things and told me to come to the nursing home the following day. I felt hopeless, and quite broke down. I told him that I had not the strength or the money to go through any more if it, and unless he thought there was still a chance that I should get well I should forestall matters and go over the pier. Ryan was understanding and sympathetic. He gave me hope that the cause of the wound not healing might be that internal stitches had not dissolved. This it proved to be, but it meant visits to the nursing home spread over months, when Ryan scraped about for successive stitches – there seemed to be dozens. Just when I had come to the end of my money, a letter arrived from Tonks enclosing a cheque for me, the money having been subscribed by himself, my brothers-in-law Pegram and Townsend, and other artists. This generosity saved the situation. I have noticed that when I had no money I was humble and slightly cringing in my attitude to others, but directly I had a bit in my pocket I became almost arrogant.

Another excerpt, this time dated August 13 1901:

*I painted another portrait of Ryan as I didn't like the first and he is very pleased with it. I am not getting on very well with the one of the Hotel keeper – I have been working nearly every day for about 5 hours. He affords me considerable amusement*

I soon realised that my surgeon, Tom Ryan, was a man with a strong character. He took me to theatres, race meetings and football matches. He gave me dinners and made me slightly drunk on champagne. If I said I did not feel strong enough for some proposed expedition, I was told not to be silly but to come along. Miss Veitch and Nurse Fitzsimons also helped me to get well, and I had interest and pleasure in a friendship I formed with Major Champion, who years before had been associated with John Burns and Cunningham-Graham, when they led dock strikers to fight with police in Trafalgar Square. I had supper with him and his wife most Sunday evenings. His wife ran a book shop called 'Booklovers Library', from which I was supplied with plenty of literature.

John Elliot Burns, born 1858 and died 1943, began work at the age of 10 and attended night school and read extensively. In 1883 he joined the Social Democratic Federation (SDF), which was at that time the only avowedly Socialist body in England, and in 1885 he unsuccessfully sought election to Parliament as a member of the SDF. Burns was tried for sedition in 1886 and was imprisoned in 1888 for his part in the 'Bloody Sunday' riot that had taken place in London's Trafalgar Square the preceding November. With Benjamin Tillett and Tom Mann, Burns was a dominant figure in the great London dock strike of 1889, which brought casual and unskilled labourers into trade unions. In 1892 he was elected chairman of the Trades Union Congress and a Socialist member of the House of Commons. The following year the Independent Labour Party (a forerunner of the modern Labour Party) was founded, and, although he was active in the new party, he did not claim to represent it in Parliament. (Britannica)

Whilst I was in Melbourne the Prince and Princess of Wales, afterwards King George V and Queen Mary, came to open the first Commonwealth Parliament. There were rejoicings and decorations in Melbourne. The decorations were many and good, and in some cases showed ingenuity. One decoration remains distinctly in my memory, a large sheet of calico stretched across a street from roof to roof. On it was printed in large letters, 'ONE KING, ONE PARLIAMENT, ONE SET OF TEETH, ONE GUINEA.' I was not surprised to find that on the door of one of the houses to which this patriotic greeting was attached was a dentist's brass plate.

Melba gave a homecoming concert to which I was taken. She sang 'Home, Sweet Home' her voice trembling with emotion.

My eldest brother (this was Sam, his half-brother by his father's first wife) was living at a mining camp on the Queensland border of New South Wales. He had gone to Australia fifteen years before because of weak lungs. The idea was that I should join him when well enough to make so long a journey. A plan had crystallised in Ryan's brain, but I trembled when he told me of it. A portrait was to be painted of the Chancellor of Sydney University, and this commission he said he meant to get for me. I knew that no power on earth would stop him. He waved aside my excuse that I was too weak. Two hundred and fifty guineas would be useful, he said. I was to stay with my brother for six months to get strong, and then return to Sydney and paint the portrait. He would arrange that it should wait until I was ready. How he managed to work this I do not know, but he did.

So after six months in Melbourne the time came for me to say goodbye to these kind people who had done so much to help me through a difficult time. Ryan, Miss Veitch and Nurse Fitzsimons came to the ship with gifts the night I left for Sydney. I have seen them all in London many times since then, and during this second world war have had presents of butter, raisins, and so on, from the ladies – forty years after my leaving Melbourne.

It was a rough passage to Sydney. I recollect holding someone's hand when the ship was entering Sydney Harbour, though I have not the faintest recollection whose, or of her face, or anything else about the journey. Soon after booking a room at a recommended hotel I received a visit from the head of the portrait committee. He was a kind looking old gentleman with a white beard. He at once took me to the Australian Club and made me an honorary member, then he marched me into various rooms and solemnly introduced me to member after member, saying 'Let me introduce Mr Ronald Gray from London.' After about fifty introductions he once more started his 'Let me introduce' – when he suddenly paused, and turning to me said 'Excuse me, sir, I forget your name.'

This is described in a bit more honest detail in a letter written on Australian Club paper and dated August 17 1901:

*I have only a few more minutes to post time, but I will try and give you a short account of my todays proceedings. Things have moved so quickly that I am almost bewildered! When I arrived at the Hotel Metropole I found an elderly gentleman had just come to see me – he proved to be Mr Smith one of the leading lawyers of Sydney and the man who has the arranging of the portrait of the Chancellor of the University. He first made me a member of this Club, which is an important one, and then fetched me to lunch here. He introduced me to about a thousand men, rushed me round the National Gallery and left me with the promise that I call for*

The committee did just as Ryan had decreed. To my relief I was to have £50 when I began the portrait, and the rest when the painting had been accepted. Should they not accept it, I was to keep the £50. The sensible reason they gave for this arrangement was that they had only Dr Ryan's word regarding my capabilities. After a few days of wonderful hospitality in Sydney, I left on the long and tiring journey to the north of New South Wales.

I tell of this journey in some detail because, with the coming of the motor car and aeroplane, all travel in out-of-the-way places is much altered. To reach the mining camp where my brother lived involved a long journey by rail and then a coach drive of sixty or seventy miles. I was tired when we arrived that night at the town where the railway ended, and a kind commercial traveller carried my luggage to the hotel and booked me a room. He woke me the following morning in time to catch the coach which left at six o'clock. On his recommendation I paid an extra 2/6 for a seat beside the driver, because, he said, coach drivers were interesting men and enjoyed a good talk. The coach was a ramshackle affair, harnessed to six or eight scraggy horses. I climbed proudly to my box seat, and the other passengers got up behind. A look at the driver was enough to convince me that he was not a man of fluent conversation. He lightly whipped the horses, and were soon away from the town. I studied him. He was a large, massive man with a heavy jowl and extremely thick lips. I hazarded a futile remark about the beauty of the morning. He did not answer but merely gave me a glance which I thought showed contempt. However, there was plenty to amuse me. The country through which we were passing was different from any I had seen before. There was no made road, and each vehicle took its own way. I could see wheel tracks side by side for half a mile or more. Everywhere, white leafless trees, killed by an early practise of ring barking, made fantastic shapes against the bluest of skies. Some had fallen. Although the scene had a weird beauty, there was about it something of a nightmare. I tried a word or two on this line of thought with the driver, but only got another of his looks.

We had taken sandwiches for lunch, and pulled up for drinks at a Bush shanty, which looked to have been built of kerosene tins. We were served by a bronzed, bearded monster, and I thought that he looked at me in an old-fashioned way and said something about me to driver. I suppose I did look ill and out of place in that setting. Then we went on again. I had given up hope of any conversation. I might not have been on the coach, for all the notice the driver took of me. During the afternoon the character of the country altered, rocky hills appeared in the distance and our way at times was precipitous. Down one steep incline the driver gave the brake a hefty pull, there was a bang, a crash and a jump, and he yelled 'Gord! The bloody brake's gorn.' These were the only words I heard him utter during the whole day, but they were worth the extra half-crown. Without the brake the heavy coach gained speed and hit the back horse which immediately sprang forward, terrified. Our driver showed great presence of mind, he managed to control the frightened horses and steer the rocking coach into a muddy pond at the bottom of the hill, where it came to an abrupt stop. It took the driver and all of us passengers a long time to drag it from the mud.

We got under way again, and towards evening arrived at the small township where I was to spend the night before starting on the last stage of the journey. The coach stopped at the only hotel, where I was expected, for a letter of welcome awaited me from my brother in which he told me that the manager of the mine would fetch me the next morning. It was afternoon before he came. He drove a light buggy with spiderish looking wheels; he smelt strongly of alcohol, and was gay and chatty. Our way took us through rocky scrub country and across streams, which he negotiated with alcoholic bravado. It was evening when straggling tents and wood fires gave evidence that we were approaching the mining camp, which I will call Fern Creek to hide its identity.

We drove down a long, unmade road on either side of which were tents and shacks. Rough looking men were cooking at blazing fires, and there was a smell of burning leaves and wood, which was pleasant. My brother lived at the further side of the camp, above a valley where one could see ranges of rocky hills fading into the distance. I had a feeling of emotion when we stopped outside a large tent and the manager said 'There is your brother.' He looked older and more of an invalid than I had expected, and he leant on a stick. The last time I had seen him was when I saw him off to Australia from Tilbury fifteen years before. In his letters to Mother he had told of his wanderings. Since then his bad health had forced him to give up a lucrative position in Sydney to come to this pure air high about sea level. He had a devoted wife, whose pleasure seemed to be looking after him.

I was installed in a wooden hut he had built for me. It was about eight feet square and raised three feet from the ground, and in it there was a comfortable camp bed. The other furniture seemed to be constructed of barrels and kerosene tins. That first night I was soon in bed, for I was tired.

The account of this journey in his first letter from the mining camp supplies a lot more detail and easily identifies where he was. I am not sure why he wanted to keep his destination a secret almost 50 years later and I have changed the name throughout for clarity:

*Borah Creek Inverell, N.S.W. Sept 8th 1901*
*My Dear Mother*

*Here I am, sitting in the shade of a little wooden cottage and Sam basking in the sun, smoking and reading his paper, about 10 feet away! A few log 'humpies' and a tent or two are dotted about the clearings made in the Bush which surrounds us for hundreds of miles – we are sixty miles from the nearest Railway Terminus! Sam is very brown and plump in the face and is better than he has been for nine years – I really think he has a good chance of getting the better of the disease which has several times nearly cost him his life. I was horrified to find how ill he has been – it is only lately that he has been able to walk about and even now he goes pretty carefully. The Manager, Mr Grant, who drove me from Inverell, told me that when he engaged him about a year ago he didn't think Sam would live to get to Borah. He thinks the change in him since then is most remarkable.*

*Alice is such a nice kind woman and evidently been most devoted to him. He has the utmost consideration shown him by everybody and I really think he leads a happy life – especially now that he feels so much better. On his pegged out claim (1/4 of an acre) he has built a small wooden 3 roomed cottage, which stands on wooden piers, and he has a tent standing at the back. I have made myself cosy in my room – the furniture is primitive, but the bed is very comfortable. I have hung up photos of Dr Ryan and some of the sweet Melbourne girls! I found the journey from Sydney to Glen Innes rather tiring. Mabel and her Aunt saw me off at the station. The train started at 5 o'clock and arrived at Glen Innes the following morning at 10. There were 4 of us in the carriage so I had to huddle up in the corner. At Glen Innes we had breakfast and then took the coach to Inverell a distance of 42 miles. The road, or rather track, runs through pretty wild country – this was most invigorating and I thoroughly enjoyed the trip. On arriving at Inverell I got a letter from Sam telling me to rest there till Thursday morning, when Mr Grant would drive me out in his buggy. Inverell is a sleepy corrugated iron town, but the district is very fertile and reminded me rather of the Sussex Down country. The late heavy rains had made everything very green – fresh grass was shooting up everywhere. On Wednesday evening Grant called and took me round to dinner at his house – they seemed pleasant people and are moving to Borah next week, where he has had built rather a nice house opposite Sam's. We started for there, next morning at 7.30 taking in a place called Tinga on our way as he had a Court Case on before the Magistrate there. It was a delightful drive and everything was so novel. We spent most of the day at Tinga which is a typical mining village peopled mostly by Chinese. Some of the charges were most amusing and the amount of perjury that went on was surprising! As the sun went down we started for Bora. It was the most exciting drive I have ever had. The track through the Bush was very rough and Grant was rather drunk and reckless and we went over boulders, through creeks and into bogs and it was certainly luck more than skill that kept us from upsetting! It was quite dark when we entered the Township, the road marked by the lights from the tents and humpies of the miners. Sam's cottage is at the further end of the Town and we soon came within sight of his light in the window. Alice came out to greet me and I found Sam sitting by the fire in the back room and my first impression was that he had altered a good deal, but it was difficult to realise that fifteen years had passed since we said goodbye at the docks. Of course we had a great yarn – in fact we have been at it ever since. I found 4 weeks letters waiting and thoroughly enjoyed all the news. You and Ken had just arrived from the country and Liz had departed for Petworth. Nothing is settled yet about the portrait. Sam thinks I look very well.*

*With my best love to you all, from your loving son, Ronald Gray*

Extract from a report on the impact of a Derelict Base Metal Mine on the Aquatic Environment, part of the MWA Proceedings 1988 and copyright International Mine Water Association 2012.

### *Mining history*

*The Conrad mine is the largest hard rock base metal mine in the New England region, and was mined intermittently between 1898 and 1957, when the mine finally closed due to low metal prices and high production costs.*

*There were two periods of significant mining activity, namely 1898 to 1913, when up to 500 men were employed, and 1950 to 1957, when 60 men were employed. Zinc, copper and silver-lead concentrates were produced, and, in the early mining period, these were smelted on site to produce silver-lead and lead-tin bullion, copper matte and arsenic oxide.*

*Alluvial tin and diamonds have been worked in the downstream reaches of Maids Creek nearby, but no production figures or when the operations were carried out are known. The bed of Maids Creek has been extensively disturbed as a result of these operations.*

## Site description

The mine is located in the valley of Borah Creek in undulating timbered granite terrain on the western edge of the New England Plateau. Only very small-scale cattle or sheep grazing is carried on in the vicinity of the mine and, apart from the attraction of the mine itself, the area is an isolated one.

Borah Creek, a non-perennial creek with a catchment of 7 sq. km, is a tributary of Maids Creek, which drains an area of 45 sq. km and flows into the Copeton Dam storage on the Gwydir River. The susceptibility to weathering of lode mineralisation has determined the position of Borah Creek to be along the outcrop of the Conrad lode.

Surface workings at the site extend over a distance of about 2km and run downslope from east to west generally parallel to Borah Creek. They comprise two main three-compartment timber-lined shafts, the Conrad and King Conrad, being 275 and 125 m deep respectively, together with eleven other single compartment shafts and four adits.

# Chapter 10

# Borah Creek

I awoke in a strange and primitive world. The life was so completely different from anything I had experienced before that I knew it was a kill or cure treatment. The food was good, if a little monotonous, my sister-in-law doing the cooking. My brother was secretary to the mine in the valley, a silver lead mine, around which this small township had grown. Also in the district were dried-up river beds where men fossicked for and found diamonds.

Shortly before my arrival there had been some bother at the mine, and a Greek miner had been sacked in consequence. Anonymous and threatening letters in red ink had been sent to the manager, who was not at all happy about the outlook. From his house to the mine was a distance of about a quarter of mile, up a rocky path through a wood. I thought it a pretty wood, but for the manager at that time it was filled with unpleasant possibilities. Two or three days after my arrival he lent me a Winchester repeating rifle and suggested that I should walk with him to the mine each morning. He carried a revolver. When we entered the wood he fired a round or two to show that he was about. He learnt somehow that the Greek and his friends intended to break into his house on a certain night, so a council of war was called. This council consisted of the manager, my brother, a mounted trooper and myself. The trooper arranged a plan of defence. My job was to lie on the floor of the doorway of my hut which was opposite the entrance to the manager's house. I was told to fire at any marauder, and not to worry if I killed him! When one has spent nine months in hospital and undergone many operations, one is not in the best form for battles – indeed, battles had never been a hobby of mine. However, as darkness fell I lay on my stomach as ordered, clasping my rifle. Hours passed, and nothing happened until I was being shaken and awoke to find the trooper standing over me. I had slept at my post! It appeared that the trooper had let it be known that if the Greek and his friends made an attack they would be shot, therefore the gang thought the best plan was to clear out, which they did during the night. None of them was seen again whilst I was there.

It soon became clear that life at Borah Creek was much the same as life on mining camps anywhere. We had the mounted trooper representing law and order, a printed news sheet called *The Digger*, a saloon, and the local bully. The trooper and I became great friends. Like most of these Australian troopers, he was a brave man, and the more I knew of the place the more I wondered how he was able to control the large district of which he had charge. This silver lead mine employed men of many nationalities, who worked in day and night shifts and were paid weekly. On pay nights the saloon became the miners' Mecca, with the result that the trooper then had his busiest time. On those evenings, when sitting with my brother, we could hear howls and screams from the saloon in the distance – a strange contrast to the calm of a lovely night. Once the trooper fetched me to see what he considered one of his best bits of work. In the garish light of an oil flare outside the saloon there were ten or twelve howling, drunken men, each with a wrist handcuffed to a strong post and rail fence. The trooper said modestly, 'I did it all by myself.'

The man who published *The Digger* was a tough fellow, bronzed from years of exposure. He enjoyed talking to me of his boyhood, which he spent in some village in England. He wished he could pop into the village church some Sunday and give them a surprise. He certainly would have surprised them. He had acquired a small hand printing press, and with this he produced his paper, of which he was editor and proprietor. It was supposed to appear each week, but circumstances sometimes hindered publication. The price of this single sheet was sixpence, and I wondered why anyone would pay so high a price for so little until he explained that it was his *They Say* column, which held up publication whilst the editor recovered from injuries received during fights caused by this column, and which made the paper worth the price. These fights were forced upon him after his outrageous references to one or other of his subscribers, and I will give one or two examples which I copied from *The Digger* at the time.

'They say that the young lady who wears her red hair tied with a blue bow should be more careful in her choice of blokes. Her present pal who sports pointed brown boots is nothing more than a dirty scoundrel.'

'They say that the cove who wears a long beard and has a bad squint would be more respected if he gave up beating his wife and devoted more attention to paying some of his bills.'

It is perhaps not surprising that both these gentlemen considered they had some cause for complaint. The number published the week after my arrival contained this reference to me. 'They say that clean-shaven Mos are being fashionable.' I was the only clean-shaven man in the camp.

One episode I witnessed concerned the bully. It reminded me of stories I had illustrated for the Harmsworth Press years before. They told me that every mining camp had its bully. He is usually a powerful man who gains his title by knocking out all who oppose him. Having accomplished this he assumes a highhanded manner towards all men; he can enter a saloon and drink another's beer or walk off with his girl with impunity whilst his spell lasts. Our bully, when I first saw him, was flabby and had a bloated face, showing that he had taken full advantage of his position. Soon after my arrival, two delicate looking young men, real Cockneys, appeared. No doubt they had come to Australia for their health, for they both looked poor specimens. One evening they were sitting on the veranda of the saloon when the bully started a row with a woman, and struck her a blow on the mouth. This was too much for one of the small Cockneys (who wore spectacles). To the surprise of the watching locals he sprang at the bully and gave him such a punch on the face that the bully was too dazed to hit back. When he recovered his poise he challenged his attacker to fight the next morning. The foregoing part of the story I did not myself see, but had it from a witness; the sequel I did see.

Early in the morning the trooper called to tell me that there was to be a fight in the clearing at nine o'clock. He was not going to stop it, but would watch from behind a rock. When I arrived there were about a hundred men, some just off night shift, sitting around on fallen trees. While waiting for the combatants I remember thinking over the strange and unexpected events which had led me to this outlandish place, where I was at the moment sitting on a fallen tree in expectation of seeing two men knock one another about. The bully arrived, big and bloated, laughing with several friends. The two small Cockneys followed. They were alone, and both were pale and nervous; my heart went out to them, for they had no friends among the audience. Time was called, and the big man came forward, smiling. The Cockney took off his coat and spectacles and handed them to his friend, and the battle began. The bully sprang about like a playful elephant, the Cockney followed stealthily with head forward and a determined look. Neither was a boxer. Suddenly the Cockney shot out his right and caught his enemy on the chin, the bully wiped it away as if it were nothing, and pranced again. Prancing is not a help when one is in bad condition, and he was breathing heavily. The Cockney bashed him again on the chin, and again and again until, in the second round, to the intense surprise of everyone, the bully gave in. We stood up and cheered. From that moment the bully's day was done – the spell was broken. Even 'half axes' as they called boys, pushed him about and took his beer when he dared go into the saloon. It was not long before he left the camp for ever.

Extract from letter undated with more detail on the fight and comments on his fellow residents.

*The next morning I had just finished breakfast and noticed groups of men going down the hill from the Township and guessing something was up, followed. Arriving at a secluded spot among the trees having for a background a magnificent view of distant hills, I found two men sparring up in professional form with seconds and a timekeeper! One combatant was tall and heavily built, the bully of the place, and the other was a thin, rather delicate looking man about three stone lighter. The fighting was not scientific but was exciting and gradually we found that the little man was getting the better of it. About the sixth round he got a beauty on his opponents chin which decked him and finished the fight. The bully amidst loud applause from the crowd had to give in! The onlookers included the schoolmaster, postmaster, all the storekeepers, miners and my friend the policeman! I was very amused to find that the champion's second was a little Cockney only just out. I noticed he was extremely rigorous as to the details and quite ready to back up his ideas with his fists. He is a typical London East Ender, pale and puny but with evidently great spirit! I couldn't help feeling that this brutal performance ill fitted the place and am sure that if the Gum Trees and rocks could think they would resent the intrusion of our civilised people who are nearer animals than any of the aboriginals could have been. In fact they are much lower down than animals – of course there are exceptions, but for the most part, they are drunken brutes. I am making some 'nice new friends' – my last being a certain Mr Ravinshaw, prospector, fossicker, writer and artist! He brought me some of what he called his 'Blacks and Whites' to look at – they were what you would expect. I have made a sketch of him and am doing a painting and tomorrow I join him in an expedition to fossick for Diamonds in the Creek!*

I was allowed to use what they called the accident ward, for a studio. It was a wooden hut of about twelve feet by eight. Here I painted the trooper and several prospectors as practise for my coming ordeal in Sydney. I found prospectors interesting men. Deep-grained optimism kept them happy during the hardest trials. In Sydney someone had warned me with a saying 'Liar, damn liar, mining expert', and I found there was reason in it. Knowing that I was from London, these men imagined I was able to interest possible buyers in their wonderful mines, and they often called to tell me of them. One prospector I liked better than most. At first sight he was a forbidding specimen, very tall and powerful; now and then he went 'on the drink' and hid himself for a week or two. After one of these bouts he asked me to go with him to see some wonderful find he had made only a mile or two away. It was a lovely fresh morning when we wandered through the rocky bush country. I could not go fast, and he seemed pleased to go slow. At each pool of water, no matter how thick with mud, my friend went down on hands and knees and sucked up a pint or two. We sat down to rest. I suggested that he seemed a bit out of condition, and asked if he always felt bad after one of his bouts. He said that he usually felt awful, and that he got the horrors. He asked if I had ever read a book called *Wormwood*, and when I told him that I had he said with conviction, 'The cove who wrote that book *drinks.*' I did not enlighten him that the book was written by Miss Marie Corelli. I always meant to tell her of this compliment, as I knew her slightly, but I did not see her again.

Marie Corelli was a well-known authoress of the time and wrote *Wormwood*, a novel about the evils of Absinthe drinking in Paris.

The editor of *The Digger* often asked me to accompany him on a visit to a lady friend who, he told me, had a large collection of diamonds. It seemed odd that any woman in this wild place should possess diamonds; I wondered who she could be, so one evening I went with him to find out. It was dark, and we stumbled along to the outskirts of the camp. Arriving at a wooden hut, he tapped at the door. After a pause the door was opened stealthily and a tousled yellow head peeped out. We entered a long, low room, lighted by a candle stuck in a bottle. The lady was fat and bloated, but there were still signs of past good looks. With a queenly gesture she motioned us to be seated, pointing to two homemade chairs. Her conversation was genteel. I gathered that she had been a barmaid at several mining camps where, she told us, the miners had always been extraordinarily kind. She talked on and on about her conquests in bygone years, until the editor suggested that she should show me her diamonds. Her manner changed at once, and she became mysterious. She said to me 'Of course you will not tell anyone about them.' She crept round the room, covered the windows with bits of sacking, put another candle in a bottle, lit it, and walked to a wooden box by her bed. She undid the padlock with a large key pulled from the bodice of her dress, rummaged about in the box and returned with two medicine bottles. Taking out the corks, she poured more diamonds than I had ever seen onto a plate which stood on a kerosene tin – her only table. I noticed that she did not take her eyes from the plate until the stones were back in the bottles. When they were safely locked in the box again she continued the conversation. Before we left I gathered that someday she hoped to retire and live in a town on an income derived from the sale of the diamonds. Walking home the editor, who was also a fossicker, told me that some of the stones we had seen were valuable. They looked pretty dull, I thought, but he said that you could not judge their brightness until they were cut.

Once or twice he took me fossicking for diamonds. The method they followed was to put a shovelful of river bed into a fine sieve and wash the sand and dirt away. With small pincers they then picked out the likely stones. I found plenty of associates of diamonds, like garnets and things, but never a diamond. When the novelty of boiling tea in a billy-can and the proud feeling of being the wild miner wore thin, I became tired of this form of activity; the result did not compensate for the sore back I got from hours of digging and peering into the sieve. Every ache alarmed me, suggesting a return of the dreaded tubercle.

I have always enjoyed getting letters, and in the out-of-the-way place the desire for home letters became a passion. The mail was brought to Borah Creek each evening in a cart, weather permitting, from the post town twenty miles away. The postman who drove the cart handed letters to callers in the wooden mail hut. It seemed that every inhabitant of the camp flocked to the hut when the cart arrived. Very few expected or ever got a letter, but they asked on principle, and felt no scruple about overcrowding the tiny space. Post hour was the social hour of the camp, and long after letters had been distributed people stood in groups, talking. At first it sounded odd to hear them greet each other with 'good night' instead of 'good-evening', although really it was equally sensible.

Once when I arrived at the post hut for my letters I noticed that something unusual had happened. The usual groups had gathered together, and were intent in something in their midst. I pushed into the crowd and found a man in the centre, talking excitedly. His hair was ruffled, his shirt was torn, and he was holding his belt in one hand, and his trousers up in the other. He said that he had been attacked when coming through the wood on the opposite hill by a wild looking man who seemed intent on killing him. Nobody had heard of a wild looking man behaving in this way before, and at once they decided to form search parties to seek him out. They continued the search, accompanied by the trooper, for several days without success, and interest in the wild man flagged. When the incident was practically forgotten, this hero again appeared at the post hut, this time more badly knocked about than before. His shirt hung in ribbons, there were knife cuts on his belt, and his arms and face were badly scratched. Again search parties went out, again without discovering any wild man. The trooper became sceptical, and told me that he believed that the man had 'invented the whole damn business,' and so it proved. This prospector lived by himself in a tent a mile or so from the camp – a lonely life which had evidently got on his nerves. To look at him it was difficult to believe that such a tough man could become an exhibitionist.

Opposite my brother's tent was wooden building where miners could get their dinner. These places were called boarding houses, although they did not contain bedrooms. The enterprising restauranteur who ran this establishment had put up a noticeboard on which he had painted 'BOREDIN HOUS'. The E between the R and D was an afterthought, so it was unfortunate that he had put it the wrong way round.

One fine day my brother took me to call on the old miner who first discovered silver lead in Borah Gully. He had built a wooden cottage on the side of a hill, where he lived by himself. It was about a mile from the mine; he could hear the noises from the mine coming down the valley, and he said it was 'his music.' He gave us 'sherry wine' and told us of his early struggles. One result of selling his mine had been to enable to him to realise an early dream, which was to be the possessor of a pair of Purdy guns. These he showed us with pride. I hope that he died before the mine failed, for it was not his fault.

Among the characters I remember was a small, pale boy, about ten years old. He delivered things in a basket from the store. Whenever I met him he said 'Fleas are very bad today, Mr Gray.' He always appeared to be scratching.

There were many Chinese people settled in the district. It was the first time that I had met them at close quarters. Two or three times a week Chinese men called with vegetables for sale. In spite of tales I heard of their methods of cultivation we enjoyed their vegetables, for they tasted good. Without their industry we should have had none. It was a pleasure to go to the little general store run by them, for they greeted one with smiles and politeness, and took any amount of trouble to please customers. On old and discarded mine workings there were always dozens of Chinese scratching about. Apparently they were able to make a living, or they would not have been so keen.

And so my time at Borah Creek hastened to its end. I was sorry to leave my brother in such a godforsaken spot, although he said he enjoyed the life. Personally I was glad to have a return ticket in my pocket. I was better than when I came, my wound had healed and no suspicious lumps had appeared, so I was returning to Sydney with renewed hopes.

My farewells over, my brother drove me one sunny morning to the township, where I was to join the coach the following day. He stayed the night. We had a good dinner, drank wine, and made the evening as merry as possible, for we both felt that it was our last meeting. He died a few years later in Sydney, where he had gone for treatment.

Years afterwards I heard that Borah Creek was deserted and that the camp was overgrown with vegetation. It had apparently risen around a fraud. The assays had been faked by the manager and assayer. Each year it was stated the mine was to pay a dividend, but the dividend never materialised, and all invested money was lost.

# Chapter 11

# Sydney

It was October when I returned to Sydney, and there was much to do. First I had to find somewhere to live, and then a studio in which to paint the portrait. I settled on a room in an old bungalow on the north shore. The house overlooked the harbour, and was surrounded by a wild garden where the trees were visited at night by screaming flying foxes, a large species of bat. To get to Sydney proper one had to take a ferry boat. There were no studios to let, so I had to content myself with a room high up in an Insurance building on the principal thoroughfare. It had a south light, which is the equivalent of the northern aspect which we require in the other hemisphere. The window was large and light harsh, and I tried several schemes to improve it.

I was nervous when the moment came for the introduction to my sitter, Dr Normand MacLaurin, Chancellor of Sydney University. He was a big man, with a fine head full of character. When I got really to know him I found that he was wise and kind, in spite of his dour, Scottish look. I spent most Sunday evenings with him and his family, who also were charming.

> Dr Normand MacLaurin was born in Scotland in 1835 and died in Sydney in 1914. He was a notable physician and held many public offices in health care in New South Wales as well as running his own medical practice. He was also appointed a member of the New South Wales Legislative Council in 1889 and Vice Chancellor of Sydney University in 1896. He became Chancellor in 1896 and was knighted in 1902 a year after Gray painted his portrait. Looking at his many business, professional and political roles it is not surprising that he had little time to sit for his portrait! What follows is an extract of a letter to his mother which gives a very clear statement of his feelings about this commission. It is worth remembering that his fee is equivalent to £30,000 today.

> *The fairy tale is again commencing – on Friday I received a letter from Mr Smith of which the following is an extract: 'At the meeting yesterday I brought the question of the appointment of an artist before the Committee and we unanimously resolved to ask you to undertake the commission of making a portrait of the Hon. Dr MacLaurin on the terms proposed and discussed between us viz £50 down and then if we find the painting satisfactory another £200 for the purchase of the portrait which if not purchased would be your property – you also to paint a replica for £100 if required.' If I fail to make a success of it the story will be spoilt! You may be quite sure that I shall make every effort – wouldn't it be splendid to make all that money – I could pay all my obligations! Really it is wonderful chance and thro' no merit of my own – they have never seen anything I have done, that was my strong point! It is rather a jump from drawing for a third rate Sunday paper to painting one of the principal men in Australia – it makes me laugh. The £50 will pay my expenses in Sydney. I shall have to get a suit of clothes as except for one suit I am ragged! I shall just do my best and chance it.*
>
> *November 1901*

My first jolt was when he told me that as he was busy at his hospitals and University, his only free time was from eight o'clock until nine each morning. This would mean very early rising for one who still felt rather an invalid. The second nasty jolt was a letter which appeared in the principal Sydney newspaper. This unpleasant reference to me read:- 'Given two men of the same ability – average mediocrity – one a stranger, and the other an Australian, the stranger always stands the best chance of getting the commission. The local artist has no chance of competing with one who has the hall mark "London". Even though he is very small fry in some other part of the world, he jumps into prominence in Australia chiefly because – he is not an Australian.' I entirely agreed with the writer that it was rough on local artists, though I felt that if he had known all the circumstances – how vitally important it was for me to gain the £250 – I should be forgiven. I longed to tell him that I had no 'London hall mark' and that it was not I, but Dr Ryan, who worked the miracle. However, I kept quiet and braved it out. The portrait progressed slowly. The doctor was patient and helpful, but I found an hour a day far too short for a sitting.

I was introduced into the social life of Sydney, and enjoyed a gay and amusing time. There were dinners, dances and picnics and pretty girls, a contrast to life on a miner's camp. I have a lively memory of the two brothers Dalley, who I had met in London with Francis Howard. At the time they were the leaders of the small group of Sydney's *jeunesse doree*. They were witty and most entertaining. One Sunday evening the younger brother threw a party. He hired a coach and four and drove a visiting theatrical company and a few friends, including me, to one of the charming seaside resorts that abound in the neighbourhood. The horses did not like the railway trains, which in those days ran along some of the streets, but Dalley managed without accident. The large party dined at a pleasant hotel, and after meandering about the sands watching the rolling breakers, we were driven back to the principal hotel for supper. During supper Dalley asked me to escort his lady friend home, her house being near my lodging. One of his friends, who overheard his request, told me that if I did see the lady home it would be as well to drop on hands and knees directly she entered the gate, because her husband carried a gun and would shoot to kill!

Another youth of whom I saw much was a poet. He had spent a good part of his life in England, and dressed with elegance. His name was Frederic Manning, and at that time he was in his early twenties. He looked delicate and walked wearily. He invited me to call, and I was surprised to find in his daintily furnished room a drawing of him by Rothenstein and paintings by Conder and other artists I knew in London. He allowed none of his family to enter his room unless invited, indeed, his attitude to them was overbearing. One evening I dined with them before we went to a dance. One of the brothers was sitting next to me at dinner. He kept me amused with tales of steeplechasing and boxing, at both of which he was an expert. Frederic sat opposite, his head wearily resting on one long, thin hand, the other drumming on the table. He was evidently dismayed by the inartistic conversation of his brother, for when we left the dining room he whispered in my ear 'Gray, please forgive everything!' In one of his letters to me after my return to England he said that he had dedicated 'a brace of sonnets' to me, but never saw my 'brace' nor have I had news of him for many years.

Frederic Manning was born in Sydney in 1882 and died in England in 1930. He moved to England in 1898 and then returned to Sydney in 1900 when he would have met Gray. He only stayed for three years before returning to England. He had showed some promise as a poet but to a limited audience and then served in the First World War where a lifestyle heavily influenced by drink made it difficult for his fellow officers to get on with him. The work that made him famous was his novel, a fictional account of his own life in the trenches, called *The Middle Parts of Fortune*. He wrote about the lives of ordinary soldiers using their authentic wartime language, something not done by any other writer before.

As Christmas approached it became unbearably hot. On Christmas Day 105f in the shade was registered, and the hot, damp air seemed to burn one's nostrils. Mother had sent a Christmas pudding which wandered round Australia until it caught up with me in Sydney. Christmas pudding is not the most suitable food when the temperature is high, but it brought something of home with it, and so it was welcome.

Each part of the world has its own pet wind. The South of France has the mistral and England a cutting wind from the east, but of all winds surely the Southerly Buster is the strangest. It comes during hot weather; after three days of intense heat, when the people of Sydney are gasping for breath, sooner or later along comes the Southerly Buster to cool the air. The inhabitants so longed for the advent of this wind that a flag was hoisted on the post office when it was known to be on the way. Before it comes the sky is heavy and leaden and there is a strange stillness, as if catastrophe threatens. Suddenly dark patches appear on the still waters of the harbour. In a few minutes the whole harbour is lashed into waves. The many ferry steamers rock and shudder and there is banging and dust in the town, and so the Buster comes to cool Sydney, and everyone is happy. As far as I remember, this magical process continues most of the summer.

The portrait still went slowly. I thought I should never get it finished. I was not really well enough for the strain and heat, but the remaining £200 had to be won. As was usually the case, I was dissatisfied with what I had done, but luckily the members of the committee who called seemed pleased – all but one. This gentleman who had been knighted by Queen Victoria, was old and infirm and came to the studio accompanied by an attendant. I assumed my most courtly manner, inviting him to be seated. To my astonishment, before even looking at the picture, he blurted out that he knew a boy of fourteen who could have done it better, adding that it was a scandal to charge £250 for a thing like that. The attack was so unexpected that I did not know what to reply. I was inclined to laugh, but realised that this was a moment for hauteur, so I walked slowly to the door and bowed them out. Secretly I thought that he possibly *might* know a boy of fourteen who could paint a better portrait, although I was not going to let on! Instead I wrote to the committee giving details of Sir H.'s visit and asking them kindly to tell him not to call on me again. I still have their reply. They expressed profound regret that one of their number had behaved so rudely, and suggested that he must have been either mad or drunk, possibly both. He *was* told not to call again.

At last the portrait was finished, and I was given the final £200. I have always regretted that I did not paint Dr MacLaurin when I was strong and more experienced.

(He kept the receipt and the original is still in his papers which the author holds today.)

I was now able to entertain some of the people who had helped to make my time in Sydney so pleasant. The weather, during the autumn I was there, was perfect.

There are many delightful places to spend a day within easy reach of the town. The Australian Club, where I took many of my meals, was extremely well run, as Australian clubs usually were, and probably still are. Curiously enough, I found the

*Portrait of MacLaurin. University Art Collection, Chau Chak Wing Museum, The University of Sydney.*

winter in Sydney very cold and trying. On Saturday afternoons the harbour was crowded with sailing boats, and one of these annoyed me, for on its sail, in large black letters, was printed an advertisement for pills. Sydney boys are certainly skilled sailors, but I hope that they have not allowed advertisements to deface their harbour.

Dr Ryan wished to see me before I returned to England, so off I went to Melbourne. The doctor had a country house near a small town named Nhil, away on the western border of Victoria – a long distance from Melbourne. I stayed there a few days. He made a careful examination with the result that he gave me the good news that he could find no sign of further trouble. He stressed the necessity for my leading in future an outdoor, healthy life. If I did this, he said, I might be free of the beastly T.B. for the rest of my life. Before I left he took me out one morning to shoot quail. There were many about, and we brought back quite a number, but I do not like shooting things unless they try to shoot me.

Nhil is a small town halfway between Melbourne and Adelaide and first visited by Europeans in 1845. The Adelaide Melbourne railway line passes through.

Winter was approaching when we left Melbourne, but the sun shone, which helped to make our voyage pleasant. Lawrence Bradbury (a proprietor of *Punch* who travelled with me) and I often talked of Burnand's high handed methods of running *Punch*. I told him how, when my brothers-in-law Pegram and Townsend sent drawings 'on spec', they were often returned folded in two without a word of explanation. The outcome of our talks was seen soon after Bradbury got back to England, when Townsend was appointed art editor of *Punch*, a post to be held by him until his death in 1921.

As we steamed up the eastern side of New Zealand calling at the principal ports, the editors of various newspapers fussed around Bradbury, and I shared some of their hospitality. I remember a pleasant day at Christchurch, with waving willows on the banks of a fine river, and a club where we had a good luncheon. It is strange how good meals remain in my memory. When we approached the North Island it became milder. I left the steamer at Wellington and Bradbury went on to visit some of the Pacific Islands.

Union Steam Ship Company of New Zealand Limited SS Mokoia, steaming between Hobart and the Bluff NZ June 29 1902

*My Dear Mother. You will see by the above address that I have said Good Bye to Australia at last – not as you may imagine, without regrets. I leave many friends whose kindness I shall always remember. Now that the curtain has fallen on my Australian experiences and I find myself rolling about on the sea again, it is hard to realise that so much has happened since I left the Waimate but certainly not difficult to see the wonderful change in my health. We left Melbourne on Wednesday last (today is Sunday) and about a dozen people came to see me off – including Miss*

*Veitch, D. (My Sydney 'pal') Kiddie and Miss Fitzsimmons. We have had a very good passage so far which is lucky, as it is winter down here and at times the Tasman Sea can be very nasty. Today she is rolling a bit but I've got my sea legs and don't mind. We called at Hobart for about 6 hours, and Bradbury (who is also travelling by this boat) and I had a walk about the town, which is prettily situated at the end of a fine harbour, with snow covered hills at the back. It was very cold and reminded me of a winter's day in England. Tomorrow we are due at the Bluff – the southernmost point of New Zealand where we remain till Tuesday when we steam for Dunedin and thence to Wellington. The Co. wrote me just before I left Melbourne that the Waimate was leaving on the 12 July so I may have to return by her. I shall just have time to see the Burrells for a few days before starting. The Mokoia is an extremely comfortable boat – very clean and well managed and the food is excellent. I stay out on deck all day and evening being determined to get as much benefit as possible from the fresh air on the road home. We have a most uninteresting crowd on board – people don't travel this time of year for pleasure. There are not many of us but as far as I can see most of them have been drunk ever since leaving Melbourne! I am afraid it will be a cold rough journey round the Horn – down there the sun rises about 9 and sets about 2 or 3, so it will also be rather dark. However I shall be on my road home, so let it blow, snow and dark!*

This is an excerpt from his last letter to his Mother documenting his trip to Australia and New Zealand. Above the letterhead Gray has written '*Bradbury has asked me to try and write something of my Bush experiences for Punch – of course that doesn't mean that they would take anything I sent, but I expect I would get a good chance if it was any good at all!*' Sadly there is no record of this happening.

From Wellington I took a train for Fielding to visit my cousin, Frank Burrell, who had a sheep run some miles from the town. A large family of Burrells had left Lincolnshire many years before and had settled in the Fielding district. They had often visited England, and Frank was not a stranger to me. His farmhouse was far larger than I had expected. It was built of brick; I was surprised to hear that he kept no women servants to look after it. Indeed, when he showed me my bedroom he said, 'If you ever want your bed made you can make it yourself!' Our meals we took together, shepherds and all, in a large kitchen.

Fielding is a small town 20 miles north of Palmerston North on the North Island of New Zealand. It was founded by a Colonel Fielding in 1871 and settlers arrived from England in 1874. From Gray's comment on the Burrells it could well be that they were very early settlers in the region.

My cousin Frank was a gay, charming person noted, I heard, for rather wild practical jokes. When I arrived he told me that he had been much distressed lately to find in the stable yard each morning a miserable little dog which looked to be famished and diseased. He had not the faintest idea from whence it came, or where it spent the night – his place was miles from the nearest farm. There he was each morning, said Frank, wagging his tail and cocking his head on one side in an effort to look bright. Frank fed him and tried to coax him into a comfortable kennel, but without success. In spite of his attentions the poor dog became thinner and more miserable looking, and the only thing to do, he said, was to shoot it. To my astonishment, this strong cousin of mine told me that neither he nor any of his men had the heart to do it, and – yes, I knew what was coming – would I shoot the dog for him? It was a damned curious thing, I thought, that since I left England people were always putting a gun in my hand telling me shoot something.

I did not like the idea of the job at all, but they all seemed so upset about this dog that I felt it was up to me to help them out. I agreed to do it the following morning. At breakfast Frank and his men appeared less talkative than usual, and seemed nervy. One by one they left the room, until I was alone with Frank. He gave me a loaded gun, saying that he thought the dog would be in the yard by now. Then he too went away, and I was alone, feeling as an old time executioner must have felt when about to cut off a royal head. I tried to be brave, and walked towards the place of execution. There was the miserable creature, with head cocked on one side, looking at me. I raised the gun to shoot, but he gave me so reproachful and surprised a look that I could not pull the trigger. He must have sensed the meaning of the gun, for he ran off and was never seen again.

Another and happier dog incident took place a few days later. Each evening at a certain time the shepherds, accompanied by their dogs, went to the hills to bring down hundreds of sheep. To show me the intelligence of these dogs, Frank told the shepherds to be half an hour late at the hut where the dogs were kept. I went there with him and he let them out, they jumped about a bit and then settled down to wait for the shepherds. After ten minutes had passed they became restless, after twenty minutes they were really worried and at last, able to bear it no long, they dashed away to the hills, rounded up the flock, and were bringing them down the hill when the shepherds met them. I suspected that Frank had made some sign to the dogs, but he assured me that he had not.

The native Maoris seemed to have got over any feelings they may have had against the settlers. I frequently saw them playing football together.

When in Fielding we always went to the Fielding Club before returning to the farm. Members had roomy lockers in which to keep their drinks. My cousin's was full up with every imaginable drink – a sight to cheer the heaviest drinker. He himself drank little, but it amused him to see others drink too much.

When I left Fielding Frank's old carter came to see me off at the station. The white-haired wrinkled tough told me that he was an old Harrovian. I should in some ways have enjoyed a longer stay in New Zealand, but had a craving to get home. I had arranged to sail in the same ship in which I had come to Australia nearly two years before, and I joined her at Wellington.

(This was the SS *Waimate*.)

# Chapter 12

# Home again

There were but few changes among the officers, and my friend the poker expert was still captain. It was winter, and very cold, and I was the only passenger for the voyage round Cape Horn. Going South, the weather became colder and the wind stronger. Ice covered the ropes and everything on deck. The ship was flung about by big waves. The noise in the saloon, where I spent most of my time reading in front of a stove, was intolerable, so loud was the creaking of wooden fittings. Meals became acrobatic for both diners and stewards. One wit, showing me the charts for Cape Horn, was careful to point out drawings of the natives who lived there, and the unpleasant bludgeons they appeared to wield. The position of food dumps buried along the coast was also shown on the chart. 'We shall be all right,' said the wit, 'if we are wrecked there will be plenty of food.' With the wind howling I thought it quite possible that we *might* be wrecked, and I did not like the idea of those bludgeons or of the wild men who carried them.

Rounding the Cape the wind became yet stronger and colder, but the sun was shining. Several sailing ships were trying to beat round in the opposite direction, and they signalled asking us to report to them. We were running before the wind and rolling heavily, and the captain gave the order for the few sails the ship could carry to be set, with the idea of steadying her. He then retired to his cabin with a bottle of whisky.

Setting sails in the gale when the ropes are frozen is an incredibly difficult job, and I wondered how the men could cling on whilst bulging canvas smacked against the swaying mast. However, they did it without accident. In spite of the fierceness of the gale the sun still shone, and it was pleasant sitting on the bridge protected from the wind, watching the plunging, rolling ship shove its way through big white capped waves, some of which broke over the decks. Suddenly there was a report like the explosion of a gun, the top sail had split in two – bang! Other sails followed and in a short time all had split to ribbons, cracking like stock-whips in the wind. Strip after strip of canvas careered from the crossbars into the distance until nothing was left of the sails. The officer on watch said, 'Well, that's that – I knew the damn sails were rotten!' He then told me the following story:- Some years before, it happened that when about to leave New Zealand in a sailing ship one of the apprentices heard that his father in England had inherited a large fortune. This news seemed to alter the boy's character; he became swanky, and walked about the deck with his hands in his pockets. Rounding Cape Horn they encountered a strong gale, and orders were given to reef sail. All the watch scrambled aloft except this boy, who stood watching from the deck. The officer yelled, 'Go up at once, you little devil, don't you see the sails will blow away?' He made no move, and shouted back, 'What if they do? Pa can pay for them!'

After three weeks of strong winds and frost, the weather improved as we got further north. I was looking forward to spending a day at Rio, but the captain told me that we had to put in at Montevideo because there was yellow fever at Rio. This was a disappointment to us all. We went back to Montevideo, where we were nearly wrecked, for your brave captain decided to approach it by the inside channel. We scraped the muddy, shallow bottom and only by luck got free.

At Montevideo the shipping agent, when he came aboard, advised us not to go ashore because they were in the midst of an election, which meant that the various political parties were shooting at one another in the streets. This was too much! After being cooped up in a pitching ship for four weeks I felt that I must go ashore and have a good meal at an hotel. The first officer felt as I did and persuaded the agent to lend one of his clerks to pilot us. This young man crept stealthily ahead and signalled when we were to bolt across a street. I think he was making the most of the danger. However, we reached the hotel, enjoyed an excellent luncheon, and swaggered back to the ship arm in arm.

And so we left our last port of call and sailed through the tropics for England. I am never happy in tropical climates, though at sea the heat is less trying than on land. The biting insects one encounters there are absent too. But even at sea the heat of the sun smashes at one out of a harsh blue sky, and if the ship happens to be travelling in the same direction as the wind, wind shutes are of no avail and one has to bear it, panting in the shade.

Nearing England we revelled in a pleasant June temperature, with a soft breeze for escort up the Channel. Most travellers experience an emotional thrill when returning to their own country – I do, every time I see the land appearing through the mist and recognise towns nestling along the coast. This voyage, we returned to Tilbury, so we had the added interest of going up the Thames.

Approaching the dock where the ship was to berth, I could see a man standing apart from the waiting dock hands. He was looking hard at the ship and I was looking hard at him, and it dawned on me that this was my brother Alfred, who had come to meet me. It was good to be home again with Mother and my kind family.

Feeling important after my travels and various experiences, I expected that my acquaintances would be as thrilled to see me back again as I was to be back. It came as a shock to hear an artist friend say, when we met in the street, 'Hello, where have you been? I haven't seen you about this last week or two!' My first visit to the Chelsea Arts Club (which had moved to the present house in Old Church Street during my absence) was hardly a success, either, from my point of view. The Club was empty when I went in, except for an old country member who was practising shots in the billiard room. I shook hands expectantly, and could not believe my ears when, wringing my hand, he said 'Hello, M. old man, I haven't seen you for ages.' This was particularly distressing because M. was, without doubt, the ugliest man in the club, if not in England! I began to realise that we are all so busy thinking about ourselves that we have little time left for thoughts of others.

---

Anyone from England who has lived abroad will recognise this experience.

---

I was conscious that I was looked upon by my relations and friends as a frail creature. They had doubts whether I had shown wisdom in leaving the fine air of Australia. Personally I consider English air as good as any other for keeping one fit if he leads an outdoor life. The necessity of being in the open air pointed to the advisability of giving up black and white work, which meant irregular hours and being indoors. I therefore accepted the Pegram's invitation to stay with them in Sussex and do landscape painting.

I still had the lease of Great Cheyne Studio which I took over when Russell married. I look on the giving up of that lease as one of the tragedies of my life. The charming old lady, Mrs Barker, who owned most of the property in Cheyne Row, had given me a new lease of the studio when Russell left. It was for forty five years at £40 a year – it would probably have lasted me for the whole of my working life. But in the uncertainty of my illness and future I thought it wiser to rid myself of the responsibility. Tonks had rented it during the time I was ill and abroad, and now was moving to Edith Grove. I knew a sculptor who wanted a studio, so I gave him my lease! Since then my regrets have been constant, for I have never paid less than £100 or more a year for studios not nearly so good.

Soon I joined the Pegram's at their farm house at Graffham – a charming village in Sussex. La Thangue and his pretty wife had a house there, and James Charles lived a few miles away. I got to work painting out of doors. I had done but little landscape, and soon discovered that I was not a Turner.

One day when I was painting in a cornfield La Thangue came along for a chat. He sat down against a stook of corn and talked generalities. He had a way of keeping back what he had really come to say until he was leaving, and it was not until then that one discovered the reason of his visit – there usually was a definite reason if he made a call. He told me on this occasion that the trials of a landscape painter had never been written. Then came the point. 'I understand, Ronald,' he said as he got up to go, 'that you intend going in for landscape painting. Well, I feel I must warn you that there is no more room at the top and none at the bottom.' I thanked him, and hoped he would call again.

James Charles was very different. He was an enthusiast, and invited me to paint with him. It was a privilege and education to work with so good a painter. Sickert once told me that Degas considered Charles one of the most accomplished painters in England. Charles was a character, and thought of little but his work. His only lapse was when he and Tubby Goodall went in for stocks and shares, and money which had been saved quickly vanished. Charles was once called to Bradford to paint a portrait of a woman, and he returned rather depressed. He had thought the portrait good, but his sitter did not seem pleased. When she saw it for the first time she said, 'But Mr Charles, you have made me yellow.' He lost his temper, and shouted, 'Damn it, Madam, you *are* yellow!'

James Charles, born 1851 and died 1906, studied at the Academie Julien in Paris and like La Thangue adopted the 'open air' painting philosophy. He established an early reputation as a portrait painter then became a talented landscape artist. In 1889 he exhibited at the Paris World Exposition and was awarded a silver medal. In 1890 he had moved to Bosham near Graffham with his large family.

During that summer there was an unfortunate incident connected with the painting of a cow which nearly cost Charles his life. He wanted a careful close-up study of a cow, and for several mornings had followed one about a field without getting a satisfactory sketch. A farm hand was persuaded to stand by and keep the cow still, but the cow had its own ideas about this, and poor Charles was getting desperate. Then he had a brilliant idea. He came to the field with a coil of rope round his shoulder; one end of the rope he tied firmly to the cow's horns, the other to his own waist, hoping that his weight – which was considerable – would slow up the cow's movements. Apparently the cow did not get the idea, for it became restless and walked increasingly quickly, with Charles stepping out manfully at his end of the rope. So far, so good, but when the cow changed the pace to a full gallop it became a different matter. Paint box, brushes and hat flew into the air, and Charles was dragged along the ground. With surprising agility the cow leapt a hedge, through which poor Charles was pulled. When, some fields away, this odd procession was halted, Charles was more dead than alive. His clothes were dragged off or in shreds, his arms and face were scratched and bleeding. The cow, freed from its burden, grazed peacefully.

After the summer at Graffham I felt so well that I was emboldened to risk the winter in London. Having given my lovely studio away, I had to look for a room in which I could paint. I found pleasant rooms in a house in Cheyne Walk overlooking the river, near the house Steer had taken.

Tonks was worried and depressed; he could not satisfy himself. The effort to do better than one can is the cause of much misery to artists. We often walked together on the Embankment after work. One evening, he was particularly miserable about his picture, a commission for a portrait of Mrs Hugh Hammersley. He said he had no doubt that Hugh had given him the commission out of the kindness of his heart, but that a matter of fact it was the unkindest thing he could have done. 'I know that before it is done I shall commit suicide,' said Tonks.

Mrs Hugh and I did all we could to brighten his outlook, but both Steer and I were relieved when the portrait was finished, because we had both suffered. Steer complained that when Tonks painted a picture it was an epoch making event, whereas when anyone else painted it was an everyday occurrence.

The Hugh Hammersleys lived in that delightful house at Hampstead known as The Grove, once occupied by Constable, and now called 'The Admiral's House'. It was, I believe, originally built by an Admiral. A flag staff and a railinged look out are features seen from a distance. There was a stone paved rose garden from which steps led up to a lawn, where a fine old chestnut trees gave shade in the summer. There were winding paths and a temple. (This garden is now ruined, for several detached villas have been built on the site')

Hugh Hammersley was born in 1858 and died in 1930. He was the third generation of a line of bankers all called Hugh. The original founded a bank in the late 19th Century and was banker to royalty including the Prince Regent. The bank ran into financial difficulties and at the first Hugh's death in 1840 was taken over by Coutts. In 1889; the third Hugh who is mentioned in Gray's memoirs, married a Mary Grant and they lived in some state in Hampstead.

Mary was painted by John Singer Sargent and the portrait was exhibited at the new Gallery where it was very well received and helped to re-establish Sargent's reputation after the debacle of Madame X in Paris. This beautiful painting is now in the Metropolitan Museum of Art in New York. Hugh sold it in 1923 when he was short of money. Mary had died in 1902. This painting secured Sargent's reputation as a painter of beautiful women and he went on to paint many famous society hostesses in London and New York. I can find no record of the painting of Mary by Tonks.

Hugh and his wife were very kind to me. They bought drawings and gave me commissions for portraits, and for a picture of their garden. The joy of being so often with them caused the past illnesses and travels to be forgotten. It was not long before I was leading the old, amusing life and meeting interesting people.

When Steer left Avenue Studios for Cheyne Walk, Harris Brown took over the Avenue studio. It is a vast studio, and Steer had been there seven years. During that time he had had but one commission, which was for the miniature of a child. Harris went to the Avenue with a reputation for party giving. At his previous studio I had first heard Clara Butt sing. She was still a shy student, but already her voice had a wonderful quality. Directly Harris was settled in his new studio, he of course gave a party. It was a gloomy, cold winters afternoon. The studio was full of smart people (Harris was very society) none of whom I knew. Whilst I was standing by the fire, feeling rather miserable, a young girl approached and asked if I were an artist. I said I was, and she told me that she also was an artist, and that she practised her art in the glow of a red light. Her voice was soft, and she spoke with an American accent. 'Won't you come' she said, 'next Saturday to see me practise my art?' She wrote her name and address on the back of an envelope, and I read Isadora Duncan, a name which conveyed nothing to me. She had been brought by Mrs Harrington Mann, to whom she introduced me and to whom I have been devoted ever since.

Isadora Duncan was born in 1877 in the US and died 1927 in the South of France. Her Mother divorced her father when she was young and school held no appeal for her. At an early age she started dancing and in 1896 she became a member of August Daly's theatre company in New York. At the age of 21 in 1898 she moved to London and started performing in the private rooms of the wealthy which sounds like the way in which Gray first saw her perform. Known as the Mother of Modern Dance, her style was the antithesis of the ballet and was free flowing and interpretive, inspired in particular by the Greek vases at the British Museum. She reappears in these memoirs later and her sad story will be completed then.

When the following Sunday arrived it was with a palpitating heart that I rang the bell at a large house in Warwick Square. From the hall I could hear music, and thumping on an upstairs floor. My expectancy was modified when I caught sight of a dozen coats and hats, some of which I recognised. On my entering a large room, Isadora – dressed in flowing white draperies – tripped forward to meet me, calling to her mother, 'Oh Momma, this is the young artist I told you about.' Sitting on the floor around the room (there being no chairs) I was annoyed though not surprised after the display of coats below, to see a dozen or so artists, all of whom had been at Harris Brown's party. I found that each had been under the impression that she had given him a solo invitation! Momma played the piano and Isadora glided about the room posturing. I did not know what to make of it. It left me with the feeling I get when listening to some modern music; not sure if it is good or damn silly. All of us were sent notices of her public performances, after this party, with the request that we should take tickets, but as I was not in a position to buy them, my name was soon taken off her list.

Years later, when she lived in Paris, she visited London and performed with her child dancers at the Duke of York's Theatre. I went with Dollie Mann to the first night. It was really a delightful show; she had gone far since the Warwick Square days. When the show was ended we went to her dressing room. We found her reclining on a sofa in a Madame Recamier pose, while her dresser dabbed her steaming body with powder. On one side of the sofa sat two elderly Victorian ladies, on the other were Ricketts and Shannon, the painters, enthusing excitedly. The Victorian ladies were full of praise – one said. 'How you must love children, Miss Duncan.' Her reply surprised even me, she said, 'Oh, yes, I do. You know, I have a baby myself.' She then named the father! The Victorian ladies visibly flinched, and one murmured, 'How nice.' Many years afterwards I met Isadora again in New York; I will tell of that later.

Tonks and I spent several summers painting together. At Wareham, in Dorset, he took rooms in the main street because he was charmed with the doorway, but by the time I arrived he had become doubtful whether he had acted wisely. The house was roomy and comfortable, but the proprietor, a retired linen draper, and his wife, though kind, were overwhelmingly genteel. A few other boarders made up the party. At meals the guests were chatty, and I had great amusement watching Tonks's expression when our host tried to entice him to talk – they were strong on 'cultured' subjects. The worst episode of a meal was our host's reiterated enquiry as to whether we would 'av any mawr'. Tonks flinched each time this kindly question was asked. The breaking point came when the draper put his hand on Tonks's shoulder in a friendly, chapel like way. No one less than a peer of the realm was allowed to do a thing like that to Tonks with impunity, and the draper immediately realised that he had blundered. It led to our making an arrangement to take our meals in our room – a far better plan.

Ancient ramparts surround Wareham, which on one side overlooks the river Frome, flowing towards Poole Harbour. I often painted on these ramparts, and it was delightful there in the summer evenings. Groups of boys bathed in the river, their pink bodies and flapping towels making a pleasant contrast to the browsing cattle. Sometimes an enquiring boy would climb the hill to discover the reason for our presence. They were mostly from the East End of London, sent by some friendly holiday fund for a fortnight in the country – and how they loved the experience! There was one, I remember, whose face was pinched and blue, and who shivered violently. I suggested that he had been in the water too long. He assured me that he had only been in the river twelve times that day, and in answer to my enquiry. 'Why so often?' replied, 'Because you don't 'ave to pay nothing!' From his conversation I gained glimpses of his home life. He must have had a good mother; on winter nights she made him do a bit of drawing before going to bed. He told me that they had been very lucky that year, because his father had only been out of work for four months. Good God, I thought, how horrible.

That summer another artist was painting at Wareham, a brother of Cecil Rhodes' friend of Jameson Raid fame. We sometimes foregathered at night, he was a pleasant man with a much wrinkled face.

Motor cars were beginning to make an appearance. It was at Wareham that we first met them on country roads. There was no tarmac in those days, and incredible clouds of dust marked their passage. One morning we were painting in a field bordering a main road. Tonks was working by a hedge which separated him from the road, I heard a car coming, and looked round to see Tonks enveloped in a sandstorm. Above the honk of the car I could hear screams from Tonks, and as the dust cleared I saw his lanky figure chasing along the hedge, waving his sketching block and hurling fearful curses after the car. His morning was spoilt, and he wandered about, cursing modern inventions.

The summer we spent at Studland Bay I remember with delight. So many pleasant things happened.

A beautiful part of Dorset with Wareham on Poole Harbour, Corfe Castle, a few miles southwest and Studland a short distance on the coast. Still a playground for the well-off holiday maker and across the other side of the entrance to Poole Harbour, is Sandbanks, home to many millionaires. Banksea Castle is the historical name of Brownsea Castle on Brownsea Island in Poole harbour. It was bought by wealthy stockbroker Charles van Raalte and he and his wife entertained lavishly there, especially during the summer.

The Hammersleys were cruising around in their lovely yacht Marcia. She was schooner rigged, and of about 200 tons register. They came to Poole Harbour, which was a walk along the sands from Studland. Tonks was a bad sailor, and feared to spend a night on board, but I was a particularly good sailor, so I spent many nights on board. The yacht was run on lines of simple though affluent elegance, and I marvelled at the comfort. We were anchored off Banksea Castle, where the Van Raaltes lived; they kindly sent eggs and fresh milk, and followed this with an invitation for our party to go ashore and bathe with them. Hugh, his friend Herbert Magniac and I went, each taking our own natty bathing attire. I fancied myself in mind and hoped to impress the onlookers, but this was not to be. Mrs Van Raalte asked to see our costumes, and said they would not do at all, because her daughters were bathing with us. We were asked to put on those which we should find in our bathing cubicles, and I was dismayed when I got into mine. It was a blue serge affair which reached from my neck to my ankles, and was far too loose. I felt horribly self-conscious when I ambled to the diving board. I plunged in, and immediately the loose costume was nearly dragged from my body. Climbing back up the steps, I was bulging with water, and must have looked like the fat boy of Peckham. I could hardly struggle up, carrying such a weight of sea water, which poured from every aperture of the ridiculous garment, but I walked back to my cubicle with as much dignity as I could muster.

> The Fat Boy of Peckham was John Trundley, who was born in Camberwell and was extraordinarily large from birth. By the age of 5 he weighed 70kg, and he was regularly appearing in Music Halls across the country. His impecunious parents continued to exploit him. He was offered a touring contract by Buffalo Bill when he weighed 210kg in 1915. And it was during the First World War that he changed his life, lost weight and was happily married for 14 years.

Returning one morning to Studland I joined Tonks at his painting pitch. He spoke of the strange quality of the light, which looked cold and was fading to a greeny darkness. We felt awed, and stood together without speaking. It was only when the sun was quite covered that we realised that we were witnessing an eclipse.

Most days we bathed from the sands away from the village so that we were able to undress in the open. When the afternoon sun threw long shadows from our naked bodies Tonks, scraping a stick along the edge of my shadow, screamed with excitement when he looked at the result; this, he said, was the correct way to draw; this was how the cavemen did it. For some time we each drew the other's naked shadow. One day a village father called to say that there had been complaints about our running naked on the sands. We pointed out that the nearest house was at least a mile away; he agreed, but said that evidently the two old ladies who lived in the house possessed very strong field glasses.

Another interest that summer was the arrival of Sir Frederick and Lady Treves and their charming daughter, Mrs Delma Radcliffe. When Tonks was at the London Hospital he had been Treves's favourite pupil and assistant, and he remained one of Treves's closest friends. Treves was writing a book on Dorsetshire and had come to explore out of the way villages. He was good looking and intelligent. Tonks admired his work as a surgeon and teacher and often told me tales of his progress through the hospital wards, when hundreds of students from all over the world flocked after him to hear his words of wisdom. He had two daughters, but one died young, a loss for which Treves never forgave the fates. One of the daughters once broke her leg, and Treves was called home to attend her. He went to her bedroom and looked at her, then he ran downstairs, went out and bought her a gold watch. In the meantime Lady Treves had called in another doctor. He told us how, when operating on King Edward VII at Buckingham Palace, he had to send a message to stop the workmen who were putting up decorations for the coronation from making so much noise. He gave up surgery when he was fifty, and travelled and wrote books, interesting books, most of them.

Sir Frederick Treves was born in 1853 and died in 1923. He was a famous English surgeon who pioneered surgical treatment of appendicitis. His most famous patient was Edward VII who contracted appendicitis just before his coronation in 1902 and was successfully operated on by Treves in Buckingham Palace. He later gained a reputation as an author with, among other books, his reminiscences of Joseph Merrick 'The Elephant Man' who he rescued from a Fair Ground display.

The book Gray mentions was published in 1908 and was called *Highways and Byways of Dorset.*

When watching the Marcia sail away I felt really sad. I had spent hours doing caricatures of people and events on board. These goings on did not seem to please Tonks; however, since I read in his life by Joseph Hone, that he had never suffered from jealousy, the memory gives me no regrets.

Back in London, my life went into fresh and pleasant channels. I lived with Mother and my sisters, and worked at my rooms in Cheyne Walk. I spent many evenings with Steer, who did not care for social functions. He was looked after with care by old Jane, his housekeeper, who had been his first nurse. When speaking of him to her acquaintances she always referred to him as 'my boy'. It was rare that an evening passed without Jane's old head popping round the door to look at the fire, and her cracked baritone saying, 'you want more coals on.' 'No, it is quite warm enough, thank you, Jane,' Steer would reply, but it was no good, Jane always picked up the scuttle and plumped on a big lump, repeating, *'You want more coals on.'* Directly she had gone Steer would look furtively at the door, creep to the fireplace and remove the coal. If it happened that at the New English Exhibition Steer had one picture out of about six unsold, Jane would say to me, 'Times are very bad Mr Gray.'

It was about this time that George Moore left Dublin to live in London. He often walked from Ebury Street to spend an evening with Steer. He was writing *The Brook Kerith*, so his conversation was always of that. He was dealing with the subject of miracles, but was not sure whether it would be better to use miracles from the Bible or to compose his own. For many evening he read us one from the Bible and one of his own, asking for our opinions as to which we preferred. Steer usually slept when Moore read any of his manuscript, so it fell to me to make the choice, and to avoid argument I always gave the palm to Moore's miracles.

Moore was a strange creature. If any of us happened to mention a woman's name he immediately asked a very pertinent question about her – the answer sometimes being one that most men kept to themselves. A witty Irish woman said of Moore that he 'Never kissed but always told!'

Steer was naughty about reading, he preferred catalogues to any novel written by his friends, who nevertheless generally gave him signed presentation copies of their books. Tonks and I did with difficulty persuade him to read one of Moore's books, but it took him a long time. His criticism was, 'Moore seems to write about very trivial subjects.'

Moore had a way of describing places and things, and verifying his statements after publication. I think it was in *Evelyn Innes* that he let himself go on about a haystack in Dulwich. After the book had appeared he persuaded Steer to accompany him to Dulwich to explore the possibility that Dulwich had one. They wandered perspiringly around in the scorching sun for some hours before they at last, to Moore's relief, found a tiny haystack and honour was satisfied.

In the early days of the New English Art Club the committee gave a party nearly every year. One remains in my memory. A singer named Shakespeare got drunk and was trying to tell Moore a story. Moore retreated and tried to push Shakespeare away, but Shakespeare stuck manfully to his purpose. At last, when he could bear it no longer, Moore screamed, 'I object to a story which takes more than a fortnight to tell!'

This period was saddened for me by the death of my old friend Brocklehurst. I went with him to Brighton for a week, where he hoped to benefit from the sea air, but as he got no better he hurried back to Cheshire. About a month later he wired for me, and I was horrified to see the change that had occurred since being with him in Brighton. Lying on a sofa wrapped in rugs, he looked emaciated and shrunken. The last time I saw him he had an open Bible in his hands. He was a truly religious man. He was in great pain. He said that possibly he had prayed wrongly when he had called on the Father to ease his agony, perhaps it was the Holy Ghost to whom he should have appealed, and he was searching the scriptures for enlightenment. A few days later he died, and I lost one of the kindest friends I ever had – and I have had many.

Conder had married a charming wife and had taken the fine old house at the corner of Cheyne Walk and Beaufort Street. He was on top of the wave, and bohemian society flocked to the many parties they gave. I gatecrashed somehow to most of them. At first we dressed faultlessly for these parties, then Sickert said it was wrong for artists to wear dress clothes, and persuaded us all to go as we were. Steer and Tonks liked the idea, and we younger sycophants agreed to keep them company. The result was that about twelve of us appeared in day clothes at Conder's smart parties, and were referred to as 'the labour party'. These evenings were greatly enlivened by Ernest Thesiger's recitations, and his wonderful impersonation of Sarah Bernhardt. Max Beerbohm did not join the 'labour party', he did not think much of Sickert's idea.

Augustus John, just beginning to climb his ladder to fame, was even then a law unto himself, and refused to be burdened with social shibboleths.

Augustus John, born 1878 and died 1961, was, as Gray says, just beginning his climb to fame. In 1908 Virginia Wolf said that the era of John Singer Sergeant and Charles Wellington Furse 'was over' and that of Augustus John was just beginning.

It was a Sunday custom at the Hammersley's house in Hampstead that if one went to tea one stayed to dinner – and dinner at the Grove was a mighty pleasant experience. Mrs Hugh's circle of frequent visitors included Henry James, Max Beerbohm, Wilson Steer, John Sargent, George Moore, Walter Sickert, Tonks and myself; some of whom were generally to be met there on Sundays. Conversation at these dinner parties was rather above my weight. I never felt of the party, always outside it – indeed, I have felt outside things all my life, and have wondered if others experienced the same sensation. I came to the conclusion, however, that if one listened enough to a witty talker one became conscious of his technique. I enjoyed Max Beerbohm's better than that of any of the others. Sickert was perhaps the most quick-witted, and did not mind hurting people's feelings. He enjoyed making fun of Moore, who was not amused. Moore did not care for general conversation, he preferred the centre of the stage with a spotlight on himself. Tonks was pretty good, but Steer and Sargent were not conversationalists. If Steer did rouse himself to say something, however, it was generally wise and never foolish. Now and then to keep my end up, I ventured a futile remark; it was dreadful if Henry James happened to hear, he was so kind, and so anxious to give any suggestion proper consideration. He would repeat one's poor little observation, examine it from every angle, give it careful thought, and regret that he could not agree.

What dinners these must have been and how the conversation of this group must have sparkled. Henry James, born 1843 and died 1916, would have been one of the oldest attendees. He was a major figure of transatlantic literature, and many of his novels concern the interaction of his American characters with the Old World. By 1897 he was living in Rye is Sussex and it was there that he wrote his famous novel *The Turn of the Screw*.

One evening Maude Allan, the first of the semi-nude dancers, was being discussed. Henry James was asked if he had been to the Palace Theatre to see her performance, he said, 'Yes, and I gathered that the dancing was intended to appeal to the sense, but I must own that it left mine woefully assailed!' He once complained that his privacy at Rye was being much disturbed by chance callers. He told us how, not long ago, a charabanc filled with 'dreadful women' had descended on him. Someone said that surely, among so many, all were not repulsive; he thought for a moment and then replied, 'Perhaps there was one poor, melancholy wanton with a certain cadaverous grace.'

Maud Allan, born in Canada in 1873 and died in the Los Angeles in 1956, was a piano teacher before in her late teens turning to professional dancing. In 1900 she appeared in her own production of *Vision of Salome* in which her dance of the seven veils made her famous and infamous. Gray mistakenly added an 'e' to her Christian name.

Max Beerbohm told me that one summer he, Mrs Hammersley and George Moore were walking on Hampstead Heath discussing a book which had lately been published concerning the relations which had existed between Lord Byron and his half-sister. Moore could not be bothered to go into the pros and cons of the matter, and dismissed the subject by shouting 'Why on earth a man may not marry his sister I cannot understand!'

Sickert was generally hard up. He had a practice of selling his pictures in bundles to dealers at about £1 a piece. Dealers bought them without looking at them. Sickert thought it better that an artist should sell all his output at small prices rather than have his studio full of unsold canvases. This theory sounds all right, but does not work out well. It was Sickert who was hard up, and the dealers who made money by his work, for they always boom an artist when they hold a big stock of his pictures – the more they hold, the greater the artist he becomes.

Whenever Hugh Hammersley heard that Sickert was extra anxious to sell, he got either Tonks or myself to go to his studio and buy some pictures. For those I bought he asked from £20 to £30, which he considered big prices. I often see these pictures now in dealer's exhibitions, priced at a hundred or two more than I gave Sickert thirty-five years ago. When Sickert was fifty he fussed because he was not well known, whereas when Whistler was fifty he was famous in both London and Paris. He often compared his position with that of Whistler, and one thing I know they had in common, they were both often short of money.

Sickert was always unexpected. I had been to lunch with him and his wife in Gloucester Crescent, Regents Park. He was in good spirits, and extremely well. A day or two later I was astonished to hear that he was dangerously ill, so I wrote to Mrs Sickert for news. This was the reply I received:-

*Dear Mr Gray,*

*Thank you so much for your kind and sympathetic note. Walter has given us a terrible fright, but is now almost well. He seemed so ill – indeed was – for ten days, that the doctors wavered between typhoid and appendicitis, and when it was proved that it could not be the first, an august specialist was summoned who pronounced it to be undoubtedly the second, and that he must be operated upon in two days. This news had such a cheering effect on the invalid, and the excitement of being waited upon by two trained nurses, who sterilised the whole house and telephoned for the entire stock of all chemists and hospital contract people in London, which arrived throughout the two days in an interminable procession – culminating in the distinction of being prayed for in church, completely dispersed all symptoms, and when the retinue, with the mysterious black bags, arrived – there was nothing for them to do. They were amazed, however, and declared him a puzzle to science, so he is to be X-rayed. I have given you a great many details but feel they fall upon sympathetic ground as you have had so much experience of doctors, haven't you? Thanking you again so much, Very sincerely yours,*

*Christine Sickert.*

Moore could also be startling. Once, in a crowded drawing room, he suddenly announced that his feet were hot and swollen, and proceeded to take off his shoes.

Walter Sickert, born 1860 and died in 1942, was a painter who had a major influence on the way art developed in the late 19th and early 20th century in England. In 1888 he exhibited a painting of a music hall artist at the New English Art Club which fascinated and scandalised, taking as it did real life, and real life as part of the gritty urban life of the poor in London.

This set him on a path that included his Camden Hill Murder paintings and others that turned their back on the romantic and sentimental. He was described as colourful, charming and fascinating by contemporaries and Gray's comments echo this description. His name is still linked with the Jack the Ripper murders which is as much a reflection of his open interest in the sordid life of the underclass of the East End of London.

Christine was his second wife and she died in 1920.

George Moore was born in 1852 and died in 1933. Moore originally set out to be an artist and studied at the Academie Julian in Paris in the 1870's. However he abandoned art and in the 1880s came to London to pursue a literary career.

His first novel *A Modern Lover* was published in 1885 and although gaining him a reputation as an exciting new literary voice, it also earned him censure from the influential circulating libraries who banned it.

*The Brook Kerith* referred to by Gray, was published in 1915 and is a retelling of the life of Christ as a non-divine figure who did not die on the cross. This would explain the discussion about miracles.

It was in 1907 that I first went painting in France with Wilson Steer. It was a Sunday on which I travelled to Montreuil-sur-Mer, and resolved never to travel to France on a Sunday again. There was much changing of trains, and I had a bicycle to cart about as well as other baggage. Steer, Brown and Coles met me at Montreuil station. When Coles saw the bicycle he looked glum, and began about 'the foolishness of bringing one – where was it to be housed? The place was small, there was no room for bicycles.' All the way up the hill from the station Coles was worrying about the confounded bicycle, he made me feel that I had spoilt the summer for the whole party. I suggested that the outlook was not quite so gloomy as he imagined, surely there was some shopkeeper who would house it for me at a small cost? But he rambled on until we reached some enormous gates. To my astonishment they pushed these open and invited me to enter a spacious courtyard, around two sides of which was our mansion. I now realised that this was another of Coles' little jokes. They had taken this fine old house for the summer at a reasonable rent. Montreuil was full of lovely houses. The first week they had spent hiring the necessary furniture and finding a servant, and when I arrived the house was a going concern. We each had a bedroom and separate studio. The rooms were all large, and Marie, our bonne, proved a marvel. She did the marketing, cooked delicious meals, scrubbed out each room every week, and did all our washing and mending, and for this we each paid £2 a week.

Montreuil-sur-mer is now more commonly known as Montreuil, the sea having retreated as the river estuary silted up. It is a small town, surrounded by brick ramparts built during the 17th century. Victor Hugo visited whilst writing *Les Miserables* and set some of the novel in the town.

It was also the base, from 1916 to 1919, of the British Army headquarters in the First World War.

It was a custom of Steer's to spend the first week in a new place wandering around looking for subjects. He was not too pleased with the trees at Montreuil, which on the plains were mostly tall, straight poles with foliage at the top. He told me that he thought it a 'damn silly landscape' and at first was disappointed and depressed. However, he was cheered when he found some good, English looking trees on the ramparts, and when once he got to work there was no stopping him. Brown was a methodical worker when he got his teeth into a subject, and whether good or bad, he never let go.

I have never liked to talk of the misery and depression I suffer when painting. Painting a picture is a personal, secret kind of job, and to bring anything to a conclusion one has to *enjoy* the misery of work.

We knew several artists living at Montreuil. Van der Weyden, whom I had known at Brown's years before, lived there with his wife and family. W. Gore, a Slade student contemporary of John and Orpen, (known as 'Ruddy Gore' because of his red hair), lived at the hotel. Fred Mayor with his family had been there for some years and felt, I thought, that he had staked a claim for all the best subjects. Other people began to arrive – Harrington Mann, his pretty wife and two small daughters, and last but not least, Frank Brangwyn appeared with a large class of students. Except that Steer and Brangwyn said 'how do you do' when they first met, the two parties passed without further recognition. Not so the students. There was a tall, elegant American girl with whom Steer became friends. She called most mornings to help him carry his painting things, and I began to fear for him. It amused us to see her struggling along the ramparts with one of his large canvases while he walked behind with paint box and easel.

Marie, our bonne, in spite of her many activities, sometimes found time to pose. One subject which Steer and I painted sitting cheek by jowl had a sequel years later. It was a picture of Marie sitting in the doorway mending a sheet. Steer exhibited his picture when back in England, and someone bought it. I hid mine, but coming across it years later I thought it good, and sent it to a provincial exhibition. A few days after the exhibition opened Steer had a letter from a man saying that some years ago he had bought a picture by Steer of a girl sewing in a doorway, and lately had seen a picture by Ronald Gray of exactly the same subject. 'Can you explain this?' he asked. Steer replied that the explanation was simple – we were sitting side by side.

Coles had not been altogether idle. It was a common occurrence to find a note on one's plate at breakfast purporting to come from some unknown person. They were usually an adaptation of a well-known verse. One morning I found the following:

*That which in Phoebe was native grace*
*In Mrs Perkins is out of place*
*He thought of the twins and wished that they*
*Were less like his old friend Ronald Gray*

We thought of a plan to get level with Coles, the idea being Steer's. Staying at Montreuil was a pleasant man with a pretty wife, with whom we had only a slight acquaintance. At dejeuner we began to put Steer's plan into practice, and one of us casually remarked that we had met the pretty wife in the market place – 'A funny thing' we said, 'she would talk of nothing by Coles.' Coles smiled fatly and said nothing. The next day we said 'Can't make it out, we tried hard to make Mrs M. come for a walk, but she kept us standing talking about 'that nice Mr Coles' for at least twenty minutes. After a few days of this we noticed that Coles began to prink himself up and wear his best clothes. He gave up working, and could often be seen hanging around the hotel where the M.'s were staying. We kept on with our part of it until one day we thought that Coles must have brought things to a climax, for he resumed his old clothes and went back to work.

There were a great many amusements to be had that summer. There was bathing at Berck, a bicycle picnic, or visiting the casino at Le Touquet. Le Touquet was far less sophisticated than it is now.

One day when at Boulogne with Dollie Mann and her children, and having half an hour to wait for our return train, we went into the casino to pass the time. Dollie suggested that I should put something on number seven, but as we entered we saw that it had just come up. In spite of that I put five francs on it, and up it came again; I tried it again, and again it won. For a last fling as we were about to leave I plumped a pile of money on red – and red it was. I was weighed down with five franc pieces.

I remember a garden where we bought roses for our friends. Even Steer bought some for his American assistant, so things were getting serious. We all gave parties; wine was absurdly cheap, so they were merry ones. Brown's gaiety was astonishing; it was a sight to see this serious Slade professor playing Oranges and Lemons with his coat off and doing high jumps with the children. Steer very much enjoyed dancing and there were many opportunities, but our dances were spoilt by an awful boy who spent his evening prying round corners and springing out with a scream whenever a moment became interesting. Steer complained bitterly about him, and we considered a hiding but in the end thought it wiser to let the matter rest. This boy, now a middle aged man, called on Steer not long ago. He was then a successful engineer.

The approach of autumn sent us back to England. To my surprise Steer announced that he was going to Paris for a week before returning home. Later he whispered to me that the elegant American and her party were also bound for Paris. It was while Steer was in Paris on that occasion that he first heard of Cezanne. There was an exhibition of his work, which Steer did not like at all.

Our visit to Montreuil was the last time Steer ever painted out of England. He said that when abroad he was a foreigner, and he did not like foreigners!

The following summer Steer, Brown, Coles, Tonks and I went to Corfe Castle. The first three went to a farm just outside the village, Tonks took rooms in the village, and I lived in comfort at another farm for 25/- a week. Jacomb-Hood was also staying at Corfe with the Cavendish Bentincks, painting one of their children.

Soon after we arrived I was surprised, one morning early, to have a visit from Steer. Knowing him as I did I knew that for him to walk from his farm to mine at that hour there must be a powerful reason, and when I read the letter he gave me I understood. It was from the father of his American friend, saying that he and his wife were staying at the Savoy, and would 'be so pleased if Mr Steer would dine one evening.' 'Now, my lad, you're for it' I said. Steer was really perturbed, though determined that he would not dine at the Savoy. Between us we composed rather a good letter explaining the impossibility of Steer's going to town. I was sorry, for the father had written a charming letter; but Steer would never allow anything to come between him and his work – not even a beautiful woman – for long.

During this summer an absurd incident occurred between Tonks and myself. He had told me about a cheeky student to whom, years before, he had given lessons in anatomy. The young man used to try to stare Tonks out, and in time it became so intolerable that Tonks determined to stop it once and for all. So one morning he sat down at his desk in the lecture room and began a staring out battle with the student, while the others watched breathlessly. The student made a good fight of it, but at last he flinched and looked away, never to try the game again. The telling of this story somehow made Tonks and me self-conscious when looking at each other. Each evening when I called I found that we looked at each other a bit longer, and the climax was reached when one evening I found him sitting, his chin resting on his hands and his elbows firmly on the table, in battle array to do me down. Seeing no way of avoiding the challenge I sat in the chair he had placed on the opposite side of the table, and we started in on this ridiculous contest. The absurdity of it made me feel hysterical, and after minutes which seemed eternity I looked away – a conquered man. We never spoke of this childish behaviour, but until the day of his death we were self-conscious when looking at each other. In after years I was consoled for my defeat when a Scotland Yard detective – one of the 'Big Five' – told me that in his experience the worst criminals were always able to look one straight in the face.

> 'The Big Four' was the name given to the four Superintendents in charge of the CID at Scotland Yard, headquarters of the Metropolitan Police, in London. This seems to have been common currency by about 1900 but Gray has added an extra one 25 years later.

Fred Brown, although at this time rather an invalid, was keen on exercise, and so, in his fat way, was Coles. They continually jeered at Steer because of his laziness, until he considered it time to put them in their place; so one hot afternoon he announced that he would walk to Swanage with them. To get to Swanage the way goes over high downs – a stiffish walk. Steer made the pace pretty hot, and kept it up until they arrived in Swanage, Brown and Coles exhausted. Steer then asked if they were satisfied, and they evidently were, for we heard no more about Steer's laziness that summer.

Steer was a strongly built man. A Swede who once gave him massage told me that with exercise he might become very powerful. When young he had a severe attack of influenza, and for years afterwards was hardly ever free from colds. He became frightened about his health, and gave up all exercise because he said it heated him. When I first knew him he rode a bicycle and often went dancing, but later, if he went for a walk, he always put his fingers through his shirt and vest, touching his chest, and at the first sign of dampness he slowed his pace.

In the days before the First World War people had more time and money to do things and go about. Wherever we went for summer there were always nice people about, and among those at Corfe were Charles Cheston and his wife, both good painters, who lived in a house designed by Voysey, who at that time was considered 'it' in the architectural world. There were also the Everetts, at whose place Tonks painted several pictures that summer.

On our return to London a friend took me to dine with some friends of his. Our hostess was good-looking, though no longer young; our host was a glum fellow, who left to attend a political meeting before the port was handed round. When we three were alone we arranged with our hostess that I should do a coloured drawing of her. I had decided to go to New York, and this was lucky, she said, for she would like me to take the drawing to a friend there; but she wished nothing to be said about it. I did not like the suggestion of secrecy, and before the job was finished I disliked it still more.

A few days later I went to their house to make the drawing, and was shown to her boudoir. Before she began to sit, she turned the key in the door and again said she wished nobody to know about it.

This secrecy business did not create an atmosphere in which I could do my best work; however, we got to work and for half an hour all went well. Then to my horror heavy footsteps sounded along the corridor and the door handle was turned briskly. Her husband's voice shouted, 'Open the door!' and I heard a growl from a big dog. My sitter put her fingers to her lips, the door rattled more violently, the dog growled louder, and still we remained silent, while I trembled. The husband had now quite lost his temper, for he yelled, 'This is a damn funny business, whose coat and hat is it in the hall?' With another furious bang on the door, accompanied by another growl from the dog, he stumped away. I said, 'What happens when I leave the house – will there by a rough and tumble in the hall, with the dog grabbing my trousers?' 'He was going to his club at one o'clock,' said my sitter, 'so stay and have luncheon with me.' But I thought it more prudent to leave while the going was good, and hurried home. Luckily the touchy fellow went away for a week and I was able to finish the drawing without further interruption. I thought it was an unfair position in which to put one who was entirely innocent of the crime her husband no doubt suspected.

I had begun a portrait of Mother. She was then over eighty, and I was anxious to finish it before leaving for America. For the last week she came every morning to sit, and on the last day was so keen to keep the pose as long as I wanted that after three solid hours the old dear burst into tears, and I had to comfort her and thank her for her pluck. I hid the portrait, but Alfred Hayward found it while I was in America and sent it to the Modern Portrait Painters Exhibition. I was astonished at the good notices which were sent to me. This portrait was afterwards bought by the Chantrey Bequest, and for years, until the pictures were removed to safety in 1939, Mother smiled at me from the wall whenever I visited the Tate Gallery.

*'My Mother' by Ronald Gray. Photo: Tate*
*The portrait was painted by Gray in 1908 and was purchased for the Tate under*
*the Chantrey Bequest for £262 and 10 shillings in 1925.*

It amuses me to recall an incident in which my nephew, Dick Townsend and this portrait figured. Mother was staying with my sister Helen Townsend; Dick was a very small boy, but was allowed to have his midday meal in the dining room. Glancing at his grandmother while eating his lunch, he suddenly said 'What an ugly nose you have, Granny.' His Granny was amused, but his mother was very angry at his rudeness and banished him to the nursery. Months later, when Dick was staying in London, Mother brought him to my studio to show him my portrait of her. He looked at it in silence for a long time, then said casually as he turned away, 'I see that Uncle Ron has made the same mistake as I did about your nose!'

# Chapter 13

# America and an Accident

Wild storms checked our progress so much that the voyage to New York took eleven or twelve days. It is difficult now to realise that in those days the first class fare was only £12. I have never in my life felt so lonely as I did during my first few days in New York. I took a room on West 47th Street, a street crowded with hotels. The weather was cold, sunny and bracing, but I found the heat of the rooms stifling. Hugh Hammersley had given me a letter of introduction to some cousins who lived in a large flat in an apartment house on Fifth Avenue. At that time London had no flats on so luxurious a scale. Hugh had warned me that his cousin was a strict teetotaller. Whether her husband was or no, I could not be sure, for he spent much time at his club. He was, however, fond of cigars, and thrust enormous ones on me whenever we met. His wife, whose portrait I was to paint, was distinguished looking, and drove about New York in an open carriage drawn by a pair of high stepping horses. They gave a dinner party to introduce me to their friends. About twenty sat down to dinner, which was extremely good. I remembered Hugh's warning about drink when a dignified butler asked if I would have ginger beer, lemonade or soda water; I caught my host's eye and thought he winked, but could not be sure. The conversation had not the quality of the food. My partner was a pretty southern girl; in her soft voice she hinted that alcohol would have put more kick into the proceedings, and I agreed. We all left the dining room together to go into a large drawing room. The ladies went to one side of the room, the men to the other, when to my surprise two plate glass screens slid out from somewhere and divided the room in half. This clever contrivance enabled the men to smoke cigars without annoying the women with the smoke – it was not then the fashion for women in New York to smoke, a fact which came home to me later.

Soon after arriving in New York I rang up an American who had been with us at Julian's in Paris, and who had lived in Chelsea for several years. He was an amusing fellow, and although thirteen or fourteen years had passed since our last meeting, he seemed pleased to see me. He told me that he had 'commercialised his art' and was running an advertising business; and he had obviously made a great success of his commercialisation. He occupied large premises in which I saw numbers of men working feverishly at drawing boards. He ran a day and night shift – the output must have been enormous. Through Etheridge I was introduced to a bohemian side of New York life.

> The late 19th and early 20th Century saw the beginnings of the modern advertising business in New York. Some iconic agencies started at this time like BBDO in 1891 by George Batten and McCann Erickson by Alfred Erickson in 1902. The only reference I can find for Etheridge is an agency headquartered in Vancouver, Canada, that states that its 'roots lie in the New York Agency world'.

Messrs Knoedler were important picture dealers who owned a good gallery on Fifth Avenue. They offered to show my six drawings of English women. I saw them hung on a panel in the corner of one of the galleries, and I sent a few invitations, at the direction of Hammersley's cousin, to people who might be interested. Later I heard that some had been to the gallery but had failed to see my drawings, so I at once went to Knoedler's to find out how this had happened. The explanation was simple. My drawings were hung on the panel of a large door which opened from another gallery, this door was constantly open, with the result that my little lot spent most of their time with their faces up against the wall!

While I was in New York an acquaintance from London was doing a lecture tour in America. She was extremely clever, and her lectures drew full houses. We sometimes dined at restaurants together, and at our first dinner we both lighted cigarettes when coffee arrived. The manager came to our table and politely told me that, 'Ladies were not allowed to smoke in public.' What changes have taken place since then.

Some years earlier this lady had suffered a painful illness which necessitated the use of drugs. I knew that she had not broken the habit, but had never seen any sign of it. An important hostess in New York gave a party in her honour, to which I was invited. I arrived rather late, and on entering a crowded room I felt at once that something was wrong. At the end of the room my friend was sitting, talking wildly. Her hat was on one side and her hair was partly down. My heart sank; how awful that this should happen here! She gave me a cheery welcome, and our hostess suggested that I should take her home. She was a strong willed creature, but the plan I followed succeeded. Servants were handing round tea and coffee, and I whispered to her that these were not much good to me, but that there was strong drink in the room below, 'so how about it?' The idea pleased her and taking her arm I was able to pilot her from the room. I felt disgraced! Driving home in a cab along Fifth Avenue she gesticulated and talked loudly, telling me intimate details of people and things at home. I met her a few days later, spick and span and as charming as ever. She made no reference to the party, and her lectures continued to be full to overflowing.

Two other painters from Chelsea were working in New York that winter, John da Costa and Wilfred de Glehn – the latter with his wife. Mrs de Glehn is an American. Her relatives were among the most charming people I met there. Wilfred gave a party to introduce Lady Somebody Something who had been dancing successfully in London, wearing practically nothing. On this night de Glehn's friends sat in a circle on the floor whilst the lady capered about in the centre. She had an excellent figure. It was an odd, and at that time an unusual performance.

> Wilfred de Glehn was born in 1870 and died in 1951. Painter of portraits, landscapes, marine subjects and figures, he studied at the Royal College of Art and the Ecole des Beaux-Arts, and subsequently assisted Sargent with whom he travelled widely. Early in his career he exhibited at the Paris Salon, the Royal Academy and the New English Art Club. He met his future wife in 1904 in the United States and they married the same year. He was elected to the Royal Academy in 1932.

With the de Glehns there I felt more at home in New York. Because our language is (more or less) the same, I did not expect to find much difference between London and New York, but there *is* a great difference. New York seemed to me like a foreign city. One felt that it was brimming over with energy – no half measures about anything. For instance, the illuminated sky signs on Broadway were an example of the thought and energy put into advertising. There was one in particular which brought a blush to my cheeks if I happened to be walking with a woman. I first saw it when walking from the Plaza Hotel; it was a lovely night, when suddenly across the blue dome of the sky, in enormous letters flashed the name of a well-known medicinal water, then, after a breathless pause, appeared 'FOR CONSTIPATION' in still bigger letters, below. However romantic one's conversation happened to be, this illuminated, huge and intimate advice would inevitably change the course of one's thoughts.

My Paris friend, Etheridge, was partly responsible for an incident in which my behaviour was not above reproach. One evening he took me to see some boxing at a club, and we went on to a party a friend was giving at Rector's, a fashionable restaurant on Broadway. The party consisted of about a dozen men and one very pretty girl, our host's friend. After supper, at which much champagne was consumed, we sat on round the table, drinking more. I remember how increasingly beautiful the lady appeared as the night advanced, and how easily, and I thought brilliantly, my conversation flowed, so much so that I was annoyed when the party rose from the table and made a move to the hall. I bravely hung on to the girl, who was smiling at my torrent of words. In the vestibule I was holding her hand and trying to quote the lines, 'Parting is such sweet sorrow,' when someone caught me roughly and began shoving my arms into my overcoat, and putting my hat on my head, and then the girl's friend, rather rudely I thought, bundled me into a cab. I came more or less to my senses when I arrived at the hotel, but I spent a dreadful night, for the room whirled round and the bed tilted precariously. In the morning I felt indescribably ill, and the conclusion was forced on me that I must have been drunk the previous night. I was not fit again for a week. I could never be a drunkard. The few times when I have drunk too much, the subsequent misery far outweighed any exhilaration of the moment. I was very ashamed of my bad manners. There is no doubt that good manners help to make intercourse with other people pleasant, and my critical self has always held in contempt my own rather smarmy ones, though I can see that these have enabled me to mix easily with many different specimens of the human race. I have never understood why wild, rough people like those in the Australian bush, seemed to take to me; they probably spot that I have a love for humanity in general!

The winter climate of New York, though very cold, filled me with energy. However late I went to bed, I never felt tired. The heat of the houses, though, which were kept at a higher temperature even than that of a life class, I found extremely trying.

New York had many well run clubs. Friends made me an honorary member of most of the good ones, for which I was grateful. It makes a great difference to a stranger in a foreign town to have a comfortable club to visit. The Player's Club in Gramercy Park I enjoyed as well as any; it was more like the Chelsea Arts Club than any of the others. I often dined at the Yacht Club and the Harvard. I must have been a member of at least a dozen. I found America so invigorating and gay that I determined to return the next year. I had managed to get enough work to make the visit worthwhile, though this quick drawing was not all in my line. In April I returned to London.

Looking back over the years I sometimes wonder whether all this going and coming helped me in my profession, or whether it would not have been better to stick it out, quietly working in London. It is difficult to know which of many possible causes influenced me to make abrupt changes in my life. I had to make a living, and I intensely disliked scrounging around for jobs among people of whom I was fond. In New York it was more impersonal, but even there I hated smiling and being pleasant to courteous people with the idea of extracting jobs. That is the worst side of a portrait painter's life – soft soaping clients. One becomes commercial, and I had no wish to be a commercial artist. I wanted to paint just whatever I felt like painting at the moment, but without private means that was impossible. My friends all had jobs, teaching at the Slade and elsewhere, which enabled them to take a haughtier stand against the criticism of their sitters. Oh, those amateur critics! 'Have I really got bags under my eyes? Aren't my eyes larger than that? Am I so fat under the chin?' How often have I longed to shout, 'Yes, damn it, you are!' Only once in my life did I so far forget myself. John Sargent's difficulty was to refuse the many people who clamoured to be painted by him. But even he practically gave up painting portraits before he was fifty, chiefly because, he said bitterly, 'there was always something wrong about the mouth.'

But I was young enough to enjoy seeing fresh places, meeting fresh people, dining and dancing, so off I went again to New York. I found the Harrington Manns and their two daughters settled in a large studio apartment overlooking Central Park. Harrington was full up with commissions. I doubt if any painter of his time could paint a family group better than he, and I am sure that many of the portraits he painted in America will in the future be cherished family possessions. He never used photographs – that ruination of portrait painting – and I was often amazed at his ability to paint children who did not keep the pose for a second.

> Harrington Mann was born in 1864 and died in 1937. He was best known as a successful portrait artist, which matches Gray's assessment of him in his memoirs. He studied at the Glasgow School of Art and the Slade School of Fine Art. He spent a year at the Academie Julian in Paris. In 1900 he opened studios in both London and New York.

It did not take me long to settle down again in New York. I had left dark, foggy weather in London, and found delight in the sunshine and bracing air. The promise of work was good also. The editress of a book which was to be published about famous American women asked me to do the many portrait drawings which would be required. This pleased me, for it ensured occupation for some time. I certainly was not out for oil portraits, over which I liked to spend at least five years!

One evening I was introduced to a tall, good-looking old gentleman who was making a pencil drawing of Dollie Mann. He talked cleverly, though rather too much, I thought. He spoke with a pretty Irish accent, and was in New York trying to make a living by painting portraits. He took from his pocket a long letter he had just received from his son in Dublin, and proceeded to read it aloud to us. The wit and quality of this letter was explained when he read out the signature – it was from the poet, Yeats.

Harrington introduced me to a very pretty, attractive young woman, Evelyn Thaw, who had gained worldwide notoriety when her husband Harry Thaw, shot and killed Stanford White, one of the best of America's architects. After a long trial, during which Evelyn was referred to as the Angel Child, Thaw was found guilty and put under detention for many years. Evelyn, when I knew her, lived in a pleasant apartment with an elderly negress servant and spent some of her time studying to be a sculptress.

> Harry Thaw was the husband of Evelyn Thaw and in the 'crime of the century' murdered the famous architect Stanford White on the roof of Madison Square Garden in New York. Thaw was the wealthy heir to his coal and railway baron Father and fell in love and married the chorus girl Evelyn Nesbit, who, before their marriage, had had an abusive relationship with White. Thaw became insanely jealous of White. He was declared guilty but insane and incarcerated in relative comfort supported by his family wealth. He and Evelyn were divorced in 1915 and he died in Florida in 1947.

The Manns also introduced me to the only real gourmand I ever met – he was also a philosopher. At one time he must have been a fine looking man, but when I met him he was fat and puffy, and his skin was red and spotty. Gout caused him to move with difficulty, but in spite of these drawbacks, I remember him as a kindly, pleasant creature. He invited us to go to a restaurant noted for its cooking of wild duck. The usual fuss which waiters make with a respected customer occurred when we entered. Our hats and coats were seized, and about three men shoved each of our chairs forward when we sat down. Our host was immersed in the menu and wine card and, concluding these important decisions, walked with an obsequious head waiter to choose the duck. It was surely the most important moment in that duck's history, this cooking and eating of its browned body, accompanied by orange sauce and burgundy. Our host in silence lingered over each mouthful, dreamily enjoying the subtle flavours. With the coffee and liqueur brandy, however, he was once more free to speak; he told us of his aches and pains which, he said, he would always bear with fortitude because their cause had given him much enjoyment. For instance, an excruciating pain in his foot was the result of drinking some lovely claret, a bad twinge somewhere else was probably caused by a well-chosen dinner the night before – and so on. He said that he willingly hastened to his end in this way, because food and drink were his delight. It is strange that this fat, puffy man whom I only saw for, at the most, three hours thirty odd years ago, should have left so vivid impression. Certainly I have come across no one like him since.

Isadora Duncan was in New York that winter, then on top of the wave. I went with Harrington to call on her. She was staying at the Plaza Hotel, so we dressed accordingly. Isadora was wearing a long silk nightgown, and seemed happy, for she told us she had just accomplished something (she did not say what) for which she had wished all her life. A bottle of whisky was on the table – a very special whisky which, she said, must be drunk without water. We pledged her in this extremely powerful liquid, and both became chatty as a result. When we left she came out into the corridor, put on one of our top hats, took our arms and made us high kick with her the full length of the corridor to the lift. We heard afterwards that this exhibition caused the management of the hotel to ask her to leave, but it was smoothed over, and she remained. It was a curious fate which, years later, condemned this gay spirit to such a tragic end. Tragedy haunted her after her fist successful years; she left a remarkable monument to herself in her autobiography. Few women have made so frank a revelation.

The new job I had been given entailed going to Washington for a month. Among the people of whom I had to make drawings was Mrs Taft, wife of the President. The time came for the first sitting and I duly went off to my ordeal, feeling that I was bearing a cross which I did not wish to carry. However, I entered the pleasant open park land in which the White House stands. Approaching a hedge which surrounds it I was surprised to see two men creeping stealthily along. Hullo, I thought, they are going to nab me! But no, they crept by, and then I went on unmolested through the gate. Then I realised the reason for this curious proceeding, for President Taft, a massive figure, was strolling thoughtfully along on the other side of the hedge. The creeping gentlemen were evidently his guards.

The White House is not large, but it looked charming. Mrs Taft had the reputation for not worrying about her appearance, and when told of this peculiarity I remembered asking a fashionable London photographer what he did when a client told him that she wished her photograph to be untouched. 'I always touch up the negative of that sort of client more than usual,' he replied, and he was a very successful photographer.

It was a pretty room in which I worked. I should have enjoyed living in the White House. During our sittings, Mrs Taft listened to the names of people invited to some function, read to her by her secretary. She asked if one or two of the listed people had left cards after the last party, and if the secretary said 'no' she was told to cross off their names. Mrs Taft was very pleasant, I got through the job all right, and I was glad of the opportunity of meeting the wife of the President.

It was lucky for me that the Attorney General, Mr Wickersham, was then living in Washington, for I often dined at his house. He admired the English poets, and sometimes read Shakespeare to me after dinner, and very well, too. One evening the Solicitor General was also a guest. He joined in the poetry reading and I spent a few delightful hours. I left the house with the Solicitor General, and as we walked home he told me that he was a lawyer in Chicago and that his first job on joining Mr Taft's government had been to give a decision on what constituted real whisky. To his surprise he found the answer unbelievably difficult, indeed he had not yet answered it to his own satisfaction. We wandered about the wide streets of Washington on this lovely moonlit night; he told me quite a lot about the troubles of office, and said he preferred his usual job in Chicago. Wickersham was one of the diminishing number of Americans who loved England and its background. He came here most summers, and often stayed at Dunster Castle, in Somersetshire.

It was getting hot, and I found the atmosphere relaxing after the bracing air of New York, but I had more jobs to do before returning. It was on one of those hot evenings that I first tasted a mint julep, which I sipped whilst lounging in a low chair at a comfortable Washington Club. I found the taste of the iced whisky and other ingredients very subtle when filtered through the bunch of mint on top of the long glass, in which one buried one's nose. They became a habit while I was in Washington.

The scene was now changed to Maryland, where I had to make a drawing of a lady who had made some invention. The house was in the country, and was a pleasant, rather large house built of wood. A double flight of steps led up to a pretty Georgian door, which was opened by the most serene and dignified servant I had ever seen. He was jet black, and his manners were perfect. I found myself among a pleasant family consisting of my host and his wife, and my host's sister – the reason for my coming. They were Southerners and all their servants were black. In the morning we had the first sitting. The fact that 'Miss Mary was to have her portrait taken' filled the household with excitement, which was expressed during the sitting by an occasional stealthy opening of the door and appearance of smiling black faces, followed by the loud chuckles when my sitter ordered them away. This became so disturbing that at last we turned the key. There is an engaging quality in these black servants.

I came back to England in that comfortable steamer the Baltic. The Manns were remaining in America, but several people I knew were travelling home. I became acquainted with one man in a curious way. He suddenly come up to me and pointed out that we had identical caps, both from Lock, the London hatters. This coincidence led to his giving me a commission to do portraits of his sisters when next he came to England. Both his sisters were married to Englishmen. I was returning home full of work and hope, but here fate upset all my plans.

> The Baltic was launched in 1903 and for a while was the largest ship of the White Star line and later sister ship to the ill-fated Titanic which sank in 1912. Captain Smith was in charge of the maiden voyage of the Baltic, as he was when he lost his life in the Titanic.

The day before reaching Liverpool I was fooling about, pretending to throw a man overboard. He retaliated and swung me round, and my rubber soled shoe stuck to the deck; I felt a cracking in my knee and fierce pain and I fell, quite unable to stand. They carried me to my cabin, and I lay in agony. The ship's doctor, not a brainy fellow, put a heavy bag of ice on my swollen joint which made matters worse. A hospital nurse who was travelling with a patient was told of my plight; she came and made me more or less comfortable, and gave me some white tablets which sent me to sleep – and I blessed her. It was a terrible business getting from the ship to the train and back to Chelsea. I was a wreck when I arrived, and felt it was hard that Mother, at her age, should be worried by so helpless a son.

The next day the Hammersleys sent a nurse and ambulance to take me to Hampstead. Their doctor, who was said to be clever, attended me, and tried every new idea, but the swelling and pain persisted. This doctor was a nervy fellow, and very short-sighted. Under his arms he always carried many books, which he read as he went along, even when crossing crowded roads. I began to worry about a commission I had in Paris to paint a fellow traveller, and wrote several times saying that I hoped to come in a week or two, but that portrait was never done.

After some weeks it was thought advisable to consult a specialist. With the aid of crutches I walked to the doctor's brougham, and we drove to Harley Street. A severe, gloomy gentleman examined my knee with care, and sent me to his waiting room while he talked to my doctor. When he joined me I asked, 'Well, what about it?' 'He is afraid it is tubercle,' he answered. I had not suspected this possibility, and the news stunned me, I pictured more years of misery, and felt it was unkind of fate to get me down again just as I had got on my feet. I pulled myself together, however, and took the nervy doctor to the Cafe Royal for lunch. At a table near ours Mortimer Menpes was sitting; he said that I looked pretty gloomy, I assured him that I was never happier. The doctor and I had a good luncheon, and both got slightly drunk.

Mortimer Menpes was born in South Australia in 1855 and died in England in 1935. His family moved back to England in 1878. At one time he was a pupil of Whistler and became famous for his skills in etching and dry pointing. He was also a successful author and publisher of some of the first coloured art books.

Then followed X-ray examinations and visits to a ruthless foreigner who ignored the agony he caused when fitting me with a new type of splint – a good splint, for in it I could stand without pressure on the knee joint. By a tricky device at the ankle a constant pull kept the bones of the knee apart. I wore this contraption night and day for more than three years; it caused me much pain.

My Australian doctor friend, Page, was working at St Mary's Hospital under

Sir Almroth Wright. They were then just beginning to use injections for tubercle. Page suggested that I should see a Dr Fleming, who was also working with Wright, and Mrs Hugh asked Page to bring him along to lunch. We expected an elderly scientist and were astonished to see a nervous young man who looked little more than a boy. Fleming (now Sir Alexander Fleming, discoverer of penicillin) treated me until I was well, a matter of more than three years.

*Cartoon of Alexander Fleming drawn by Gray in 1911 and which refers to Fleming's role in the London Scottish Regiment and his use of 'compound 606' or salvarsan in the treatment of syphilis.*
*By permission of the Alexander Fleming Laboratory Museum.*

Sir Almroth Wright was born in 1861 and died in 1947. He was an early proponent of vaccination and promoted the efficacy of immunisation in preventing deadly illnesses, especially typhoid. In 1902 he started a research department at St Mary's Hospital in Paddington. One of his protegees was Alexander Fleming who had enrolled at the Hospital Medical School in 1903, where he qualified in 1908. He joined the research department and became an assistant to Sir Almroth as he then was, as he had been knighted in 1906. Fleming would gain worldwide fame as the discoverer of penicillin, albeit accidentally. In 1928 he was studying influenza and noticed that mould had grown on a set of petri dishes used to grow the influenza germ. This had created a bacteria free circle around itself and was to be named eventually as penicillin. But it was only developed further by two other scientists Howard Fleury and Ernst Chain and was produced commercially in the 1940's during the Second World War. Fleury, Chain and Fleming were awarded the Nobel Prize after the war.

Fleming became a close friend of the extended Gray family and he and his wife rented a flat in the Gray home at 20 Danvers Street. A blue plaque commemorates this today. He also stayed often with Gray's brother in law Fred Pegram and his family where he was a favourite with their daughter Marjory who was Gray's heir.

Mrs Hugh usually drove me to St Mary's for my injections; sometimes we stayed to tea with Sir Almroth Wright and his young men, a remarkable team of youthful enthusiasts. They worked late into the night at his bidding, counting blood corpuscles, or doing any job he wished. The all took an interest in my case.

I found that, lying in a long chair with my legs up, I could paint and draw again, and many people gave me commissions. During warm summer days I painted pictures in the Hampstead garden, and there were interesting visitors to keep me amused. When the time came for the Hammersleys to go to their house in the Isle of Wight I moved to Pegram's studio as he also was away. My sister Elizabeth acted as my devoted nurse, which I remember with gratitude. My plight was a signal, it seemed, for my friends to try to make my time pass pleasantly. Indeed, Elizabeth complained that she was weary of opening crates of flowers which were frequently sent to me from the country. It amuses me now to remember how I accepted these attentions as a matter of course. Hardly a day passed without callers or sitters. I made drawings of all conditions of people. Most afternoons I was taken for motor drives into the country, though after a time Fleming stopped this activity, for vibration of the car inflamed my knee.

When it was realised that this illness would be a long job, it was decided to get a man to look after me and pull me about in a bath chair. Mrs Hugh found a pleasant young man in the Isle of Wight, and I engaged him.

I took rooms in Trafalgar Square (now renamed Chelsea Square) not far from Mother's house; she was too old to have an invalid on her hands, although she protested. The house in Trafalgar Square was run by a retired butler and his wife, the latter having been a cook. They were pleased when I entertained friends to dinner – they seemed to enjoy the extra work. The old man kept chickens in the back garden, and I was surprised how interested I became when, towards Christmas, he began expecting them to lay. I enquired each morning, but always got a gloomy 'No'. However, one night when I came home late, the old man was at the door to greet me, and his eyes sparked as he said, 'The speckled Wyandotte has laid an egg.' I said, 'Thank God,' and slept peacefully.

During the summer I stayed with friends at Lancing and Bosham, and at both places I did much painting with my leg up, usually sitting in a bath chair. My attendant, Johnson, was a smart looking young man and evidently had a way with him, for at some of the houses we visited there were complaints of his goings-on with the maids – indeed, one affair was considered serious, and I was asked to speak to him about it. He waved the incident aside. 'If anything happens,' he said, 'it couldn't be me, I was only with her a moment!'

Mrs Hugh had never been strong; her lungs were delicate and for the last year or two she had spent much time lying on the balcony which overlooked the rose garden at Hampstead. Her friends were saddened to see her gradually losing strength, and most of us realised that she would never be well again. Her interest in things did not flag, and she welcomed visitors in the same gracious way. Mr and Mrs Grant, her parents, were often at The Grove. Mr Grant did not like the way Tonks treated his opinions, to which he paid no attention whatever, and the old gentleman was once so much annoyed that he burst, 'Tonkey rhymes with donkey,' and this cheered him up so much that he chuckled away to himself for some time. Tonks angrily left the room. It must have been the first time since his school days that he had been called Tonkey, and certainly the first time that his august name had been coupled with donkey. However, he was forgiving, and they made friends again, though we often heard the old muttering under his breath, 'Tonkey rhymes with donkey!'

My accident prevented my returning to America to get on with the drawings of well-known women. It being a good commission Pegram went in my stead. He was able to do the drawings far better and quicker than I – indeed he had such success that he continued to visit New York until the First World War stopped him.

Years passed and my leg was still encased in the fearsome steel scaffolding. Continued reaction to the tubercle tests almost forced me to give up hope – but not quite. I did at one time beg Fleming to take my leg off and have done with the pain; I remember him standing at the end of my bed and telling me it would be foolish to do this because tubercle might appear at the part where the leg was cut off. 'Stick it out,' he advised.

During the winter of 1911 Mrs Hugh died. Her coffin was carried on a bier down the hill to Old Hampstead Church, and afterwards to the grave where her little daughter was buried. Many of her friends were there to pay homage, and carry away and keep a happy memory of a remarkable lady and friend. I felt very lonely when I hobbled back to the car.

Lady Agnew had built a lovely house in a corner of Smith Square, Westminster. Detmar Blow had designed it, and I drove about with her, helping with the furnishings. An apartment for bachelor friends had been arranged at the top of the house – an ideal apartment, consisting of bedroom, sitting room and luxurious bathroom. Lady Agnew kindly said that I was to be her first bachelor guest, and invited me for the first week after she had settled in. I remember well the first night of my visit; Johnson had helped me to bed, loosened some straps of the splint and left me cosily buried in soft pillows, reading and happy. After about an hour I heard horses gallop into the square below, soon followed by more. There were sounds of commotion and champing of bits. I was puzzling over this when the door was flung open and Johnson, very excited, shouted, 'The firemen say there is just time to get you downstairs!' 'All right,' I said, 'then get on with it.' He fumbled with the straps and I grabbed at clothes, but we were not getting on very fast and I was relieved when a gruff voice boomed up the stairs shouting, 'It's all right, we've got it out.'

Lady Agnew gave a large house-warming dinner party and asked me to bring A.A. Milne along. Milne was beginning to make his name with plays and with his contributions to *Punch*. I knew him through my brother-in-law F.H. Townsend, the Art Editor. Milne was fair haired, good looking, and moved wearily. He had rooms in Westminster, and I picked him up there. There were about twenty five guests round an enormous circular table, mostly well-known people. A reception and music followed, during which I noticed Milne curled up in a window seat, apparently asleep; how wise, I thought.

Towards the end of 1912 Fleming gave me good news; the latest tests showed that I was free from tubercle. I was relieved and grateful, though the condition of my leg was nothing to brag about. It reminded me of an Indian famine leg, bone with no flesh, the knee joint would not bend. Although I had worn the splint for more than three and a half years, night and day, it was nearly another year before I could walk properly without it. Fleming sent me to a patient Swede who massaged and gradually bent the knee until the joint worked freely and strength came to my emaciated muscles. The only exercise I was allowed when I got stronger was slow dancing, so I joined a dance club and sometimes persuaded victims to go with me. I have harped much on my illness on the chance that some fellow sufferer may read these lines and be given hope.

During the last years Chelsea had been changing its character. The Vale had lost its country village atmosphere, for the old houses had been pulled down; Tonks and Stirling Lee had combined to build a house containing studios and rooms for themselves, and Harris Brown had built a large place opposite. An architect named

*Gertude, Lady Agnew, established a reputation as a great beauty with the portrait painted by Sargent in 1892, entitled 'Lady Agnew of Lochnaw'.*
*The Agnews moved into No 10 Smith Square as described by Gray where she hosted sumptuous dinner parties and dances.*
*The painting is now in the National Gallery of Scotland. Wikicommons.*

Williams rebuilt the rest of The Vale, and also some of the houses in streets leading from there to Church Street – streets which covered the garden where, as children, we had watched the fallow deer. Williams was also responsible for the houses in

Chelsea Park Gardens. I do not think that his architecture was great, but personally I feel grateful to him, for his houses are varied in design, and the streets he built have a cosy feeling which architects since the war, with their copies of Swedish and other foreign styles, fail to give. I showed a Swedish architect round London just before the Second World War, and his comment was that we seemed to have copied all their mistakes!

In the summer of 1914 I again stayed at Bosham. Steer and Brown took lodgings in the village and Tonks was staying with friends a few miles away. Our enjoyment of the lovely weather was spoilt by rumours of alarming events in Europe, and the news became graver as the days passed. Anxiety to get the morning papers increased and villagers and visitors waited at their garden gates for the boy who brought them from the station a mile away. When England declared war the excitement became intense, and we all began to walk along the road each morning to meet the paper boy, who was quick to take advantage of our anxiety; he walked slower and slower every day, and we had to walk further and further to get our papers.

The village was stirred by fantastic rumours, and at first I believed all I heard. When an old yokel told me that six spies had been shot, and he himself had seen them lying dead on the Chichester Road, I went off to have a look for myself. I could not find the bodies, and assumed that they had been removed to the mortuary, so I asked at nearby cottages. No one knew anything of shooting or spies, and yet the old yokel had seemed such an honest man.

A small, pale man arrived in Bosham, dressed in black and wearing a bowler hat. He spent each day sitting in the same place on the quay, always looking towards the end of the creek. He never said good morning or spoke to a soul, and local fishermen and sailors were quite certain that he was a German spy. His landlady said that letters continually came to him from foreign parts. I wondered whether this little man realised that he was always being watched and followed. They dogged his footsteps, and discussed him in the pub, but when the police made investigations they found him to be a respectable London clerk on a fortnight's holiday!

It was Goodwood Week, and many people were down for the races, but one by one they left for London. Reservists began to be called up; we often saw the sad sight of a farm labourer walking to the station on the way to his depot, accompanied by his wife and children to bid what often proved to be a last goodbye. It wrung one's heart, for it takes time to get used to slaughter and misery; we were now witnessing the ringing up of the curtain for the great tragedy.

# Chapter 14

# Artists at War

It was not long before Fred Brown left for London and Steer was alone at the lodgings. For a studio, Steer had taken a boathouse which overlooked the creek. The outbreak of war had dulled his enthusiasm for work; he was irresolute and undecided what to do. Talking things over in his studio one morning we heard unusual noises, and Steer went to the door and looked out. There were many soldiers outside, and one said, 'It's alright, grandpa, we're only putting down a bit of barbed wire.' That settled it – Steer determined to return to London the following day. I helped him pack. He had lately taken to carrying his painting things in a cricketing bag, because, he told me, porters treated him with more respect when they took him for a sportsman.

Back in Chelsea he became a special constable. His first beat was in Manor Street, outside the electric power station. Thinking to gain a more comprehensive view of the building he walked up and down on the opposite side of the road. A sergeant on his rounds asked why he was not on the correct beat. Steer explained what he thought his good reason; the sergeant said, 'Oh, we live and learn,' and ordered him back. Cold winds gave him bronchitis, and he was persuaded to go back to his painting.

A day or two after Steer had left Bosham, Tonks appeared at the house where I was staying. He was in an excited condition, for he had quarrelled with his host and hostess about the war and had left them without warning. Tonks was always quarrelling with someone, and then making it up again. I was now the last of our Bosham party. A young officer had come to say goodbye to his mother before leaving for France. He told me with confidence that the war would be over by Christmas, and that the Germans were in for the biggest hiding they had ever had. Shortly afterwards this boy was in the retreat from Mons.

I was caught in the prevailing restlessness. When I heard that my brother Kenneth was joining the Royal Flying Corps I could not work and soon left for

London. I was forty-six. And remembering that I was considered too old for the Boer War I hardly expected an active job in this; and besides, I was groggy in one leg. Soon after my return I dined with Lady Agnew. Temple Franks was there also, a tall good-looking barrister who was at that time head of the Patent Office. He told me that a corps was being formed to protect London from Zeppelin attacks. It was to be a part-time job for professional men, with pay. Franks had been enrolled as Chief Petty Officer, and said that he would try to get me into his crew as an A.B. A few days later I took the oath and was enrolled as a member of his crew.

> Zeppelin attacks against Britain were launched by the Germans on January 19 1915, and bombs were dropped on towns in Norfolk including Great Yarmouth and King's Lynn. The first London attack took place in May 1915. September 2 1916 saw the largest Zeppelin raid on London with 16 Airships taking part. Until then there had been little opposition to the raids due to the inability of ground based guns to reach the craft and there being no planes able to fly at the altitude of the Zeppelins. This was to change as the Germans moved to deploy heavy bi-planes as bombers. The first Gotha raids took place on May 25 1917. Londoners took to using Underground Stations as shelters for the first time. This was to become essential behaviour in the Second World War.

Our first pitch was on top of the Cannon Street Hotel, where a Boer War pom-pom gun had been fixed to the chimney pots. These guns fired shells which exploded only on concussion – not much good for aircraft work, and decidedly tiresome for people in the streets below.

For some extraordinary reason, the lieutenant commanding our gun made me his secretary at £1 a week. He could not have chosen anyone with less knowledge of secretarial work! This lieutenant was a barrister, a kindly man who took his position seriously. When we walked together I, being an A.B., had to walk behind him. The crews were mostly composed of barristers and lawyers. Time worked was six hours every other day. Naval petty officers on the retired lists were attached to each gun, and were responsible for drills and lectures on the gun. The admiralty had no tables worked out of trajectories for any angles above forty-five degrees, so some of the mathematicians among our crew got together and worked out the higher angles, for obviously all aircraft shooting would be high.

On my way to Cannon Street one morning I was handed a ten shilling note instead of a ten shilling piece when buying my ticket for which I had put down a golden sovereign. I was surprised and rather shocked. A sovereign was a good coin with which one could do much; we had used them all our lives, and they were to be replaced by paper money. This, I think, was the first big change caused by the war.

In case of an alarm, gun crews not on duty were told to report at the gun station. This was sometimes not easy during a raid, for omnibuses stopped running and one could hardly get into the underground stations because of London's East End population, which surged there immediately the maroons sounded. I am writing this in 1943. The knowledge of the great devastation caused by raids during the last few years makes the raids of the First World War seem trivial; at the time, however, they were a new experience. No one knew what would happen, and the defence was at first rudimentary. Rumour spread that London would be destroyed by the mighty Zeppelins. I had the feeling that I wished they would get on with it, so that we might know the worst.

> Maroon rockets were fired as air raid alarms. They were fired by spotters round the city to warn of aerial attack.

It was only during the fine weather and in moonlight that Zeppelins risked a journey to England. On one such night the maroons first sounded, and with some difficulty I made my way from Chelsea to Cannon Street. On arrival, we off duty crews were given rifles and ammunition and stationed on the roof of Cannon Street railway station, with instructions to fire at the enemy! However, we were in a position to enjoy the beauty of the night. From our high stand we could see, through a misty atmosphere, the domes and spires of London, lit faintly by the moon. In the distance searchlights flickered. Suddenly nearby searchlights jumped like solid tubes of light into the dark blue sky. One beam lit an object shaped like a cigar which was coming towards us – so this tiny thing was a dreaded Zeppelin! It glided nearer, and though at a great height, soon looked a dreadful monster. Guns opened up, and I could hear the rat-tat-tat of our little gun. Some of the men fired their rifles, a futile performance. All this noise was suddenly eclipsed by terrific explosions, and the station roof shuddered. The Zeppelin was dropping heavy bombs. One result was the appearance of a few scattered fires, which very soon became an incredible blaze. I thought that surely the whole of the city was on fire, but we were told later that it was the glare from burning warehouses in Wood Street. Flames forked high into the sky and lit up everything, including the Zeppelin, on its way home, untouched!

I had no sketch book with me, but on the back of an envelope I drew the church spires and large buildings, marking the height of the flames. This activity was stopped by our chief petty officer, who marched his crew off to the scene of the fire, where we mildly helped to keep the crowd back, by this manoeuvre obtaining a good view. Being off duty, I spent the next day painting a small picture from the scribble I had made the previous night. This painting was bought by Rex Fry, who, with his brother John, was a member of our gun crew.

During the course of the war I painted several raid pictures for Rex and other members of this affluent crew – indeed, most raids meant the sale of a picture or two for me.

*Cannon Street Anti-aircraft gun painted by Ronald Gray 1917.*
*In the collection of the Imperial War Museum.*

*King's Cross Anti-aircraft gun in action, painted by Ronald Gray in 1917.*
*In the collection of the Imperial War Museum.*

Full accounts of the raid were given in the morning papers, and one item of news caused the Cannon Street crew some concern. This was that some small bombs had been dropped from the Zeppelin with the result that several people were killed in Mile End Road whilst getting in and out of an omnibus. Our gun had fired in this direction, and the men who had worked out the trajectory tables considered that Mile End Road would be about where our shells would have fallen, and these shells exploded on contact!

It was not long before the organisation of the anti-aircraft defence began to improve, and we became less of a 'Harry Tate' army.

'Harry Tate' army and 'Harry Tate' navy were expressions used in the First World War to describe an outfit that was incompetent, despite thinking it had everything worked out. This came from a well-known comedian of the time, Harry Tate, whose most famous sketch was based on his inability to look after a car, something at which he expressed expertise. He added another catch phrase to the language, 'good-by-ee', which remained popular in song through to the Second World War.

The Cannon Street crews were moved to the grounds of the Water Board in Rosebery Avenue, King's Cross, where a French 75 gun had been installed. The hours were increased to twenty-four hours duty in four hour watches, and twenty-four hours off. Among the new recruits were two of my friends. H.P. Hansell, tutor to the Princes, also joined, and became permanent cook's orderly. We slept in army huts on wooden bunks; and the crews showed much ingenuity in making these hard bunks comfortable. The two crews which formed our watch were pleasant, amusing men, and the lieutenant in command of the station, Finnis, was popular, so I felt myself lucky to be there. It was on this station that we witnessed the first destruction of a Zeppelin.

A spell of fine weather and a full moon made an attack probable, and I well remember that lovely evening. My friend Colyn Thomson, an artist, MacDonald, a lawyer, and myself, were lounging on the gun platform enjoying the mystery of the moonlight, which made gaunt buildings appear like fairy palaces. We had been there for some time when the alarm sounded, and the gun crew scampered to their places. That night I was ammunition number. Shells, already set at different ranges, were in pigeon holes. My job, when the officer in charge called the range, was to hand on the necessary shell to the next man, who handed it to the loader. We waited; searchlights were reported in the distance, and messages were shouted by a man at the telephone. 'Zeppelins approaching London. Zeppelins over Harrow. Zeppelins approaching your station, get ready.' Then we could see it lit by searchlights, coming towards us, and the order was given to fire. Guns flashed from all directions, shells looked to be bursting pretty close, and the Zeppelin changed direction. We had fired several rounds when the gun layer shouted,' Misfire.' The shell was extracted, and Finnis, the officer in charge, said it must be thrown into the reservoir, into which he threw it with no ill effect or explosion. I regret that I was not much more heroic!

Whilst this byplay was in progress someone shouted that the Zeppelin was on fire, and the crew broke from their gun positions to watch. Sure enough, in the distance we could see a slowly descending mass of flame. Everyone shouted wildly, and cheers came from nearby streets until it seemed that a roar of joy went up from all over London. For hours cars carried sightseers to gloat over the burning wreck. It fell at Cuffley, shot down by a young airman.

Our night's work was by no means over, for we spent the rest of it taking off fuses similar to those which had misfired (made by a foreign firm) and putting on others. From this first success it became quite common to bring down Zeppelins, and on favourable nights crowds waited in the streets hoping to see one fall.

One night, when on my way to the Chelsea Arts Club, I found it difficult to get onto the pavement at Queen's Elm because of the crowd. I shoved through the first line, and a man told me angrily to get to the back, because they had been waiting for a long time and meant to keep their places!

The last time Zeppelins came to London they tried a new technique, which did not work well About a half a dozen came together, travelling very high, and when approaching London they stopped their engines and left it to the wind to carry them across the town. Our listening posts lost track of them, but luckily someone in command gave orders that no searchlights were to be used, and the Zeppelins, drifting in the cold air, were not sure of their position, though I think they dropped one or two bombs. When they tried to start their engines they could not because of the cold. They were helpless, and drifted in the wind, they were blown about all over the place, only to come down and be captured. One came down in the south of France, and the crew gave themselves up to a peasant.

After this failure the Germans gave up the attempt to crush England with Zeppelins and tried what could be done with planes. The beginning was modest enough. A plane got to London in daylight and dropped one small bomb, which exploded in Brompton Road somewhere near Harrods. Not much harm was done, but in this war we have seen the devastating power which has grown out of this first idea.

The Prince of Wales and his brother Prince Albert came one morning to visit their tutor Hansell at King's Cross gun station. The Prince of Wales, then on leave from France, looked healthy and boyish. He had charming eyes. Prince Albert looked delicate, but they were both full of life, and interested in everything about the station. They watched a gun drill, and had shots on our miniature range. Temple Franks loaded the rifles and another A.B. and I stood at attention. The Prince of Wales had the first shot and got a bullseye and when Franks offered another loaded rifle he refused it, saying that it was always best to let well alone! Prince Albert also made some good shots. They played around the station for at least two hours, and left in a taxi.

While at King's Cross I made many caricatures, including one of Hansell. Being six foot four, he was an obvious subject. I drew him on sentry duty outside a sentry box. He was living at Buckingham Palace at the time, and my caricature amused the Court, he told me. Shortly afterwards I was commanded to make a drawing of Prince Albert, who had been ill and was on leave from the navy. Hansell was excited, and so was I. He gave me so many hints as to my behaviour at the Palace that I wearied of it, and told him that I could only be myself and take my chance.

At the first sitting I do not know whether Prince Albert or I was the more nervous! He was always very polite and courteous, helping me each time to put my table in position. He was in naval uniform, and asked me to keep his cap well up in the front. While I worked he told me about his visit to the West Indies with the fleet.

Once, when I was arranging the next sitting, I heard him whisper to Hansell, 'I can't have him that day. I have another old man coming!' Although approaching fifty, it somehow came as a shock to be thought old. I certainly did not feel it. I then remembered that when, years before, a friend told me that he was thirty-five, I had considered him done for.

One morning a brother was with Prince Albert when I arrived at the Palace. The Prince said, 'Let me introduce you to my brother, generally known as Henry.' Then turning to Prince Henry he said, 'Now get out of it,' and pretended to kick him from the room. I remember Princess Mary being there one day with a lovely dog, which was trying to pat a piece of sandwich from a hot fire bar. One or two memorable mornings Queen Mary came to Prince Albert's room, and was, of course, charming.

Having been asked to do so, I made the Prince's cap stand well up above the badge. When the drawing was finished and delivered, I was told to call. Apparently when King George saw it he said the cap looked too German and I was asked to flatten it!

I do not think they cared for the drawing. It certainly was not one of my best, as I wished it to be, but commissions never have been. For me it had been a privilege and an interesting experience to meet our much loved Royal Family so informally.

Our crew had been moved from King's Cross to a new gun station at Highbury, and after a month or two of foggy winter weather we were again removed, in January 1917, to Hyde Park – a more up to date station, for we had two three inch naval guns with improved high explosive shells. Our late officer, Finnis, had joined a Guards Regiment, and new people were in command. The whole organisation had been gingered up, and life became more strenuous. Hyde Park was a kind of clearing centre, and we A.B.s were kept for hours loading lorries with ammunition, which I found was as much as my weak leg could stand. Some of my friends left, the young ones to join the army. It was an intensely cold winter, the Serpentine was frozen over until April and the wind blew continuously from the north east.

*Drawing of Prince Albert, the future King George VI.*
*Royal Collection Trust / © Her Majesty Queen Elizabeth II 2021*

The uniform of the R.N.V.R. was unattractive, indeed, we were continually taken for railway porters when travelling by train. One of my friends, seeing his son off to school from Paddington, was so pestered with questions that when two old ladies asked whether a train went to Marlow he said, 'Yes, jump in, madam, you're just in time,' and when it had gone he found that he had put them into a nonstop for the West of England!

Certainly the uniforms which had been given us when we joined were poor things. Soon after I had mine I met Sargent in a restaurant. He looked astonished when he saw me and said 'What on earth have you joined?' Some of us felt that we must look a bit smarter now that we were stationed in the West End; Balfour at

King's Cross had his uniform made at a naval tailors in Bond Street. Certainly they made us well cut clothes, but we still got no peace on railway platforms, and, added to this, I was several times taken for an omnibus inspector. Vanity made me wish I had been mistaken for something more warlike.

The Germans bombed London continuously; of course not with the intensity of this present war, but often our guns were hardly cool before they had to be fired again the following night. Seven Gothas once came by day, in V formation, and bombs were dropped on the city. They went where they liked, for we had no planes capable of tackling them, and all our barrage could do was to keep them high. In contrast to the present war, we always heard an hour or so before the planes arrived that they were on the way. They then had further to travel, and our spies were able to watch their preparations.

I do not remember that there was any civil organisation of air raid wardens or fire watchers. The fire brigade and police tackled what had to be done. The blackout was not so drastic, though the streets seemed very dark to us. It was a continual interest walking about after an air raid. I always fancied there was a smell of gunpowder everywhere. London was a hushed city, the only traffic being ambulances and fire engines. It was amusing to drink a cup of coffee at a stall, for the strangest companies gathered round them, drinking hot drinks and eating 'doorsteps' or a 'slab of seedy'. I admired the public spirit of a friend of mine who, both during and after a raid, walked about the streets gaily whistling – a cheering sound in times of stress.

For my first few days leave I went to stay with Steer at a village near Painswick, where we painted happily and forgot the war.

It was during the war that Mother showed signs that her strength was failing. She was approaching ninety, and she was tired and wanted rest, although her brain and memory were unimpaired. Air raids had not frightened her – indeed, when an alarm sounded and my sisters wrapped her warmly for a descent to a lower floor, she was always particularly anxious that they should not put her stocking on inside out! She enjoyed hearing the All Clear because she liked the idea of small boy scouts being driven round, blowing trumpets and shouting, 'All Clear' at the top of their voices. When off duty I often sat with her and told her of any amusing events at the gun station. At first she would smile and be amused, but gradually she became less and less interested and seemed hardly to recognise me. My time for another few days leave had come. The doctor said that Mother might possibly continue in the same condition for weeks so I went to stay in the Isle of Wight with Hugh Hammersley and his new wife. The following morning a telegram told me that Mother was worse, so I caught the first train, which arrived at Waterloo soon after an air raid warning had sounded. There was only one taxi, and I grabbed it. I tried to get another for an injured airman who had travelled with me, but had no success, so I invited him to come in mine, and dropped him at the Berkeley. When saying goodbye he was profuse in his thanks and begged me to lunch with him on a certain day, I went, but he was not there, and I lunched alone!

I arrived in Chelsea too late by some hours. Mother was dead. It was a great grief to us all, and I felt that part of myself had gone. We were left with the memory of her devotion and knowledge that, in a small way, we had atoned for the worry we must have caused her when we were young. In her old age she was happy.

The monotony of life on the gun station, and frequently standing all night by the gun when raids were expected, rather frayed one's temper. An unfortunate incident occurred which nearly resulted in my being put under detention. A fussy and rather foolish Chief Petty Officer was marching us to our posts as sentries. We were always friendly together, and I was rather surprised to hear the C.P.O. say, 'Step out, A.B. Gray.' I thought he was joking and said, 'I am stepping out.' 'How *dare* you answer back,' he said. 'Don't be a bloody fool,' I said. 'HALT! Fall out, A.B. Gray, and follow me.' He marched me back to the officer's hut and tapped at the door. 'Come in,' said he and we entered. 'Please, sir, A.B. Gray has called me a bloody fool.' The officer turned quickly away and pretended to light a cigarette. I saw that he was laughing, because his shoulders shook. He then tried to look serious, and said that such a remark was shocking, and that I must apologise. I replied that I could not honestly apologise, because candidly I did think him a bloody fool. The officer again turned away to light a cigarette. Then he spoke seriously, and said he supposed that I knew he would have to send me to Chatham if I did not apologise. That was a different matter! 'Oh, well,' I said, without looking at the C.P.O., 'to please you, sir, I will say that I am sorry.' Honour was satisfied, we were dismissed, and I was marched to my sentry go, this time I stepped out so vigorously that the silly little C.P.O. could hardly keep the pace. He had a bad time after this, for hardly a soul would speak to him.

I moved from my lodgings in Trafalgar Square to a studio I rented from John Tweed in Avenue Studios, Fulham Road. The old butler who had looked after me came each morning to get my bath ready and give me my breakfast. I had my other meals at the Chelsea Arts Club when not on duty. Most of the Artists were in uniform. The few whose health prevented their being called up were reaping a harvest. Among these was McEvoy, who blossomed into one of the most successful portrait painters. Unlike the majority of these he was a good artist as well. He had been through difficult times, and was surprised and delighted at his success. Our way being the same, we often walked together when leaving the club. He talked of his sitters. I remember that he said he had painted most of the Duchesses and was then starting on the actresses. Orpen and Augustus John went to France to paint for the War Museum, Orpen told us that John had a charming way of always answering a salute, which pleased the Tommies.

Derwent Wood born, 1871 and died 1926, was an established sculptor before the First World War, and as Gray states, he volunteered to work in hospitals as an orderly, being too old for active service. Here he saw many men with horrific facial injuries and he persuaded the authorities to allow him to make masks to help the injured return to society with confidence. The masks were made of metal and then painted to match the recipients skin tones.

Derwent Wood, the sculptor, and some of the older members worked as orderlies at Wandsworth Hospital, and tough work it was. Later, Wood modelled masks to cover horribly maimed faces.

It was pleasant dining at the club, for one was always sure of an amusing time. George Henry's acid but kindly wit was a delight. George Lambert astonished those who did not know him with tales of his own remarkable prowess, but one forgave him because he was witty. He could mimic any accent, and told funny stories perfectly.

H.M. Bateman joined up early in the war. After six months training he was discharged because of bad health. He had no work, and felt altogether depressed. He took a room and tried to make a fresh start. Among the drawings he made at that time was one showing the various phases through which a recruit passed when learning bayonet fighting. First a weary looking soldier was softly jabbing a swinging sack, then the series showed him gradually warming to his work until at last he was seen rushing through a village, furiously stabbing at everything and everybody. This drawing was published in some journal, and Bateman forgot about it. One winter he was sent to France to make drawings for propaganda, and was lodged in a Chateau with other correspondents. One day he got a message that a Colonel Campbell wished to see him, so he hired a car and was driven to the village named. When he arrived he was cold and miserable. The car stopped outside a large building where enormous soldiers stood on guard, and as he mounted the steps a man even bigger than the rest came forward to meet him. Taking Bateman's hand and patting him on the back he said, 'Bateman, my boy, you've been the spirit of bayonet fighting in the British Army!' Bateman, who is small, looked up surprised and said, 'Oh, have I?' He was taken into a large hall, and there on the walls hung reproductions of his bayonet fighting drawings. Colonel Campbell told him that the army had been trained on those drawings.

H.M. Bateman, born 1887 and died 1970, was a well-known cartoonist from an early age. He had contracts with *The Tatler* and other magazines like *Punch*. He is best remembered for his 'The Man who...' series that ran in *Punch*. A well-dressed man makes a social mistake of relatively minor proportions but would produce an over exaggerated reaction from an upper middleclass

One of the strange jobs which I undertook during the war was the curing of a child who had a habit of squinting so badly that her guardian became distracted, and asked me to help. He sent me a photograph of a pretty little girl of which he wished an attractive picture made of all but the left eye, which I was to make squint horribly. When it was finished, the awful squint I had painted looked so appalling that I was loath to let the picture leave my studio. However, I sent it, and here are extracts from a letter I received soon after.

*The girl was* terrified *and at once dashed to her bedroom to see if her eyes had gone at all crooked yet! There were copious tears and good resolutions enough to fill a small ledger. For once, I was the unsympathetic stern guardian, and notwithstanding this, was given a most embarrassingly affectionate farewell greeting, with assurances to the last that never, never, never again, etc. etc. I have, thank goodness, and thanks to you, seen the end of that worry, of that I am confident. And meanwhile the portrait, in a North of Ireland nursery (where it had been purposely skied) squints on all and sundry! With boundless gratitude, I am etc.* (Farewell greeting sounded a bit Irish, I thought.)

I also remember having a commission to paint an old man of eighty-six who lived at Eastbourne. He caught an eight o'clock train each morning to arrive at my studio for ten o'clock sittings. I was astonished that he showed no sign of fatigue after so early and long a journey. I was also somewhat startled when, at the first sitting, he said that he would like to show me his foot. However, I behaved as though it was quite usual to examine a sitter's foot, and told him that I should be delighted to have a look. He proceeded to take off an elastic sided boot and a thick woollen sock and then held his foot high for me to examine. It certainly was a remarkable foot for an old man, an arched instep, long straight toes with no bumps or corns, and well-kept toe nails. I sincerely congratulated him, he thanked me, and we got on with our work. He told me that he had just married a young girl of twenty-six. 'After all,' he said, 'King Solomon when old took virgins unto himself, and what was good enough for King Solomon is good enough for me.' After a sitting he liked me to go with him to the Cafe Royal for lunch, and then on to a picture exhibition; indeed, the old man tired me out whenever I accompanied him.

The war went on and on. Many of my friends and relatives had been killed and wounded. Philip Connard had come back from France to join the navy as a war artist. His war record is remarkable. At the time war was declared he was about thirty-six.

His one-man exhibitions at the Goupil and other galleries had been most successful, and his future was assured. Then the war came. Passing Fulham recruiting station while out walking, he went in without further thought and joined up as a private. He became a corporal, and he said that he never felt prouder than when he was given his stripe. Later he was sent to an officer's training corps and drafted to the Artillery as a lieutenant. Connard went to France with his battery in time to take part in the Somme offensive; when that petered out he was lent to the Royal Navy as a special artist, and joined the Harwich Patrol, where he was happy, and painted those interesting pictures which, before this present war, were to be seen at the War Museum.

It was towards the end of the war that Marie Lohr and her husband, Tony Prinsep gave a dinner party to which John Sargent and I went. I remember it especially because that evening I first met Lillian Braithwaite, and began a friendship which I much valued. I had always wished to meet Miss Braithwaite because Steer told me that he had danced with her years before, and that he thought her the most beautiful girl he had ever seen. Among the guests at this dinner was that most delightful actress Miss Lottie Venne. She was then over seventy, but was still acting and very much alive. Conversation got onto the subject of the colour of hair; Miss Venne's was red, and she told us that her 'dear son' had said to her, 'Mother darling, as long as we have sixpence in the house you shall never want for henna!'

On the way home Sargent talked a good deal about Miss Venne. He was surprised that anyone of her age should be so witty and attractive.

> Lillian Braithwaite, born 1873 and died 1948, was primarily a stage actress. She made her first professional appearance in 1897 in a company touring South Africa, followed by her first London appearance in 1900. A high point of her theatrical career was in the first staging of the Vortex with Noel Coward in 1924. Lottie Venne was born in 1852 and died in 1928. She had a fifty year career as a comedy actress of great renown. If she was over 70 at the dinner party, it would mean that the dinner was in the 1920s and not during the war. A rare mistake in Gray's memoirs.

The next time I met her was at a first night, where I found myself sitting near her. I told her that I was sorry she was not acting in the play we had come to see, because she always made me laugh and feel happy. The dear old lady's answer was, 'It is a curious thing that it is often sad people who are able to make others laugh.'

Walter Greaves, one of the brothers whom I mentioned earlier as owning and hiring boats on the Thames, had been a noticeable figure about Chelsea for years, and during the war he was still to be seen, wandering about with a large portfolio of his drawings of Chelsea in hopes of selling them. He continued to dress in the style of Whistler, indeed, he tried to look as like him as possible. I find it hard to believe that the same man painted some of the pictures ascribed to Greaves and also made those drawings which we know are his work, and which were most incompetent. I think that there is no doubt that he painted the picture of *Hammersmith Bridge* which was hung in the Tate Gallery. When that picture was bought for the Tate he said to me that it 'really made him hot to think that that picture was to be hung in a public gallery'. I said that I liked the picture and then he told me that he painted it when he was sixteen, and was getting on nicely with his painting until, some years later, Whistler came along with his new-fangled ideas. It appeared that when Whistler came to Chelsea, Walter Greaves and his brother became his devoted assistants when not working at their boat business, and one or other of them rowed Whistler about the river when he was getting material for his nocturnes. One of Greaves' stories about Whistler was a propos the portrait he painted of his patron, Naylor Layland. Whistler was having great trouble with this picture and for months he wiped out each day what he had done the previous one. At last, in desperation, he painted a nude figure with the idea of putting the clothes on later. It was at this interesting moment that his mother, fearing that her son was becoming lazy, insisted on seeing the portrait. Greaves said the old lady was horrified when she saw the picture of this important client sitting completely nude, looking quite happy and as though it were his accustomed state.

Marchant, of the Goupil Gallery, sometime after Whistler's death, gave an exhibition of pictures by Walter Greaves. It was much written up and had an instantaneous success. Until then Walter had been very poor. Marchant had him rigged out in new frock coat and tall hat, and gave a party in his honour. The party included Augustus John, William Nicolson and several others. They sat so long enjoying their luncheon and drinks that they ordered dinner. After dinner Marchant took them all to a box at the Palace Theatre and put it about that Mr Walter Greaves was there. In the interval some of the audience gave Greaves a clap, which he gracefully acknowledged. After the show they went to a restaurant for supper and sat late into the night. Marchant told us that the only one of the party who was entirely unaffected by the feasting was Greaves. He was at the gallery next morning early, quite fresh. Not a bad performance for a man of well over seventy.

Walter Greaves, born 1846 and died 1930, was a Thames boatman. He and his brother befriended Whistler and for 20 years were his apprentices and students. He tried to emulate Whistler's success but fell into obscurity in the 1870's until he was rediscovered by William Marchant. His fame after the successful exhibition lasted a few weeks as he was accused of plagiarism of Whistler's work and he fell back into poverty. His fellow artists did what they could to support him in his later years, and he was a Poor Brother of the Charterhouse in London.

I had always regarded Tonks as a man of high courage, and during the war he proved this more than once. First he was at a French dressing station working as a doctor; he then went to Italy with another medical unit, but complained that the young men composing it were too intellectual for him! He and John Sargent went to France together to paint for the War Museum. When in Arras they were in a house close to a big gun emplacement, and every time the gun fired he and Sargent swore at each other! Tonks also went to Russia. Before the war he had been made Slade professor on Brown's retirement, but to enable Tonks to do war work Brown continued at the Slade until the war ended. At the Royal College of Surgeons is a remarkable collection of anatomical drawings Tonks made when working with Gillies, the surgeon, who did so much for soldiers suffering from facial injury.

Walter Russell also went through tough times in France when working in the front lines at camouflage. He was in several bad blitzes, but luckily was not wounded.

During the latter part of the war anti-aircraft stations were taken over by the War Office, and regular soldiers took the place of us older men. Some of us joined an organisation formed to plot the course of planes raiding London; the control room was in the old County Council building near the Admiralty Arch. In this room were many telephones connected with observation posts in and around London. A large map covered an end wall, and another large scale map was fastened to a table in the centre of the room. During raids all telephones were manned, and messages received were shouted to an officer seated in the middle of the room. This officer sifted important news, and the course of the planes was plotted on the maps. I often marvelled how he could make sense of the noisy shouting.

One night, during a raid, I was on a telephone connected with Shooters Hill. The observer said, 'German planes overhead.' A pause – then, 'Plane dropped a bomb, I think it will get me.' I waited, and over the telephone I heard a loud explosion and feared the worst. I asked, 'Are you alright?' and was answered, 'Yes, but there is a fight going on overhead.' Another pause then, 'One is falling in flames.' 'English or German?' I asked. A weary voice said, 'Oh, English I expect.' But this time it was the German who crashed.

We were told one night that a German plane had come down in one of our aerodromes, and an overgrown German boy had jumped out, saying that he was only sixteen and had flown over and bombed London. 'Oh have you?' said one of our airmen, 'then come and have a drink.'

Rex Fry and his brother John had also joined this control room. Rex commissioned me to paint a picture of the room during a raid. I enjoyed the job, painting in the mornings. There were many figures in the picture, and there was great competition among the men to sit. One little man importuned me a lot to be allowed to pose. I wanted a figure up a ladder, leaning over pinning flags into the large wall map – a most trying pose to keep. The little man said that he would be delighted to do it, but before I had finished he regretted his offer, for he nearly fainted once or twice whilst perched on his ladder. When this picture was exhibited, the London Museum wanted to buy it, but Rex wouldn't part with it.

*Metropolitan Observation Room* ©*The Cecil Beaton Studio Archive*

This picture, now known as *The Metropolitan Observation Room during an air raid* was sold at Sotheby's for £10,000 in May 2013. This was Gray's first Royal Academy exhibit.

After the raid it was generally a case of walking back to Chelsea in the early hours of the morning, as the only vehicles about were fire engines and ambulances. The lights on the street lamp posts were shaded with conical covers which threw curious shadows on the pavement and caused me to play with the idea that I walked through streets peopled by giant figures from pictures by Longhi. If it were possible for a member of a present rescue squad to walk through London after a raid in the last war, he would wonder what all the fuss was about. But to us it seemed pretty grim and there were some horrible incidents, though on a smaller scale than now. A head man from the fire brigade who lectured to us one day, gave us figures of the fires the raiders had caused which surprised us. However, the Germans left it too late, luckily for us, to have much effect on the first war, and it was not till 1941 that they were able to try out the idea with real success.

The first member of the Chelsea Arts Club to be killed was Bill Baynes. He was so anxious to join up that though over age he persuaded a sergeant to pass him, with the aid of £1. He was in the early fighting at Ypres, and I remember that when he returned to the club on his first leave, he and his rifle were covered with the mud of the Ypres trenches. He said that he expected to be killed, and not long afterwards we heard that he had been blown to pieces.

John Cameron, our wild Highlander, joined as a Tommy and was soon promoted to Colonel. Hennings, the sculptor, was on General Rawlinson's staff, and Dugdale, Charles Cundall, Dyson Smith and Hogg were more of the members who acquitted themselves honourably. Artists seemed to make good soldiers.

It was a sad shock when I heard that Percy Gethin had also been killed in France. He was one of the most romantic and charming men I ever knew. He had the perfectly natural manners of a well-bred Irishman. We first met in 1892 at a dinner party at Hurlingham. He was then about eighteen, and had been studying at an art school and wanted work. I introduced him to my friend Gerald Moira, who wanted an assistant to help with his large decorations, and Gethin worked successfully with Moira for some years until he was appointed an art master at Liverpool.

After Liverpool he came to London to teach drawing at the Central Schools. He had a natural gift, and as the years passed he improved so much that when war came he was doing the most interesting drawings and etchings and holding successful exhibitions. I have had two of his drawings hanging in my room for years. I like them better and better. He need not have joined the army. He was at least forty, but I suppose, born of a military family, it was in his blood. We dined together just before he went, and he told me that an aunt had died and left him a small property in Ireland with enough money to keep it up. He was delighted to think that he could now give up teaching and give his whole time to painting after the war. I have a pencil note which he wrote in the trenches. He said, 'Here we are, playing at being soldiers and really doing it remarkable well.' The next news was that he had been killed.

> Percy Gethin was killed on the Somme on June 28, 1916.

I admired the brave show which Ernest Thesiger put up during the war. When we were young we knew him as a student at the Slade School, and having always looked on him as an amusing playboy, I was astonished to hear that he had joined the army as a Tommy. To one so carefully nurtured, life at a training camp must have been a sore trial. However, he went to France with his regiment and endured the rigours of a cold winter in the trenches. He was badly wounded, and when well again he treated the whole experience as a joke. He told me that when coming round after an operation on his wounded hands his first words to the nurse were 'Is it a boy or a girl?'

> Ernest Thesiger, born 1879 and died 1961, studied at the Slade School of Art before taking to the stage and making his first appearance in 1909. He was wounded in January 1915 and invalided home. His interest in embroidery led him to found the Disabled Soldiers Embroidery Industry. His needlework interest resulted in him becoming a friend of Queen Mary.

At the beginning of November 1918 I was ill with a sharp attack of influenza. On November 11, that memorable day, my sister Elizabeth came to my bedroom to remind me that the maroons would be fired at eleven o'clock as a signal that the Armistice was to be signed. She stood looking out of the window. I lay in bed. We waited without speaking. An expectant stillness had fallen on London and there was no sound of traffic. As the clock on Old Chelsea Church struck eleven, the maroons boomed their message that the war was ended. Elizabeth kept very still, she was crying. There was a big lump in my throat. My reaction was a compelling restlessness. In spite of feeling weak, and of Elizabeth telling me to stay in bed, I dressed and made my way to the Mall. I have a vague recollection of shouting crowds in front of Buckingham Palace and lines of captured German guns along the roadside. People had run from business into the streets. Taxis drove aimlessly about, filled inside and out with hatless people. All were shouting. It was like a mad dream. I felt weary, and made my way home to bed.

And so the door slammed on an epoch in which it was my good fortune to have lived.

# Chapter 15

# 1918 to 1951

The memoirs sadly end in November 1918, but Gray lived on until 1951. At the end of the war he was 50 and what I have been able to learn about his later years is mainly from letters to him written by his many friends in the art world and elsewhere. In his papers are over a hundred letters from friends including Muirhead Bone, Philip Connard, Charles Cundall, Gerald Kelly, J.A. Mullard, Walter Russell, A.R. Thomson, William Russell Flint, Fred Brown, D.S. MacColl and members of his family.

It is clear from comments in the memoirs and in the correspondence from his friends that Gray was missing the high summer of life in late Victorian and Edwardian England and the world that he had enjoyed so much, and his travels were now limited to the Continent for painting trips, primarily in France, Switzerland and Scandinavia.

He was also very out of sympathy with the artistic trends of the '20s and '30s and this is clearly shared by some at the highest levels of the artistic establishment in their correspondence with Gray on Royal Academy letterhead.

As mentioned in the introduction to the memoirs written by his niece, Marjory Pegram, he participated in a hoax. His scorn for what he called the 'nonsense' which was being foisted on the public led him into perpetrating a successful hoax which made him unpopular in certain quarters for many years. He persuaded a doctor friend who had never in his life held a paint brush in his hand to paint a large picture in oils, which naturally looked like the painstaking effort of a ten-year-old. He himself with immense gusto, did an absurd picture in the prevailing fashion of the day; and these two masterpieces, signed with assumed names, were sent to a London exhibition which featured modern art. Both were hung on the line and caused a considerable stir, and it was some time before the hoax was discovered. His triumph at having 'got away with it' amply compensated him for the anger that his crime aroused. 'There you are' he would say. 'I told you the whole thing was a lot of nonsense!'

Notable events are few, but in 1923 he became a member of the New English Art Club and in the same year held a one-man exhibition at the Goupil Gallery. In 1925 his portrait of his mother was bought by the Chantrey Bequest for the Tate Gallery and in 1934 he became an associate of the Royal Watercolour Society, becoming a full member in 1941. Throughout this period, he exhibited at the Royal Academy and at the Paris Salon where he won a Silver Medal.

It is impossible to recreate a chronological story, so I have concentrated on important times and events in his remaining life. There are 'The Chantrey Bequest', 'Summer painting trips', 'Modern Art', 'The Second World War' and finally the last few years of his life.

## The Chantrey Bequest

On 7 January, 1924 Gray received a letter from Sir Muirhead Bone. He had talked with Gray at the New English Art Club exhibition and had seen Gray's portrait of his Mother:

*What I wanted to know was if the picture of your Mother in the exhibition was for sale, and if so what would be the price for it to the Chantrey Bequest? I spoke to Steer and Tonks about it and they both hoped very much that it would be possible to have it purchased by the Chantrey. I thought £250 might strike you as a fair price. What do you think?*

*The procedure is that the Chantrey Selecting Committee meets and considers various suggestions of their members for purchases. This committee is composed of three Academicians and two appointed from the Trustees of the Tate Gallery (at present these are the Director and myself). Our recommendations then go to the Council of the Royal Academy who hold the purchasing power under Chantrey's will.*

*One or two of the Selecting Committee would like to see your picture bought but the matter still has to be discussed by the whole committee. As I am anxious to name a definite price to them before our meeting on Friday, I should be very glad if you would kindly give me an answer by return to this enquiry.*

(It states on the receipt in his papers that he received £250 and 10 shillings in the end. I wonder where the extra came from?)

The picture was much admired by his contemporaries, and it was exhibited in 1948 as part of a Chantrey Bequest exhibition. Connard wrote to Gray on 13 December on Royal Academy letterhead.

*My dear Ronnie,*

*Further to my letter of yesterday, I have today taken a closer look at the Chantrey pictures and what I said in my first letter is more than confirmed in my second and third visit to the exhibition. In my opinion your portrait stands above all others in the show including Steer's portrait of his housekeeper, and not only portraits, it is of a higher standard than anything in the show.*

At the time, Connard was Keeper of the Royal Academy School, and principal tutor, a position he held from 1945 to 1949.


# Summer painting trips

Painting trips to France were an important kind of therapy for the artist friends of Gray. On 12 July 1926 Connard writes to Gray:

*I am very tempted to join you, but to be quite candid I am afraid of it. I want to go to the coast somewhere to pull myself together – fancy going to Le Havre as a kicking off ground – if it was possible to get accommodation quite near St Cloud I would be with you like a shot, but I am thinking of hot days, long walks or bus rides and the thought of them wilts me rather – I may suddenly turn up in any case.*

There is a postscript: *I leave here tomorrow Tuesday even if my destination is hell – perhaps by the night boat for Havre.* A decision was made.

His next letter is from Hotel du Commerce in Dieppe, of which there is a painting by Sickert done in 1914. Sadly, he does not seem much happier:

*My Dear Ronnie,*
*I was glad to get your letter. We are in it so to speak just now. Over 2,000 people slept on the beach and in any old place last night, but in spite of all these drawbacks Dieppe is one of the most inspiring places I know. The colour is beautiful. All it requires is the ability to put it down – I shall not be able to do much for a day or two as the crowd is too dense – I've worked hard since I've been here and it all counts though I've little to show – and if I had the ability there's nothing I would like better to do than stay here. Night is made hideous by a beastly fair just opposite, roundabouts with the vilest organs which go on until midnight. It is just awful.*
*Shall stay here for a bit to see what I can do. The country round about seems*

*dull after Dieppe. It has an attraction that is unexplainable – I hear Orpen is here*
*at the Royal Hotel. I haven't seen him – I believe he plays tennis a lot.*

(William Orpen was a successful portrait painter before the First World War and an
official war artist during it. He was knighted in 1918 and became a Member of the
Royal Academy in 1921. He died aged only 52 in 1931.)

And on 8 August he writes again, having heard from Gray, and he is not finding
his fellow visitors any more congenial:

*I want to get somewhere fairly quiet and attractive if so be there such a place in this*
*world. All the people here seem to be of the midland of England type who, without*
*being in the least bit snobbish – have more money than becomes their station, and*
*they most certainly ought to eat in the kitchen. I sit at a long public table and I speak*
*feelingly – I'm lonely and I want companionship and shall leave here in a day or*
*two. If your place is all right and there is room for another, I wonder if you would*
*let me know at once. I did think of going further south, but as all France as well as*
*England go near the sea the first 2 weeks in August, it seems to be taking a leap in*
*the dark. I am writing this so you will get it on arrival at Sangatte. Poor old Steer,*
*he has all the luck. If some poor benighted fool would do the same to me, I would be*
*rather pleased. It sells pictures.*

*I'm now going to brave the terrors of the crowd again, Cheers, Philip*

A year later in 1927, the year his wife Mary died, he is near Sisteron at the Hostellerie
Castel-Bevons, from where he writes to Gray on 15 September:

*It is raining like smoke my dear Ronald and this gives me another opportunity of*
*telling you where we are and what we are doing.*

*We had a rotten journey arriving at Lyons at 4.30 am and waiting until 9.55*
*for a train to bring us on to Sisteron where we arrived at 6.30 pm or thereabouts,*
*having passed in the train most beautiful country between Grenoble and Gap to*
*find ourselves on arrival at a place as much like Clapham Junction as makes no*
*matter. Noisy, dusty, literally millions of motor cars, lorries, babies, cats, dogs, rats,*
*white mice, all on their way to or from Nice – and dear old Adrian was difficult*
*to move, as at the inn are two very nice waitresses who attended to the dear thing's*
*wants and he did want some!!! I scoured the country in a car, and I eventually found*
*this place 3 or 4 miles from Sisteron and here we found ourselves a week after our*
*arrival – I came a day earlier than Adrian, the only way to get a move on.*

*This hotel is beautifully situated quite alone in the hills. Lovely, lovely country*
*if we had time to do it with river, hills, trees and all within easy reach and in the*

*hotel grounds. The hotel is good, cooking excellent. We have two bedrooms, sitting room, own bath and own W.C. It is 55 francs a week, and among other things the wine is good and cheap, made here red and white for 5 francs a bottle. Rarely meet a car. Sometimes see them in the valley and work to the music of grasshoppers. Such lovely things. Magpies and woodpeckers create a constant drone of pleasant sounds with occasionally sheep bells coming in as cymbals. Butterflies my dear Ronnie, that send one into an ecstasy of joy with their radiant and delicate beauty. A real place to live in and dream of the beautiful pictures one will do. The weather so far has been lovely – (confound the week at Sisteron) and the rain is a welcome relief. It began at about 11 and is still going on at 3.00 pm and I hope for the rest of the day – the river and stream are drying up there not having been any rain since March. I'm hoping for some lovely gorges all within 2 minutes from here and then old thing we shall have the ripple of the brook which will harmonize admirably with the deep heavy voice of Dear Uncle Adrian.*

*I shall make an effort to come here in the spring with blossoms and spring flowers, the scent of thyme, just think of it.*

*This is something like the view we get from the terrace where we drink our coffee. Immediately behind us are pinewoods where we sit and drink as may be. Hope you're having a good time. Give the nicest message you can think of to MacColl from me. Uncle Adrian sends you greetings. For myself let me remind you in case you might forget of the omni axiality and the diagonals. Cheers. Philip*

In the original letter there is a pencil sketch of the view he describes. A very superior version of a post card. On 17 July 1928 Connard was writing to Gray who was staying at the Hotel Vieux Moulin in Saint Jacut-sur-Mer, a commune in the Cotes-d'Armor department of Brittany in north-western France.

*Dear Ronnie,*

*Your letter is not very encouraging. The impression it conveys is there might or might not be one other place that is worse but since no one has ever returned or even written from it (the other place) we are left more or less in the dark as to whether it might be a suitable place to stay and paint in. Steer might make something of it. David Murray has said 'it was hardly the sort of place that would suit his style of painting' and from what you say St Jacut-sur-Mer doesn't sound too promising for a bloke like myself. I was or rather had intended going out to you tomorrow, but it seems a long way to go, besides being somewhat of an expensive journey to find at the end of it my choice limited to that and Hell. England my England is all right but for the ever-sordid lodgings and food. I may go to Boulogne and look about there, or to somewhere in the hills. Steer is going to Framlingham. He dislikes Aldeburgh, besides which he can't get in. I spent last weekend at Felixstowe. Jane was acting there. All London seemed to be there, poor fretful mothers with families so hot and clammy – all England is in the same condition and from what you say France is in the same condition. To quote the French book, 'I haven't seen her blow her nose on the napkins nor spit in the teacups but she's got a face that shows she would.' Well Ronnie I don't know what to do but must be off tomorrow or the day after. I may in spite of all blow in on you. Blessings on you old thing from Philip.*

One further letter dated 2 March 1936, finds Connard working in Scotland at Skelmorlie in Ayrshire. For once there are few complaints as he is staying in a large country house with views of the Kyles of Bute.

*My Dear Ronnie,*
*How are you? By you I mean the community – Freddie, Jane, Marjory, Steer and Tonks. As you have them all in hand more or less clinging to you round the neck, it is to you we must look for any information regarding their state. At the moment I am gazing on a lovely scene looking across to the Kyles of Bute. In the meadows immediately in front are sheep with newly born lambs, innumerable rooks, sea birds and little birds all in a delightful setting of sunshine with long tree shadows. It being early in the year the sun is very low – really when one looks upon such loveliness it seems impossible there should be such a lot of bickering and trouble in the world.*

*True it is, I am writing in the room of a wealthy man who can afford a house in a lovely district but then it isn't necessary to live in a luxurious house to enjoy these things.*

*I've been in bed with a cold for two days. Am getting all right again and then hope to get at it on the Queen Mary. The lighting has been altered so I shall have to make the painting fit the lighting.*

Later he writes:

*Shall leave here on Thursday so as to miss the King. There is a lot of bustle now, but it will be worse later.*

'Freddie, Jane and Marjory' are the Pegram family. Jane is Gray's sister married to Fred and Marjory is their daughter. The reference is to the Cunard ship RMS *Queen Mary* where he was painting a large panel on the subject of England. The famous transatlantic liner sailed on her maiden voyage on 27 May 1936 only a few months later. The new king Edward VIII must have been visiting the area. He had become king on 20 January 1936.

# Modern Art

In her introduction to Gray's memoirs, Marjory Pegram refers to a hoax perpetrated by Gray to expose the folly of modern art. I have not been able to find any public record of this apart from perhaps a reference to it in an undated letter to Gray from Sir Gerald Kelly from his home at 65 Gloucester Place, Portman Square, and it concerns a painter called Guevara who was Alvaro Guevara (1894-1951) and who married Meraud Guinness (also a painter and member of the famous Guinness family).

> *Dear Gray,*
> *Guevara wants to remove his pictures.*
> *He bothered the folk at the gallery then went to Lander who didn't want to see him but I telephoned there and had him directed on to me. He is very young and exquisitely sensitive!!! I did my best to point out that his contention that his pictures oughtn't – nay couldn't remain in a room contaminated by insincerity was all balls – but he's rather slow and oh so young. I seemed to detect in him a real fear and anger that this spoof would ruin sales for all exotic 'expressionist' pictures. (I'm delighted to think this may be so!!!)*
>
> *I told G. that as far as I was concerned, he could remove his pictures as far as hell – tho' as I like them, I should regret it for a minute or two but that no one bothers his neighbour for long, and that a month hence he would just be known as troublesome and touchy. I asked him to go and see Tonks and get advice. If Tonks thinks the child has been badly treated and should remove his pictures – then we'll let him have them.*
>
> *The van came for them and two photographers to take pictures of Guevara shaking off the dust of the M.S.P.P. What a subject!!*
> *See Tonks and let me know what he told the child.*
> *Kelly*

It is tempting to assume that the MSPP refers to a society of Portrait painters but the only one I have found is the Royal Society and Gerald Kelly was a member in the 1920s. But it does not seem to fit.

There is another letter from Kelly to Gray, this time dated 20 April 1950 when Kelly was knighted and President of the Royal Academy.

> *My dear Ronald Gray,*
> *I have for years been increasingly apprehensive at the encroachments of the civil servants and the government machine into the realm of the arts. The British Council*

*seems to be entirely run, if I may so express it, by homosexuals; their antics in foreign capitals redound to our discredit. The interference of the layman, however cultured, in the arts has always been a menace.*

*Neither Lutyens or Munnings took any notice of my croakings: I think it is too late to do anything very much but all my endeavours as President will be to undermine this ~~damaging growth~~ stronghold, but I don't expect to have more success than I had when I tried to defend the Masterpieces in the National Gallery from the harsh treatment approved of by Sir Philip Hendy and executed by that nasty German Ruheman.*

*You and I may be old, but I think that our lives were passed in happier times. All good wishes to you – and thank you for your letter.*
*Yours sincerely,*
*Gerald Kelly*

When the British Council decided to hold an exhibition of war-time paintings by Picasso and Matisse in London, by way of establishing a cultural interchange between France and Britain, they threw a fair-sized chunk of 'fat in the fire.'

Evelyn Waugh, writing in a letter to Nancy Mitford, described the exhibition as 'disgusting', and Charles Cundall, Fellow of the Royal Academy, writes to Gray on 15 December 1945 as follows:

*The Picasso show at the V&A has attracted thousands out of curiosity. The pictures should go on to Blackpool now. Still to be really honest I must say I am glad to have seen them, horrible as they are (though I thought the colour good) but they should not be shown at the V&A. We shall get more and more French paintings now with the help of the British Council. Perhaps one day the English painters, especially the water-colour painters, will get a show in Paris but the present British Council will not do it.*

The British Council is referenced in a letter from Connard to Gray dated 7 June 1945. Gray has written to Connard about his friend Olga's comments on a British Council-sponsored visit to Stockholm in Sweden by the Director of the National Gallery, Kenneth Clarke, later Lord Clarke. Olga was a long-term friend of Gray's and he painted in Sweden quite often before the war. Connard writes as follows:

*I suppose K. Clarke was sent out by the British Council. Have you told McColl about Olga's letter – it is deplorable that people such as K. Clarke and other glorified shop walkers of museums should be the guardians of taste and knowledge in pictures.*

MacColl is Douglas Sutherland MacColl, painter, art critic, lecturer, writer and Keeper of the Tate Gallery for 5 years. He appears quite often in Connard's letters to Gray, but his name is always spelt incorrectly.

On 7 July 1951, 4 months before he died, Gray wrote to the Editor of the Daily Telegraph, stimulated to do so by a letter from his old friend A.J. Munnings published on the same date:

*The Chelsea Arts Club*
*Sir,*
*I have lived nearly 84 years, most of them spent in a struggle to make a living by drawing and painting. I have known intimately many of the best painters of the time and have watched some efforts to gain notoriety quickly. These efforts still continue and to appreciate modern painting and sculpture one has to know all the 'back chat' written by the 'intellectual' critics. Many intellectuals seem to have a vein of silliness. The vocabulary they use – 'ultimate truth', 'negro intensity', 'significant form', and 'ultra-dynamical', etc. surely prove this.*

*There is only good and bad art. Ancient and modern have nothing to do with it. Very few men of genius are born in a hundred years – but I read now of a fresh one every week. Painting is just a job of work like any other of the crafts: a gifted man does it better than a silly one. An enormous 'top hamper' crushes this art and directors of galleries, writers on art, art masters, art councils, etc. all get a better living out of it than most of the painters. I am certain that pictures have no cultural value whatsoever – a few cultured people enjoy good pictures – others don't enjoy them but get an uplift by pretending to know. Artists were better in the days when it was a struggle to get there, unassisted by government aid. I do agree with the very good letter from my old friend A.J. Munnings which I read in today's Daily Telegraph.*
*Ronald Gray*

# The Second World War

Like all Londoners, Gray and his family and friends were affected by the Blitz which started on 7 September 1940 and raged for 57 days and nights. Damage was widespread. Bombs rained down on the City, the Docks and the East and West Ends. Buckingham Palace, The Palace of Westminster, and Westminster Abbey were among those well-known buildings hit and Chelsea and Kensington, where many of Gray's artist friends lived were no exception.

Although many Londoners sheltered in Underground stations, the majority stayed in their homes and again Gray's friends were no exception. Over 20,000 Londoners were killed and 2 million houses were damaged or destroyed.

Six days after the Blitz started, Gray's brother Alfred wrote to him from the family home at Danvers Street in Chelsea, still used as the headquarters of the family business. The main house had been divided into flats, one of which was occupied by family friend, Alexander Fleming. Number 67 Earls Court Square was the Pegram family home, now inherited by daughter Marjory. Dick is Dick Townsend, son of Fred, so they are niece and nephew of Alfred.

*My Dear Ronald,*

*Thank you for your letter of the 9th. Do not worry about us, we are all right.*

*Last night a bomb fell on the house behind 67 Earls Court Square and levelled it to the ground and all the windows of 67, at the back, have been blown in, the rooms covered with dirt and glass and the house is unfit for occupation. They are all fortunately sleeping in the basement and although 'jumped' a bit, all is well. Captain Woodhouse was there and Marjory says he was a tower of strength to them. The back of Dick's house, number 45, has been badly damaged also. I am sending round a man tomorrow to help clear up at 67 and I have been up to the Kensington Town Hall to get a Claim Form – which we will get filled in and return.*

After more family and business news the letter ends:

*Maggie and I are well and except for want of a little more sleep have not much to worry about – although the bombs are dropping rather faster than we would like.*

Alfred writes to Gray again on 25 September:

*My Dear Ronald,*

*Thank you for your letter dated 18th. Marjory is getting a little straight now but everything done is temporary only as other bombs may follow.*

*Dick and his wife had to leave their studio as it is uninhabitable, and they are now at Bill Hill.*

*Don't let the Hitler worries affect you at all – there is nothing you could do if you were here. When I got here this morning, I found the Germans had dropped an incendiary bomb on the roof of the house – there was no one in the flats and the flames were seen coming from the roof and the fire brigade broke in at the front door – and at the door of the flat – and put it out. They are not too careful. The roof and the woodwork of a lot of the centre flat and the house is burnt out and worst of all the hose shot so much water that it has drenched Alex Fleming's flat and furniture. We got Alex at St. Mary's but sadly had not heard the news yet!*

*To crown it all, I called on a Miss Kingsley yesterday and arranged for her to call this morning at 11.00 am to see the large flat with a view to taking it on a long lease – she called, and being Irish, she could not help being a little amused at what I had to show her.*

*Last night was the worst one of the lot; there seemed to be a steady stream of planes from 8.00 pm to 5.30 am dropping bombs all over London.*

*Maggie has a cold and as she is sleeping under the stairs, she finds it difficult getting rid of it.*

The final letter from Alfred is dated 4 October:

*My Dear Ronald,*

*Thank you very much for your letter of 28 September – with regard to the house we have got the roof covered with tarpaulins, have cleaned away most of the burnt wood and rubbish from the top floor and are now with our own men repairing the central heating, the CW supply and the HW supply and after this we have to get the electric wiring put right, as until these are all done the poor Flemings cannot go back. I was awfully sorry for them when I saw their possessions all smothered with water and several of their ceilings down. There is no knowing when we can get the rebuilding done and at present, I have no idea what the 'demmed total' will be.*

*We made one claim for compensation, but claims are not considered until the war is over!*

*It has been very lively here day and night – though last night I was undisturbed and slept from 10.30 pm to 5.45 am – I don't know if it means more for tonight, but I don't care.*

*When I look round here I come to the conclusion that London has had its face badly scratched – nothing more – and Hitler can do nothing more.*

*I called on Steer yesterday and we had a long talk. At first, he did not know who I was and asked afterwards, 'Are you Alf Gray?' Alf was able to assure him on this point.*

*I found him quite well, very irritable, and fairly philosophical.*

*He complains because every one of his friends says he ought to go away, and no one makes a concrete proposal. He told me one friend did offer to take him in – but as he found the house was full up already, he felt he would be a nuisance and would not go. He says if anyone would offer him a quiet spot –*

*a sitting room, 2 bedrooms, a bathroom and a W.C. for himself he might take it provided it was not too far away.*

*He has already had an incendiary bomb dropped just outside the house, but a man from the garage nearby put it out.*

*He tells me he spends a lot of time in the passage under the house.*

*I could not help feeling full of pity for him knowing that he cannot see.*

*Maggie's cold is much better – but she is worried – I want her to go to the Menzies at Haslemere, but she won't leave me. It is no use for me to remind her that she is far more valuable* well, *than she would be if she stays in London and becomes ill. I still hope to get her Haslemere way.*

Steer had started to lose his sight in 1927 and by 1940 was no longer painting. He died 18 months after this visit in March 1942. The letter has more family news and then finishes:

*Be of good cheer – you will get some more fine weather in St Martin's summer – and now join me in a good British cheer. Hoo bloody ray!*

And Hitler thought the morale of Londoners would be easily broken.

Another letter dated 16 November 1940 is from Connard in Richmond:

*My dear Ronnie,*

*Your letter was awaiting me on my return from Queensferry where I've been making studies for a picture – it was bitterly cold at times and very windy. I went to do a balloon barrage for the Ministry of Information. There are I should think 5,000 in London and environs and less than 50 on the Forth, usually about 5 – bright boys these museum boys.*

*Saw Steer yesterday and we are in complete agreement about this war. My windows are broken and my roof coming down. Last night was very noisy and many bombs were dropped hereabouts. Am very proud of Jane who sticks at her job of driving an ambulance. She has been in the worst of the night raids, and also been bombed out of her own home, with a direct hit on next door which blew her place to pieces. Found herself with blue sky overhead. I haven't seen her since, but she is going on with her work – am going to try and find her this afternoon.*

*Brown who I saw yesterday is looking frail but is optimistic as ever and hopes it will be over by Xmas. He doesn't go out now.*

Jane was his daughter.

Connard's next letter is dated 10 February, 1941:

*My dear Ronnie,*

*I was glad to get your letter. Things are grim hereabouts to put it in its mildest form. I see Steer about every 10 days. Riley Street is down on both sides from end to end, in spite of which he has no intention of moving. We've had very bad raids hereabouts and my windows are broken and nearly all my ceilings look like coming down any moment they are so cracked. So are the walls.*

*There were only 5 all told at Brown's funeral. I represented all the societies – he was moved to hospital a few days before he died and I didn't see him after he was taken away. I saw him about a week before he died; Mawson is very cut up about it. I spent an afternoon with him a few days ago.*

*I've been trying unsuccessfully to do some panels for the Ionides. I've spent 6 months on them and today I've taken one entirely out and I shall have to begin again. This wretched war, when it is over, won't bring any happiness to anyone. I've no confidence in any politician of this or any other country.*

*I may see Steer tomorrow. All good wishes from Philip.*

The reference to 'Ionides' is probably to the pioneering art deco designer Basil Ionides and his wife the Hon. Nellie Ionides, a well-known art connoisseur and collector who had a home at Riverside House at Twickenham. She bequeathed her collection and the Orleans House to the Borough of Richmond where the Richmond art collection is held and there are several Connard pictures in this collection.

The final war letter comes from France and is dated 7 January, 1945. In his memoirs Gray recalls a summer spent with family friends at their chateau at Montataire in northern France. He and Tonks visited in the late 1880s and had a wonderful time. The chateau was then owned by Agnes Anna Cecile Schultze, Baronne de Conde and second wife of George Baron de Conde who had died in 1886.

When she died in 1891 the chateau was inherited by her brother Naylor Dunbar Schultze who died in 1895 and left the chateau to his three children, two daughters and a son, Alfred Dunbar Schultze. Alfred was a good friend of Gray's who must have visited regularly after the First World War, as Alfred was high on the list of people to contact after the liberation of France in 1944. Alfred was an interesting man, having been born at Kandy in Ceylon as it then was, and was a child prodigy violin player and composer under a nom de plume 'Stefano Khardys'. Sadly he had to sacrifice the development of his talent to attend to the many other responsibilities that he had inherited from his father.

# Chateau de Montataire, Oise, France

*7 January. 1945*

*My Dear Ronald,*

*What a joyous surprise to see your friendly handwriting & remembrance after all these sad years of silence. Your kind lines, dated 16 November last, only reached me yesterday.*

*We were truly distressed to hear that both your Chelsea home & Marjory's in Earls Court are both knocked about. As you do not speak of anyone else of your family we greatly trust that you are all there 'to answer the call', our call of friendship of course?*

*As regards our dear old historical house of Montataire, it has suffered greatly alas at the hands of the hated Huns, since their arrival on the premises on 15 June, 1940, after which arrival full occupation took place till 5 December, 1940 when my dear wife & self were taken off at 6.00 am as civil prisoners (without the slightest warning) to Besancon (Doubs) where we finally arrived in the deepest of snow at 5.00 am after a train journey of 54 hours. I was in the barracks of the Vauban Camp where 4,600 other British-born subjects were interned, and my wife, happily, was taken off straight to the beautiful old historical hospital where she was a great favourite with all (invalids like herself and the charming nuns taking care of them).*

*For 3 mortal months she never left her bed, but after a time I was allowed to visit her, & her doctors (French officers also interned) handed her over to me for treatment and thanks to God I was able to pull her through as I have done many a time & am still doing now. After 2 months at the camp the doctors found me so pulled down and fearing a second attack of 'Angina Pectoris' that 7 doctors signed our joint liberation, and on 7 March, 1941 we were both en route to Montataire. To our distress on arrival we were told that the new general staff of the enemy, installed during our absence would not hear of our re-entering the chateau so that till we could get installed next to 'Peter the Hermit's Cave' where we still reside, our faithful servants, past and present, welcomed us & fed us, God bless them!*

*Owing to the Germans' ill usage of the castle itself & all its contents – & the mounds of dirt they have left inside and out & and also their pillaging of the chateau and the Petit Chateau (Khardys). These houses are uninhabitable for a long time to come. Apart from our internment at Besancon we have never left Montataire at any time during these years of danger since the beginning of the war. During the bombardments night and day at the slightest alert 1,800 to 2,000 people would rush up for shelter in our caves, etc., though ourselves never bothered about the danger. Early June 1940 the chateau was for 5 hours between the firing of the French troops retreating and the Germans advancing. Bits of the burst shells were in our ceilings and on our beds, etc. Creil was already badly destroyed by the Germans early June 1940 & since then all the towers all around including ours have had to suffer* heavily *by the Allies' inevitable bombardments & our home has also had its share – hardly a single window left. The day of our liberation, 31 August, 1944 the cursed Huns had placed canon, etc. round the Park and down the beautiful Chestnut Avenue leading up to it with the idea of defending themselves. In the afternoon one of their carts full of munitions, was 'su panne' & as they could not move it from where it was (Place de L'Eglise) just above us, they set light to it & shells, torpedoes, etc. shot all over the place – one torpedo hit our beautiful chapel – the resting place of our ancestors, & my Uncle and Aunt, Baron and Baronesse De Conde, with the result that much of its beauty and its lovely stained glass windows are destroyed for all time alas!*

*Played out though I am I still keep going & never have a moment to myself what with the numerous invalids and others that I cure or keep alive. My dear wife's health has also given me much anxiety although many a time I have been able to restore her to health.*

*You naturally heard of dear Lilla's passing away on 20 September, 1938? Violet and her children (save Pearl) and grandchildren are now all in Paris – Pearl is now with Mrs Mowbray Marras at Newquay (Cornwall). Pearl's husband, Frank Coates, is also in England. Violet's daughter, Beryl (Babs), is married to a Frenchman with an English name of origin: Jaques Sydenham. Their home, bombardments permitting, is in Amiens.*

*My wife has lost 2 of her relations as far as we have heard so far during the war, i.e. a sister, Milly, & brother, John. We are still without news of many of our dear ones & friends. Our cousin, Baron de Conde (Etienne) & his family are settled at Le Bouscat, near Bordeaux.*

*Lilla's (now Pearl's) & Violet's charming villas at Le Touquet-Paris Plage have been at the mercy of the war since mid-1940 and must be wrecks by now.*

*Our beautiful walks and woods at Montataire, thanks to the population heating themselves at our expense, hardly have a tree or shrub standing therein. It kills me with sorrow when I have to pass through them & conscience and honesty are non-existing nowadays. Everyone seems to have subscribed to the Germans' manner of 'honouring' these principles.*

*There is no need to put Creil when addressing your letters to Montataire. It only has to be scratched out by the post office & delays delivery, Montataire having its own PO.*

*At the beginning of the war, Lady Decima Moore Guggisberg begged me to take on my old duties as chairman of the Entertainment Committee*

186

*of the British Army & Navy Leave Club in Paris, which she was reforming. That Club in 1917-1919 did wonderous work as you no doubt heard, but I was already too full of work responsibilities to be able to accept as much as I would have loved to. Its life was short owing to the arrival of the foe in Paris. My wife, as a child, remembers Taunton well. She and her sisters loved being at Miss McLacy's (?) school 'Wildoak'. We also had some very charming friends, the Misses Winifred and Rosie Hains, met at Spa, who also had a reputed school at 'Gardenhurst', Burnham-on-Sea (Somerset).*

*You will be tired deciphering my hurried writing, so 'Au revoir' dear friend, till we meet again! Our love to you all,*

    *Ever yours*

    *Alfred*

    *This is to help the Censors:-*

*From Alfred Cecil Dunbar-Schultze, O.B.E. known as an infant prodigy Violinist & composer years and years ago under the nom de plume 'Stephano Khardys'. British-born subject, born on the Island of Ceylon.*

Lilla was Alfred's elder sister and Violet his younger sister who inherited the chateau on the death of her brother in 1951.

'su panne' means broken down.

Lady Decima Moore Guggisberg was originally the actress Decima Moore and made her first appearance in December 1889 on the London stage in the premiere of The Gondoliers by Gilbert and Sullivan. After a successful career on the stage she married her second husband Brigadier General Sir Frederick Gordon Guggisberg and they travelled together to the Gold Coast in West Africa where he was Governor. She continued to appear on the London stage and then in World War I she was Director of the British Navy, Army and Airforce Club in Paris where she worked alongside Alfred. At the outbreak of World War II she re-established the club and fled on 11 June, 1940 one day ahead of the German arrival in Paris, and left a note on the Club door, 'Temporarily closed'.

By the outbreak of the war, Gray was living in the Charterhouse in the City of London. He was one of the brothers and in the past had helped several artist friends to join including Walter Greaves and Joseph Mullard. At the outbreak of the war, Gray went to live in the village of High Ham in Somerset, and he regularly received letters from Mullard chronicling the progress of the Blitz and its impact on the Charterhouse.

The Charterhouse has a scrapbook dated 1939 which includes sketches made by Mullard of many of the Brothers and by Gray of wartime preparations. There were four letters from Mullard to Gray in the Gray papers, the first dated 1 January 1940.

*Dear Gray,*

*A happy new year. I hope it will be happy* because *we have downed the gangster Germans – well we had last Sunday, the second Great Fire of London. Dante's Inferno isn't in it. The first fire of 1660 may have been more impressive – there was more wood, but this was more widespread – and more devilish. Down came hundreds of incendiaries, 20 about on us – mostly in open ground. One on the roof of the doctors and on the masters. If it had got hold it would have been goodbye to Charterhouse.*

*Barts medical school was soon in full blaze and finally gutted. Behind that was a chemical works which burned fiercely for hours.*

*The whole of Barbican except the Post Office is practically burnt down.*

And later he continues listing further damage:

*8 City Churches destroyed and the Central Telegraph building where your post arrived on Sunday was in full blaze on several top floors when I saw it at 2.30 Monday morning. Newgate Street was blazing like hell. The whole area between Barbican and Old Street, about 300 yards, was one mass of burning material, a tremendous inferno. Then later:*

*The Guildhall Hall is ruined, but not the Picture Gallery nor the library. St Lawrence Jewry the adjacent lovely church is gone. St Brides has gone, so has Christ Church where the schoolboys used to worship and which is the next building to the General Post Office.*

*The biggest fire was Waterloo Station. It lit up the whole sky over London.*

This letter then goes into detail of who amongst the brothers is not getting on with whom, so normal institutional life continues in the midst of mayhem.

Gray used his time at High Ham to do two things that have benefited this book enormously. He decided to write his memoirs which he completed in 1945 and worked closely with D S MacColl on his biography of Philip Wilson Steer written after Steer's death in 1942. The book sheds interesting light not just on Steer's last days but on Gray's life at the time. He was also one of two executors of Steer's will.

Gray, as these memoirs record, first met Steer in 1886, and they remained close friends all their lives. There is a quote from a letter from Steer to Tonks in September 1921, quoted by MacColl in his book.

*Gray has been a perfect brick and has done for me all that any human being could possibly do. All I regret is that I have made him waste a great deal of his time.*

*One of his last paintings of High Ham in 1945 © The Charterhouse*

Further tribute to Gray's ability to make very good friends is well encapsulated in this next quote from the same paragraph by MacColl.

> *I have tested his sociable qualities in long painting spells, Welsh and Cornish, and watched with admiration his easy gift for getting into friendly relations with men and women of every rank and kind.*

In 1939, and now resident in Charterhouse, Gray was engaged to paint a portrait of the Master, Mr Schomberg. He was struggling with the background and appealed to Steer for help, and he answered as follows.

> *He asked the colours I was using, and I said 'Black, Golden Ochre and Yellow Ochre.' He said, 'Of course you won't get it with those. Don't use black; try deep chrome and ash blue and glaze it down. Why on earth will you paint with about four colours when there are so many! If a wall is yellow, you must make it look yellow and luminous.*

Gray commented rather peevishly in a letter to MacColl 'Years ago, however, he used to say, the fewer colours one used the better'.

Sadly, Charterhouse have no record of this painting and it has disappeared.

# Charterhouse and Death

The last years of Gray's life were spent in the Charterhouse, an ancient institution in Smithfield in the City of London. The site was originally a Carthusian Monastery but at dissolution was purchased as a private house by Lord North who did extensive renovations. In 1611 Thomas Sutton, a successful merchant, bought the property and at his death he left money to establish a foundation to support a school and a home to 60 'Brothers' and a chapel.

The school moved to Godalming in 1872 and now the alms house consists of accommodation for 40, common rooms including the Great Hall and the Great Chamber, gardens and a chapel. Despite severe damage in the Blitz in May 1940, the Charterhouse still functions according to the spirit of the original endowment and reminds visitors of what a Tudor mansion looked like and which once were common all over London.

Gray died in the Charterhouse infirmary on 16 November, 1951 at the age of 83 after a long battle with cancer.

His obituary was published in the Times on 19 November and what follows are excerpts:

*Ronald Gray, who died in London on Friday, was one of the last surviving painters of the small but select 'Steer circle' in Chelsea, and probably the most faithful disciple of the master.*

*He studied at Westminster School of Art under Professor Frederick Brown who was principal there before his appointment as Slade Professor at University College in 1892. Under Brown the Westminster, as later the Slade, was a nursey of genius. Among Gray's fellow students were Henry Tonks, David Muirhead and Walter Russell. Gray was in close contact with the moving spirits, consisting of Brown, Steer and Tonks of the New English Art Club though he did not become a member of the Club until 1923.*

*As a painter he was distinguished by subtlety and refinement rather than by force. He seemed to be content to work in the background as a member of a school, and seldom made any public appearance, preferring the appreciation of his colleagues to more general recognition.*

# Acknowledgements

Many people around the world have helped me prepare these memoirs for publication: archivists and curators of the Royal Collection Trust, Sydney University, the Alexander Fleming Laboratory Museum at St Mary's Hospital in London, the Charterhouse in the City of London, The Imperial War Museum, the Cecil Beaton Studio Archive, the Tate Gallery and the owners of the Chateau de Montataire.

Special thanks are owed to Julie Petersen, who read the manuscript and gave me many useful comments and corrections, and to my nephew Robert Coombs, who dug out the Gray family history for me.

Last but not least, I would like to thank the team at SilverWood Books who were very patient dealing with my inexperience as I made this, my first venture into the world of publishing.

Richard Gocher